IOSCO COUNTY, MICHIGAN

FAMILY HISTORY

Turner®
PUBLISHING COMPANY

Nashville, Tennessee

TURNER PUBLISHING COMPANY
412 Broadway • P.O. Box 3101
Paducah, Kentucky 42002-3101
(270) 443-0121
www.turnerpublishing.com

Compiled 2002-2004
Copyright © 2006, Iosco County Historical Society
and Turner Publishing Company
Publishing Rights: Turner Publishing Company

Library of Congress Control No.
2005921417

ISBN: 978-1-68162-217-0

Printed in the United States of America.
Limited Edition

0 9 8 7 6 5 4 3 2 1

Photo, this page: Gustave C. Graf's 40 acre farm on Rempert Road in Tawas Township, 1887.

On the Cover: The Lumbermen's Monument

One of the most outstanding scenic and historical sites in northeastern Lower Michigan is the Lumberman's Monument. It is a statue in bronze, nine foot high, of a sawyer with an axe and crosscut saw, a river driver with a peavey, and a timber cruiser with a hand compass—dedicated to the lumbering era of Michigan. This monument rests on the south bank of the AuSable River—a river which plays and essential role in the lumber business in this area.

At the present time 1800,000-200,000 visit the site each year. It is located approximately 15 miles from East Tawas, and in a central location from the existing camping and picnic areas.

Robert Aitkens of New York City, a sculptor, suggested that the three-figure monument be accepted and was awarded $50,000. Mr. Aitkens drew material from photographs of early lumberjacks, and the photographs of a person standing on the exact site chosen for the monument.

TABLE OF CONTENTS

Early History of Iosco County

In April 1840 the Michigan Legislature, then in existence only three years, parceled out the whole territory of the lower peninsula into counties and attached them to Mackinaw. The second Governor of Michigan was William Woodbridge until 1841 when he resigned as governor to serve as U.S. senator. J. Wright Gordon became governor of Michigan. There were thirty-six counties in Michigan at that time. One of them was this county which was christened Kanotin, the name by which the Indians called it. Kanotin means "In the path of the big wind." According to Indian Legend a terrible wind swept through this area uprooting trees and leaving great devastation in its path. The Indians considered that the Great Spirit had shown his displeasure. They avoided this area, after the great storm, for many years. Schoolcraft, seeing the beautiful tall hemlocks and pines and the more than 250 lakes within the borders of the county gave it another Indian name. He called it Iosco, meaning "Water of Light," indicating that it had been blessed by the Great Spirit. After that Indian villages sprung up again along the Huron shore near the AuSable and on Van Ettan Lake. The first explorers of this area were French fur traders who landed near the mouth of the AuSable, and Jesuit missionaries who landed frequently at this spot and also all along the Huron shore wherever there were Indians to teach. The first records of the Huron Shore came from these early missionaries. One wrote describing this county, as it was 250 years ago. Written about 1720 a Jesuit wrote: The forests amid which their lot was cast filled them with wonder and admiration. The great inland lakes appeared to them like oceans along the borders of the wilderness. Flocks of waterfowl of varied plumage streamed along the shores of the lakes and the waters swarmed with fish. As they traveled the Indian trails through the wilderness they found extensive tracts of oakland that seemed to them like cultivated parks. These tracts of plainsland were studded with little crystal lakes. The ground in the spring was covered with beautiful flowers-blue violets-the largest they had ever seen were everywhere. Great numbers of moose and elk bounded through the thickets. Deer were seen in groups of five or six feeding upon the margins of the watercourses. Flocks of wild turkey and other game filled the woods. The plains were alive with grouse. Carrier pigeons swept along like clouds above the forests in numbers so great as to almost obscure the sun. They beheld great quantities of wild fruit. The great clusters of wild grapes growing along the rivers reminded the Jesuits of the champagne districts of France. At this time all of this area was under the French flag. The early explorers found the Chippewa Indians here. Old legends told by Sodney Mucklepoosh and John Silas tell us that a powerful tribe called the Sauks lived here and were very hostile and war-like. The Sauks once occupied the whole of this territory from Thunder Bay on the North to the head of the Sheawassee on the South including the Saginaw River and its tributaries. The Sauks were always at war with the Chippewas and Ottawas who occupied the Lake Superior region and with the Pattowattamies on the South and with other Indian nations in Canada. At last a council was called consisting of the Chippewas, Ottawas, Pattowattamies, Menominies and six nations of the Algonquines and planned a defense against the Sauks. At an appointed time they all met at Mackinaw Island where they filled out a large army and marched against the Sauks, completely overpowering them by their superior numbers. Their greatest battles were fought on the Saginaw, Cass, Shiawassee and Flint Rivers. The few remaining Sauks were banished west of the Mississippi River. Sodney said that although the Chippewas and Ottawas could now live in peace in the Land of the Lakes, so many Sauks had been killed here that their spirits hovered over the battlegrounds and brought a great sickness. Smallpox visited the villages and many Indians in the Saginaw Valley died of it and were buried along the Saginaw River where Bay City now stands. In 1908 a water main was put through one of these cemeteries against the warning of the Indians. Although the epidemic had been more than a century earlier, a small pox epidemic broke out in Bay City shortly after the cemetery was dug up.

After the Sauks were driven out this area became the common hunting ground of the Chippawas and Ottowas. The early settlers found them in the AuSable River Valley all along the Huron Shore and in the Saginaw Valley. The white man wanted the land that the Indians occupied. The Indians were tricked into signing a treaty with General Lewis Cass by which the Indians ceded to the U.S. Government all but 40,000 acres of their territory. This land was to belong to the tribe in common and was to be permanently the hunting ground of the tribes. In 1837 this land was surveyed and put on the market for sale at $2.00 per acre. It was held at that price for some time; then, was reduced so that the few acres remaining could be sold. That sold for $1.25 per acre. After deducting the cost of the survey and sales costs the Indians received the remainder or so the treaty of 1837 stated. Actually the Indians were to be paid $1.25 per acre but received much less. Iosco's first white settler was probably Louis Chevalier who was a French fur trader and settled on the mouth of the AuSable before 1800. The American fur company had an outpost at the mouth of the AuSable in 1828. Before that at the time of the massacre at Mackinaw which was in 1763 there was an Indian settlement at the mouth of the AuSable post. An Englishman by the name of Henry escaped the massacre of Mackinaw and in August 1764 as a captive of the Ottawas who had saved him came to the Indian camp and brought Henry. He wrote of this: "The Indian, Warvatium and family were to go to their winter quarters. They proposed much to my joy to take me along. We proceeded to the mouth of the AuSable hunting all the way," said Henry in his account written to his government after his release. He continued: "I enjoyed a personal freedom of which I had long been deprived and became an expert in the Indian pursuits of hunting and fishing as the Indians themselves." Henry stayed at the Indian camp at the mouth of the AuSable until April 1765. When Wawatam and other Indians prepared to return to Mackinaw Henry persuaded Wawatam to return him to Ste. St. Marie where Cadotte was the Indian Chief. Cadotte was friendly to the English and turned Henry over to them. So, probably Henry, the only Englishman who escaped death at the Massacre of Mackinaw was the first white man to live for a while in this county. Another early settler in Iosco County was a man named Simeon. His last name is not known. He divided his time between a hut on Tawas Lake near what is now called Sim's Creek and a rude shanty near the mouth of the Tawas River. His wife was a woman of superior intelligence but she did not like her solitary life. After the first white child born in Iosco Co. was born to her she left taking her infant daughter with her. Her husband soon followed. There was left, however, on Tawas Bay an old pioneer who long preceded his family here. His name was Peter Hart. The first real settlement or village was made at the mouth of the AuSable River. Curtis Emerson and James Eldridge of East Saginaw had located there and Benj. Pierce had a trading post. This land was divided into lots and sold to Benj, Pierce, WLP Little, James E. Smith Enoch Olmstead, Hulett Duell, Patrick Perrott, and Horace D. Stockman. This first settlement in Iosco Co. was founded in 1849. Some of these men were undoubtedly of French origin but most were Americans.

This first settlement was a fishing village and fishing was its main enterprise for many years. Many thousands of barrels of fish were shipped from AuSable to southern cities. It was a common sight to see a fleet of fifty or sixty vessels emerge from the harbor and set out with their crews. Mr. O'Toole kept supplies for the fishermen and their families. When prices were low, he advanced money and clothing to them and helped them in many ways until prices for fish came up. It is said he never lost by his kindness. The river on which they settled was named by the French. It was spelled Aux. Sable and meant "The Sand." One of the Jesuits writing of this river said "The AuSable River is by far the most beautiful river I have seen. It being 100 feet or more in width, 22 feet deep and more than 200 miles long. The banks of the river are 150 feet or more high and the scenery is sublime." Soon after the fishermen, the lumbermen came. Immense quantities of pine were cut along the AuSable and for miles back and were floated down its waters to the cities on the shores of Lake Huron. In 1865 the first mill was built at the mouth of the AuSable before a dock was built. Steam boats and sailcraft landed supplies on the River. Small fishing boats carried them in. Backus and Bros. built the first mill but it burned in 1867. It was rebuilt and operated by them, until 1875 when Potts and Co. bought it and added many improvements. In 1883 the mill cut was 40,000,000 feet of lumber and employed about 200 men. A salt block was added and brine supplied by a pipeline running from East Tawas. Afterward salt wells were opened up in AuSable and Oscoda. This mill afterward became known as the Oscoda Salt and Lumber Co. with Henry M. Loud as leading spirit of the enterprise. In 1877 the immense salt block was burned and later rebuilt on a smaller scale.

Two villages had now sprung up—Oscoda and AuSable. Henry Loud was an important man in both towns. He had four sons and one daughter, all of whom played an important part in the early history of the two towns. Henry M. Loud was the first to visit the AuSable River Regions in the interest of the lumbering business. His lumbering enterprise was first known as Loud, Priest, Gay & Co. but afterwards as Loud and Gay, the latter being his son-in-law. With the coming of lumbering came wealth and prosperity to these towns. Loud owned vast tracts of pine timber. So also did Ex-governor Alger, T.F. Thompson and others. T.F. Thompson was a native of Ireland and came to this country at the age of 15. In 1866 he came to Iosco Co. to engage in lumbering. Thompson, now called South Branch, was named for him. At one-time he owned 15,000 acres in Iosco and Alcona. He built a large hotel or halfway house on the South Branch of the Au Sable one-mile from the main branch. Here Mr. Thompson cleared a farm of about 200 acres to raise hay and grain for his horses and vegetables for his hotel. Mr. Thompson became a legendary figure because of his great physical strength. Many tales were told involving this characteristic. He had a son also very powerful but of a kind and generous nature. The Thompson Farm became known as a harbor of refuge for hunters, weary land lookers, and lumberman and teamsters. With the coming of the mills and settlers to Oscoda and AuSable churches sprang up. The first church organization there was the Methodist church. H.M. Loud assisted in establishing this church. He was a graduate of a theological seminary in the East and often times preached in the church. He was an orator of no mean ability. The first minister to visit Au Sable and probably the first to preach in the county was Rev. Marchant who walked from Harrisville to AuSable in 1861. It was his custom to walk to the mouth of the AuSable, then call for someone to row him across the river. Before the church was built he preached in the homes of the fishermen. After the service someone would row him back and he would begin his long trek back to Harrisville. In 1865 H.M. Loud, Priest, and Gay organized a Sunday school. Their S.S. library boasted 200 volumes. In 1867 a Methodist church was built in E. Tawas with Rev. Jared Copeland of Tawas as pastor. This church was a part of the Flint River Conference and was the first church building in the county. In 1868 a Congregational Church was organized and afterwards a Presbyterian. Catholic and Baptist societies followed, also a Hebrew Church (synagogue). In 1872 AuSable and Oscoda were incorporated as one village with Nelson Lipscombe as president. In 1877 the first paper was published. It was called "The AuSable and Oscoda News." The editor was P.D. Bissell. In 1879 the village borrowed $6,000 and built an iron bridge across the AuSable River connecting the two towns. From then on they had a phenomenal growth.

With the coming of the lumberman and when the great drives of logs came down the river bringing the Rivermen to town, and camps broke up in the interior Oscoda and Au Sable were anything but quiet towns. The saloons were busy and many a lumberman spent his entire winter wages drinking and having a good time. These men were hard workers and hard drinkers but at heart they were generous and outgoing. Many of the early churches owed their existence to the generous donations of the lumbermen and rivermen. AuSable and Oscoda both grew to towns of considerable size and finally became separate cities. In 1882 a railroad was built along the shore from Bay City to Alpena. A branch from it was built into the lumbering areas in Alcona Co. This was called the Loud Line. It was famous for the many accidents occurring on it. Crewmen were inexperienced and the rails were narrowly gauged and poorly constructed. The engineer was often reckless and could not control his engine. In 1870 the first Masonic lodge was built in AuSable. The first Masonic meeting was held in 1867. Oscoda and AuSable grew and flourished for about 30 years. Then lumbering began to decrease and business fell off. On the 27th of July, 1911, the two towns were completely destroyed by fire. Oscoda soon began to rebuild but without the lumbering interests it never got as large or prosperous as it had been. Fishing once more became the main industry. The first settlement at the mouth of the AuSable began in 1849, but not long afterwards Tawas City was settled in 1854 by Gideon O. Whittemore of Pontiac, Michigan. Mr. Whittemore was a lawyer who had been prosecuting attorney and judge of Oakland Co. In June 1853 he landed at Tawas Point and was hospitably received by Captain Graham, keeper of the lighthouse, which had just been completed having been erected in 1852. Mr. Whittemore and members of his company located a tract of 5000 acres of pine and secured a front of about a mile along the shores of Tawas Bay. They purchased the site that is now Tawas City and erected a sawmill here in 1854 which was the beginning of Tawas City.

The name Tawas was adapted from the Indian name Ottawas which was an Indian tribe living here. It was obtained by dropping the first two letters of the name. The name of the chief was "Tawas" an abbreviation of the tribal clan. At this time there was no post office south of Mackinac. Mails were carried to Mackinac by boat then loaded on dog sledges and carried south. In the winter when boats could not sail, dog sledges carried the mail both ways. Mail was also brought from Bay City by sailboat in the summers. In 1865 the first post office was opened at Tawas with James O. Whittemore, eldest son of G.O. Whittemore as postmaster. The office was a box in his dwelling for eleven years. When lumbering opened up in the interior of the county, like Oscoda and AuSable the growth of Tawas was rapid. G.O. Whittemore lived ten years after he settled Tawas. His sons James Charles and William carried on the work begun by their father. Iosco was organized as a county in 1857 with only two townships: Tawas and Sable. These were the first organizations in the county. The first county officers were chosen the same year (1857) and were as follows: Sheriff, Charles H. Whittemore; Clerk, James O. Whittemore; Treasurer, Chas. P. Haywood; Register of Deeds, James O. Whittemore; Prosecuting Attorney, G.O. Whittemore; Probate Judge, G.O. Whittemore; Surveyor, Henry Daggett. G.0. Whittemore sowed the first crop of grain ever planted in Iosco Co. It consisted of ten acres of wheat and was sown on plainsland. He also took measures to have the Iosco and Ogemaw State Road opened. This road was a great benefit to the new county. G.O. Whittemore used his influence to see that other roads were opened through the wilderness to be used as tote roads upon which to carry mail to the interior. He built a larger sawmill on Tawas Bay, erected large docks, laid out Tawas City, cleared the numerous streams of rubbish so that logs could be floated down them. The hardships of pioneer life and his excessive labors late in life proved too much of a strain. One peaceful summer evening in 1863 he sat on his son's porch admiring the moonlight on Tawas Bay and quietly passed away, evidently of a heart attack. The record does not say. The first church in Tawas City was the M.E. church. It was organized in 1868 with Rev. E. Barry as pastor. The first school was opened in 1863 with Miss Graham as teacher. She was the daughter of Capt. Graham the lighthouse keeper. The schoolroom was over the Whittemore store. This room also served as a courtroom. Court was held here when the judge could catch a sailboat coming here from Bay City. Early records show very few cases in the early days. It was in this room that church services were held when missionaries came to town. Communion was held here at that time. It was the "Upper Room" for many travelers and transient preachers. When settlers first came to the Tawas shore, there was an old Indian burial ground across from where the depot now stands on Tawas River. The early settlers buried their dead nearby. In 1875 the present cemetery grounds were purchased one and a quarter miles from Tawas, also on the river. Another cemetery was laid out and used by the Lutherans two miles from Tawas on Cold Creek. Nearby the Lutherans put up a two-story building, which they used as church and school for their members. The first lodge in the county was the FreeMasons organized in 1872 with nine Charter members. The first newspaper in Iosco Co. was started by the Whittemores in Tawas City but afterwards was purchased by C.R. Jackson and moved to East Tawas in the year 1881. In 1877 this paper was the only official organ for the two counties Iosco and Alcona and was called the Iosco Co. Gazette. The first railroad in the county was built in 1878 by Sylvester Hale. It ran from his mill in Tawas Township to township 21-north range 4 east in Ogemaw Co, a distance of 21 miles. It was called the Lake Huron and Southwestern R.R. As a business venture it did not prove successful. In 1879, it was purchased by C.H. Prescott, who had also purchased extensive mill property in Tawas City. The railroad was organized under Prescott and given the name of Tawas and Bay Company Railroad. While the road never made very much money for its owner, it helped to open a large tract of good country to settlers and gradually farms were cleared along it. In 1867-68 at a cost of $12,000 the first Iosco County courthouse was built with the jail in the basement. The courthouse had a fine location facing Tawas Bay. In 1869 the Board of Supervisors purchased 320 acres of land from J. Schaffer to be used as a county farm and poor house. Good buildings were erected. The first County Fair was held in 1875 on the courthouse grounds. It was a decided success and proves that the soil in the farming areas could produce good crops. In 1879 the Fairgrounds between Tawas and E. Tawas were laid out. In 1876 the LifeSaving Station at Tawas Point was built with George Haskins as keeper. Many more saw mills were springing up along the Bay and back from Tawas in the adjoining country. In connection with the Tawas City Mills salt blocks were operated, the first salt block was built in 1880 by Wm. Nisbet & Adams who operated what had been the Whittemore Mill. In that year they produced about 200 barrels of salt per day. The Hale Mill and Salt Works had the same capacity.

Probably the men who did the most in a financial way to build up Tawas was C.H. Prescott and Sons who bought the mill property of Nisbet, Green & Sons and expended $8,500 in improvements. Prescott built a large store and immense docks out into the Bay on which great piles of lumber were stacked to be shipped away on the numerous Lake schooners. As lumbering commenced in the interior of the county, roads were opened up. Farms were cleared along these roads. The roads took the names of the settlements, thus the Wilbur Road into Wilbur Twp. The Hemlock Road was named for a large Hemlock tree that marked it. The Plank Road, which runs on an angle Northwest, was once planked its entire length, about five miles, and was used by lumbermen to haul their logs to the mills. East Tawas started with a mill built by C.F. Adams, Valkenburg & Co. Mr. S. W. Chillson drove piles for the mill foundation. The first logs for this mill were floated from both the AuSable and Rifle Rivers. The mill was started in 1862. During the next year they built a dock 500 feet from the shore with a boom for raft of logs attached. This firm was afterwards known as the East Tawas Milling Co. Soon after East Tawas was granted a post office. C.C. Parker was appointed Post Master. The first bank was established in Iosco County in 1870 by the E. Tawas Milling Co. Among the many mills in E. Tawas were the Emery Mills with a large salt block attached. The salt well was 905 feet deep and the capacity in 1882 was 80,000 barrels per year. The M.E. Church of East Tawas was the first church organized in Iosco County. It was started by Jared Copeland in 1866 who held meetings in a schoolhouse. In 1873 a church edifice was built and dedicated at a cost of $5,000. Dr. Reeves was the first physician in Iosco Co. He settled in E. Tawas in 1868. He was a very skillful physician and in that early day possessed the largest private Masonic library in the country. Dr. Reeves' daughter married the congressman George A. Loud. In 1870 Dr. Goodale began the practice of medicine in E. Tawas. The early businessmen who helped to build E. Tawas were Benj Richards and sons who came here in 1874 and entered the hardware business. W.H. Clough came in 1875 and opened a grocery. James La Berge, a dealer in boots and shoes, came in 1875 and built a store block. Dr. T .A. Gates built a store block and was a practicing physician. Alabaster is the only town in Iosco County that did not have its origin in lumbering. From the first its limestone and gypsum beds have been its chief resources. The quarries were discovered first by the Indians and then by fur traders who noticed the outcropping in the Bay. An Indian fur trader Wm. C. McDonald who was employed by the American Fur Company, owned a mile along the Alabaster Shore. In 1841, he sold portions of his interests to James Fraser, Harvey Williams and Alfred Hartshorn who, supposing it to be of great value, explored the land along the shore. They made the mistake of boring in hollows instead of on the ridges so the limestone quarries were not opened until 1861. In that year Wm. St. Patrick of Flint found gypsum in large quantities. With the discovery of gypsum came a settlement of people and Alabaster Township was formed from Tawas Twp. Then came Grant Township and others. Plainfield Township split off from Sable in 1868. Then Wilbur Township and Burleigh Baldwin already contained E. Tawas. Sherman between Alabaster and Raleigh came next. AuSable and Oscoda were among the first townships to be formed. In 1906 capitalists from the East discovered that the AuSable River had wonderful waterpower that could be chained and put to work. They set out to purchase the land and water rights to build dams to furnish electric power to Saginaw, Bay City, Flint and other large cities. Five dams were built.

Iosco County Historical Society

For many years there were people in Iosco County who felt it was of vital importance to preserve certain records, books, documents, etc. of historical interest, also various items which were in common use by area residents in years gone by, and to have a central locations to store and exhibit this collection. Joseph Barkman, a local lumber businessman, had a vast amount of memorabilia of the area, which he collected over the years. His grandfather, Abraham Myers, arrived in the Tawas area by boat more than 100 years ago and was one of the first merchants, operating a general store in East Tawas. The memories of not a few people were stirred when they had occasion to stop at Joe's lumberyard and viewed the articles from his collection, in which he had on display. This no doubt played an essential role in why the local people established a museum of exhibit items, which they had kept over the years for future generations to view.

In late 1967, a few people met to discuss their common interest, and in 1968 regular town meetings were held to discuss historical Iosco items at the Iosco County Court House. Among the organizers were Albert Buch, Neil Thornton, Joseph Barkman, Edna Otis, Helen Hertzler, Marion Jenkins, Jack Weible, Arthur Dease, Mary Jane Hennigar, Leon Putnam, Norman Sibley, Arthur Leitz, John Hennigar, Cleopatra Shelp, and Helen Curtis. They called themselves the Iosco County Historical Society and became incorporated on November 28, 1975. The first president was Jack Weible, and Marion Jennings was secretary.

In late 1975 Joseph Barkman died and bequeathed his collection of artifacts, together with $10,000, for the establishment of a museum. The surviving members of the Barkman family matched the amount with another $10,000.

In May of 1977 the Iosco County Board of Commissioners authorized purchase of the McKay family home at 405 West Bay Street in East Tawas for the establishment of a museum. The county was to pay $30,000 from revenue sharing funds for that portion of property. Iosco County Historical Society was to be responsible for the development and operation of the museum. One of the finest frame houses in the city remaining from the lumber era, the two-story building fronts Tawas Bay. It was built sometime before 1890 and was originally owned by a Detroit and Mackinac Railway Company official.

On June 17, 1978, formal opening of the museum was held. The guest speaker was John Cumming, director of the Clarke Historical Museum and trustee of the Historical Society of Michigan. The program was held on the lawn in the back of the museum, overlooking the Bay, and was followed by an open house and guided tour.

There have been several exhibits in the museum which drew interested visitors of special interest and very popular were replicas of four historical ships that sailedthe Great Lakes. These were loaned from the Michigan State University Museum. Another interesting exhibit was a large collection of dolls, many of which were over 100 years old and originally form Germany.

Since the museum has been open the visitors have numbered in the thousands and from practically every state in the union, as well as foreign countries, namely England, Germany, Belgium, Australia, South America and Canada.

A dedicated group of members and volunteers continue to operate the museum for the preservation of the history of Iosco County.

Daniel McFarlane, MD and Margaret McFarlane at the
A.J. Bradshaw Photo Studio, c. 1880.

ABBOTT FAMILY. Eben Farnsworth Abbott, born 1844, died 1929, next to youngest in the family of Anson and Huldah Collins Abbott, was born in Pierpont, New York. Soon thereafter the family moved to Thamesford, Ontario. There he spent his boyhood, receiving a good education in the public schools

In the 1860s, they moved to Michigan, to be nearer the married children living on farms near Saginaw and Midland. When crossing Lake Huron, a fierce storm was encountered. To lighten the ship, the captain ordered the freight thrown overboard. Eventually, he made it safely to port in Bay City.

Eben and younger brother Lucius were not on the boat, however. With the help of the farm dog, they were driving the cattle from their old home, crossing into Michigan at Port Huron. With their own cattle they had two steers that a neighbor was sending to his brother in Michigan for a yoke of oxen. Nights they stayed at farms along the route. Soon after reaching their destination, Eben met Samuel Chilson of Plainfield who told of the wonderful opportunity to secure a home in the plains region of Iosco County.

In October of 1866, he took up a homestead north of Gordon Creek. The light soil proved unsuitable for farming, however, and one by one the entire plains community moved to better farmland.

After his father's death in 1876, Eben, with his mother, moved to the pioneer community later known as Wilber. There he circulated a petition to have Wilber Township organized. This was accomplished in 1878, taking one township from Plainfield and one from AuSable.

In 1886 he married Alice Jennie Falls, born 1862, died 1950, daughter of Melvin and Amanda Hobson Falls. This couple raised nine children, teaching them by precept and example honesty, thrift, the joy of sharing, self-worth and the dignity of honest labor.

Front Row, l-r: Mrs. Abbott, Jennie, Mr. Abbott, Alton, and Edna. Back Row, l-r: Amy, Hollis, Eugene, Beth, and Harvey

Alice, a skillful, ingenious homemaker, was a born nurse. Good judgment coupled with use of home remedies and herbs made a doctor's services seldom required.

Both Eben and Alice were sensitive to the needs of others; hospitality was the key-note of their home.

In various ways Eben supplemented the farm income; he operated a horse-powered hay baler. In partnership with William Phelps, he was engaged in lumbering several winters. He also carried mail with horse and buggy from E. Tawas to the Wilber Post Office. Active in community affairs, he held offices of public trust at different times.

EDWIN RICTOR "RICK" ANDER-SON. Rick was born on Good Friday, April 14, 1933, on Washington Street in E. Tawas. His father, Edwin Arthur, a lifelong resident of E. Tawas and Iosco County was born February 1, 1900. Ed worked one year at a General Motors factory in Flint and then for the Iosco County Road Commission. His mother, Luella Sophia, was born December 15, 1909 in Greytown, Ohio and moved to E. Tawas in 1923. Luella finished the thirteenth year of school, County Normal, and taught for two years in the Laidlawville School District. As a young teacher, she was introduced to Ed through his sister, Esther, while she was boarding with the Anschuetz family.

Rick's parents were married on May 19, 1932. Luella worked as a homemaker and raised Rick, William Mitchell, born December 7, 1934, and Michael John, born May 12, 1949. Luella was Sunday School Superintendent for many years at the Grace Evangelical Lutheran Church.

Rick resided in E. Tawas until his marriage. He enjoyed all the boyhood fun of growing up in a small town community, including fishing and swimming in the bay. He remembers the economically lean years. He tells of how he and brother Bill both got their tonsils removed, even though Bill didn't need surgery, because two could be done for the price of one.

Rick and Christine Anderson

Rick attended E. Tawas schools and was saddened when the old E. Tawas high school was razed in 1997. He went to Central Michigan University and earned a bachelor's of arts in history in 1955. He completed his master's degree in history at Wayne State University in 1968. Rick taught one year at Ithaca, Michigan High School in 1956 and joined the U.S. Army and served two years, spending time in Japan and Korea.

While in basic training, Rick met Christine Anne Hunter, a native of Grand Cayman Island, BWI, who was pursuing her nursing education in the U.S. They married on June 28, 1958 and lived in Rockwood for 10 years before moving to Grosse Ile, Michigan. Rick taught social studies at Riverview High School until he retired in 1987. Chris continued to work in nursing, earning a master's degree in women's health care in 1988. They were proud of their children, Allison Marie, born in 1958, a physical therapist who has two children. Darrell Arthur was born in 1964, and is a corporate jet pilot for Ford Motor Company. Erik, born in 1965, is an electrical engineer and he and Darrell both have three children.

After Chris's death in 1989, Rick continued involvement in his Lutheran church on Grosse Ile as well as volunteering for the YAF, Greenville Village and Habitat for Humanity. He married Martha Galvin in 1997, a retired OB/GYN nurse practitioner. They reside in Clinton Township and are active members of Hope Lutheran Church in Warren. They continue to build with Habitat for Humanity. They enjoy traveling, visiting with grandchildren, and keeping touch with Anderson and Gackstetter relatives when they stay at their condo in Oscoda, Michigan.

WILLIAM MITCHELL "BILL" ANDERSON. Bill was born December 7, 1934 in East Tawas, Michigan, was the middle son of East Tawas native, Edwin Arthur Anderson, born February 1, 1900 (died May 29, 1982), and Louella Sophy Gackstetter Anderson, born December 15, 1909 (died March 19, 1989) in Elmore, Ohio.

Louella and her siblings came to the area when her father, Peter Gackstetter, a widower, moved to Alabaster seeking work in 1923. (See Peter Gackstetter).

"Ed" worked for the Iosco County Road Commission for 40 years before retiring in 1970. Louella taught school prior to their marriage on May 21, 1932 in Bay City, Michigan. Ed and Louella were married for 50 years and eight days. They were members of Grace Lutheran Church in East Tawas and resided on Washington and Westover Streets in East Tawas and on Anderson Road in Baldwin Township until their deaths.

Bill's siblings are Edwin Rictor Anderson, who was born on April 14, 1933 (See Edwin Rictor Anderson), and Michael John Anderson, who was born on May 12, 1949, and married native, Kathy Jean Palmer. They have three children: Shawn Warner, Shelby Christine and Shannon Lee.

Bill is a graduate of the old East Tawas High School, Class of 1952. Following two years of military service in the 2nd Armored Cavalry Division of the U.S. Army, Bill attended Central Michigan University in Mount Pleasant, Michigan. where he majored in accounting. He later became a revenue agent for the Internal Revenue Service and was transferred to Jackson, Michigan in October 1965. Upon his retirement in Jackson, Michigan in November of 1990, he ended a career of 31 years of government service.

He married Joyce Jeanne Werkema, a native of Grand Rapids, Michigan, who was born on January 19, 1937, on April 24, 1965 at Faith Lutheran Church, in Grand Rapids. Following their wedding, they moved to Jackson, Michigan, where they continue to live. They have two sons, Michael William Anderson (Kim), who was born on December 11, 1966 and Jon Lamont ("Monte") Anderson (Amy), who was born on December 24, 1968 and, at this point in time, they have two grandchildren, Deanna Hudson-Lee and Kaleb Edwin Anderson. (Another grandchild, a boy, is due on July 18, 2002.)

In his retirement, Bill keeps active volunteering on various committees at St. James Lutheran Church in Jackson, Michigan, and has served on its Church Council as well. He also volunteers to deliver meals to the shut-ins and to do odd jobs for "Habitat for Humanity."

Bill is currently working part-time at the Cascades Golf Course and Ken Douglas Driving Range in Jackson, which he managed for a number of years following his retirement.

ANSCHUETZ CENTENNIAL FARM.
Our farm was homesteaded by Johannes L. Anschuetz who was born in Germany in 1829 and married Margaret Zorn who was also born in Germany in 1836. They were married in Frankenmouth, Michigan.

After their marriage they came to Tawas Township, Iosco County to homestead. On December 14, 1875 he received the sum of $4.00 and permission to homestead 160 acres of Section 23, part of which is still owned by Harold Anschuetz.

Johannes and Margaret had five sons: George, Henry, Ernst, Herman and John, and one daughter Annie.

John had two sons, Elmer and Arnold, and one daughter, Adella.

Arnold farmed 80 acres for many years and then the farm went to Harold his son, who still lives there. He also farmed for many years and now has a saw mill there.

It was recognized as a Centennial Farm in 1968, the first in Iosco County by the Historical Society.

Now after all these years the Centennial Farm is still in the Anschuetz family.

JOHANNES L. ANSCHUETZ.
Johannes was born in Germany in 1829, married Margaret Zorn, also born in Germany in 1836. They were married in Frankenmuth, Michigan in 1855. After their marriage they came to Tawas Township to homestead. In 1875 he received for the sum of $4.00, permission to homestead the SW 1/4 of Section 23 in Tawas Township containing 160 acres, part of which is still owned by members of the family.

When he had completed building a house for his family, he built a shed in which he made and repaired guns. Many of his customers were Indians who came on foot from the county line where they had a settlement. For supplies, he met the boats at the dock and pushed his supplies home through the woods with a wheelbarrow.

Johannes and Margaret had five sons and one daughter. One of the sons, John, was a farmer, and he and his wife Augusta Kobs, had two sons and one daughter. Their son, Elmer (Shorty), married Edna Daley. Their daughter, Judith, is married to Kenneth Thibault. Their children are Lisa and Julie. Judith Thibault is owner of Century 21 Tawas Realty. She and her husband are also owners of Tawas RV Park on Townline Road.

BARKMAN FAMILY.
Abram Barkman was born in Poland in 1862. He came to Detroit with his parents when he was 13 years of age and was engaged in business in this community for more than 60 years. His activities included merchandising, lumbering, banking and extensive operations in development of resort property.

When he came to Tawas, he was a clerk in T. Simons Store in Tawas City and continued in the employ of Mr. Simons for seven years. He then started in the dry good business for himself in the Myers Block in East Tawas. Several years later he purchased the Urquhart building. He was in the building business until his retirement from the dry goods and banking business.

In 1912, he started the manufacture of box shooks and crating in a plant located in Tawas City along with retail sales of lumber and building supplies. He was also interested, with the late W.M. Gardner, at the Hardwood Mill in cutting and sawing of second growth timber. He was also interested in the private banking business (Tawas Exchange Bank) in East Tawas and the private Bank of Beckman and Barkman in Lewiston, Michigan. This was later sold to Herman Lunden. He was the owner of the Barkman Lumber Company and retained an interest in the Barkman Outfitting company which was operated by his sons.

Abram Barkman was married twice. His first wife passed away in 1901. He later married Clara Barkman, daughter of pioneer A. Myers. The family consisted of six sons and two daughters: Joseph, Nathan, Julius, Harris, Aaron, Milton, Helena, and Regina Barkman.

The Barkman family has always been involved in community affairs. A. Barkman was always concerned about people that needed help. Clara Barkman, in her own way, without either the family or public knowing about her involvement, made certain that those in need received food, clothing or whatever for Christmas and Thanksgiving. The gifts were distributed anonymously by someone who never revealed the whereabouts of the source.

Joseph Barkman who was in business with his father took over the Lumber Company after the death of A. Barkman. He continued this operation until he passed away in 1975. He was a person who in his entire life contributed to many causes. Land was given to the Tawas St. Joseph Hospital and the Masonic Lodge. Financial contributions were made to all of the churches in East Tawas and Tawas City. He was always the first to make his contributions to the United Drive. His interest in saving things and pictures of the area are now on display in the Historical Museum in East Tawas. It was his desire that a Museum become a reality. He also established a scholarship for the Tawas Area School District which will be in existence forever.

Nathan Barkman was very much involved in the promotion of the area. He served on several boards--The East Tawas Dock, Silver Valley, and the Chamber of

Commerce. He promoted and was a partner in Tawas Industries and Northern Construction Builders. Being located in the Tawas area, he became buyer for many companies that were commercial fishing outlets. The cities were New York, Philadelphia, Chicago, Detroit, etc. The fish that were purchased were from the Great Lakes. Both Joseph and Nathan Barkman were in office for the city of East Tawas and the American Legion.

Julius Barkman and both sisters, Helena and Regina, reside in New York City.

Aaron Barkman became the manager of the Sherwin Williams Paint Company and lived in the Chicago area. He now is living on the West Coast.

Harris Barkman has been involved in civic affairs for many years. He was a director of the Tawas Area Chamber of Commerce for four years before heading that organization for another four years; he was secretary of the Iosco County Centennial Committee in 1957 and served on the Planning and Award Board; he established the Iosco County Economic Development Corporation which is a funding vehicle for industrial development in the business community; he established the Barkman Outfitting Company and in 1961 the Three C Vending and Amusement Company in Oscoda, Michigan. In 1976, this business was sold, and he became interested in other community affairs. The artifacts and other items left by Joseph Barkman made it possible for him to bring about the Museum in East Tawas and complete a dream of his brother Joseph.

A. Barkman passed away in 1941, Clara Barkman passed away in 1957, Joseph Barkman in 1975 and Nathan Barkman in 1960.

BEATRICE ANNE (PETERS) BERNARD. Beatrice's maternal grandparents, Henry E. and Mary A. (Shaw) Rittenour, were born and lived their lives in lower Michigan. They were married on December 24, 1915. "Erroll" and Mary had 10 children but three died as infants. Daughter Frances Irene was the oldest child, born on December 25, 1916. After graduation from high school, she married Arthur Carl Peters on November 10, 1934.

Beatrice's paternal grandparents, Archibald C. and Wilhemina C. (Katt) Peters lived most of their lives in the Midland and Hemlock area of Michigan. "Archie" was born in 1872 on the ship USS *Europa* bringing his parents from Germany to New York and eventually to Michigan. "Minnie" was born near Midland, Michigan in 1885

and was raised in that area. Archie and Minnie were married on April 16, 1902 in Bay County, Michigan. They had five children and son Arthur Carl was born on April 5, 1908 in Midland County, Michigan. After Art graduated from the eighth grade, he helped his father on the farm and got a job at the Chevrolet Motor Plant.

Arthur C. Peters and Frances I. Rittenour were married on November 10, 1934 near Hemlock, Michigan. They had four daughters and the second daughter, Beatrice (Beatty) Anne Bernard, was born a twin on January 22, 1938.

Art, Frances and daughters first moved to the Hale area in 1946 for a year, living between Long Lake and South Branch. Art had relatives in the South Branch area and felt it would be a good place to live. The daughters attended the Hale and Goodar Schools. In 1950 they again moved to Long Lake and have lived in the community most of the years since then. All of the girls graduated from the Hale Area School (then called Plainfield Township Rural Agricultural School).

Beatrice A. Peters and Berkley B. Bernard were married on July 11, 1954 and they have four children. See "Berkley Bruce Bernard" history for more.

BERKLEY BRUCE "BERK" BERNARD. Berk's maternal grandparents, William H. and Katherine C. (Klinck) Rahl moved to Hale from Samaria, Michigan in 1900. They purchased and cleared a farm one mile north and one half mile east of Hale. Berk's mother, Alice Roosevelt Rahl, was born there on January 13, 1906, the youngest of five children. In 1920, William, Katherine, daughters Pearl and Alice moved to the residence behind the former Cowie building in Hale where they had established the Rahl Confectionery

Berk's paternal grandparents, Franklin Ellsworth and Amy Lorinda (Turner) Bernard, were from Hatton, Wood County, Ohio. Their only child, David G. Bernard, was born at Hatton on August 19, 1902. The Bernard's first came to Hale in 1902 and purchased grazing property for their sheep in 1903. Franklin farmed, raised sheep

and bought and shipped cattle. In 1916 the family moved to Hale permanently and purchased a home one eighth mile south of town on M-65.

David G. Bernard and Alice R. Rahl were married on June 17, 1923. David was partners in farming with his father until he became postmaster in 1934. Berkley Bruce Bernard was the youngest of their five sons. He was born on February 17, 1934 in the living quarters behind his grandparents' confectionery store.

After Franklin's death in 1937, David, Alice and sons moved to his home just south of Hale. Mother Amy lived with them until her death in 1943. Berk and his brothers were raised in that home and attended Hale School. David and Alice lived there until her death in 1986 and his in 1994.

Berk married Beatrice (Beatty) Anne Peters on July 11, 1954 and they have four children. Berk built a small home for them on a corner of the Bernard property south of Hale. With later additions to the home, that is where Berk and Beatty currently live in 2002.

In 1958 Berk and Beatty started a business, Bernard Woodworking, and manufactured wood windows. In 1969 they purchased a lumber yard one half mile south of Hale. This was the beginning of Bernard Lumber Company. In 1966 the business was moved to the Bernard property next to their home and the name was changed to Bernard Building Center. They have enjoyed many years of steady growth.

Daughter Debra Anne was born on March 6, 1955 and attended Hale Area Schools. She lived in Hale until graduating from nursing school in 1976. Debra married Randolph Raymond Fisher in 1977 and has lived in Bay City, Michigan since graduation. Randolph and Debra have three children: Amy born in 1978, Nathaniel born in 1980 and Jennifer born in 1982. Currently, Amy lives and works in Chicago, Illinois. Nathan and Jennifer are still living at home and are attending college.

Son Bruce Edward was born on July 10, 1956 and attended Hale Area Schools. He lived in Hale until after college graduation and was married to Ann Marie Thrall in 1976. After working out of the area for a short time, Bruce and family returned to Hale and have lived there since. They currently live north and west of Hale on Loon Lake. After working in the family business for many years, Bruce recently purchased it with his two brothers. Bruce and Ann have two children, Christopher Alan born in 1977 and Douglas Aaron born in 1979. They both attended Hale Area Schools. Chris and Doug have also joined the family business and currently work in sales. Doug is engaged to Julie Gibson and they are to be married on August 3, 2002.

Son Bryon Arnold was born on January 27, 1960 and attended Hale Area Schools. After graduation from college, he joined the family business. After working there many years, Bryon recently became part owner with his two brothers. He married Susan Kay Ruckle in 1987 and they have one child, Kaylee Lorraine Ruckle-Bernard born in 1997. Kaylee will be attending Hale Area Schools this fall. Bryon and family currently live one and one half miles south and one mile east of Hale.

Son Daryn Jay was born on May 3, 1961 and attended Hale Area Schools. He worked elsewhere for a short time after graduation, then joined the family business. After working there for many years, Daryn has become part owner with his two brothers. Daryn married Melissa Helen Clayton in 1982 and they have two children. Angelique Erica was born in 1983 and is currently attending college. Antoni Michael was born in 1985 and will be a junior in high school this fall. Both Angelique and Antoni work summers in the family business. Daryn and family currently live four and one half miles south of Hale on State Road.

Berk and Beatty recently sold Bernard Building Center to their sons and have retired. Berk enjoys his favorite hobby of working with wood and Beatty is active in community service. They will celebrate 48 years of marriage on July 11, 2002.

BERRY/LAFRAMBOISE FAMILY.
Henry Berry (nee Nere LaFramboise) was born in. Quebec, Canada, on June 9, 1851, and as a young man, like many of his countrymen, came "west" in search of opportunity in the United States. Alvina Filion, also Canadian born (1857), met this young Frenchman in her widowed mother's boarding home where she waited tables, and in 1874 the young couple were married at James Church in Bay City.

Henry built the family home in 1876 at 109 Pearl Street Ad all but one of the 17 children born to the couple arrived at what is still the "Berry House" in Oscoda. The oldest son was also born in Oscoda, so all claimed Oscoda as their birthplace.

Mr. Berry was a hardworking man and soon had progressed from laborer to millwright to master carpenter and in the last capacity could number among his building credits the new dock, built after the July 11, 1911 fire, and Van Ettan Lake Lodge the same year. He built the old Oscoda Inn,

later renamed the Welcome Hotel, the Iosco County Bank, later known as the Oscoda State Savings bank, now Myles' Insurance. When the dams were constructed along the AuSable River, Berry Senior built many of the temporary homes at Foote Site in addition to the gas station, theatre and grocery store there. Sons Ernest and Cleophas contracted to build four houses at Five Channels dam site and two houses at Loud Dam. Another son, Emory J., served as camp cook on many of these power company dam site jobs.

The Berry home is still in the immediate family, now owned by William and Marjorie Hallas Bailey, daughter of Florence Berry Hallas.

Alvina died in April 1911, the year of the big fire. In June of 1926 thirteen children gathered at the Berry home to celebrate Henry's 75th birthday. Seated around the birthday dinner table in order of their ages were Charles, Cleophas, Arthur, Leo, Sam, Ernest, Rex, Louis, Eugene, Florence, Josephine, Lillian, and Emory. Two feature events of that 1926 reunion were recounted in the Oscoda Press. Charlie, the eldest, noted for his boxing abilities and classed at that time with Kid LaVigne and Battling Nelson with whom he'd fought to a draw, was matched with his brother Rex who had done some boxing in Canada, Sudbury being his home, and the two brothers put on a fine show of "...two rounds of skillful but fast and furious mixing which was pronounced a draw." The second feature of that June afternoon over 50 years ago was a baseball game between the Berry Boys and a team made up of old ball playing friends and classmates. From the Press: "... Henry Berry was a critical spectator of the game and proudly saw it finish with his sons the victors-16 to 18."

Henry Berry died May 12, 1932, and is buried in Sacred Heart Cemetery in Oscoda beside his wife and four infant children. Son Emory, the youngest, is the only surviving member of the family, and at 76 years of age, lives in Dearborn, Michigan. Baisel Berry, son of Cleophas, lives in Oscoda and, like his father and grandfather, is a successful builder.

During the past several years, Emory, Marjorie, and recently Baisel have passed on but many in the family visit Oscoda, some regularly on summer vacation. Bill Bailey still lives in the old family home. In July 1991 a large family reunion was held complete with a commemorative ballgame and the sharing of family stories with members from all over Canada, Ohio and Michigan. Both family names are still in common usage.

FRANZ RUDOLPH "FRANK" and MARGARET (KRUMM) BERTSCH.
Frank was one of four children born to August and Lena (Korner) Bertsch, both were born in Germany. Their children were orphaned at an early age and Frank was sent to live with relatives in Reese, Michigan.

Frank returned to Tawas City to find work, and on April 4, 1922 was employed by the Detroit and Mackinac Railway Company until his retirement.

Frank married Margaret Martha Krumm on September 4, 1927. They had two children, Frank Richard "Dick" and Mary Catherine.

Margaret's grandparents, the Ernst Shoenbeck's walked across the ice from Port Huron to settle in East Tawas. In 1877 Ernst helped organize The Emanuel Lutheran Church in Tawas City. Both Frank and Margaret were active in the Church until their deaths.

Frank loved to rabbit hunt and garden. He planned his garden all winter, looking in all of the seed catalogs. The produce was abundant and the excess was sold to local housewives who ordered bushels of tomatoes for canning.

Frank's passion was the Detroit Tigers and win or lose he was one of their greatest fans. A trip to Detroit to see a game was something to anticipate for weeks.

Margaret was a homemaker except for working as a welder at the gas mask factory during World II and the Midas Truck Stop for a short time. Margaret was an excellent baker and her cinnamon rolls and butterhorns could be smelled for blocks when she baked. Her grandsons, Richard "Rick" and Rod Bertsch, teased her that they could smell them baking in school five blocks away. Margaret love to play cards and Bingo.

KENNETH and GENEVIEVE (LOVELACE) BIRDSEY.

Kenneth (born 1904, died 1978) was born in Detroit, and used to summer at the Birdsey cottage on Van Etten lake every summer when he and his sister Virginia (later, Hans) were children. Around 1946, Kenneth, his oldest son, Gordon, and Ken's mother, Ann Birdsey, became full time residents in Oscoda. Kenneth moved a log cabin on South US23, to the corner of Lake and Bank streets, and built six small cabins to rent out. The Holiday Cabins remain to this day.

Genevieve Lovelace (born 1920, died 1980) was born in Coleman, Michigan. Her father and mother, John and Mary Lovelace, moved to Oscoda in 1929 during the depression. John helped Mr. Loud build their lodge on the island on Van Etten Lake and paid John with property on Loud Drive. Genevieve went to grade school in the one-room school house near the Indian Reservation, west of F41. She had to cross over the Pine River on her long walk there. Sometimes the boat was on the other side, and she had to wade! After there were school buses, her bus driver, Bill McQuaig, used to meet her when there was deep snow, and let her walk in his footprints. Eventually, County Line road was better, and made life easier for all. Gen graduated from Oscoda High in 1939. Gen, like the male members of her family, was excellent with the rifle, and could provide game for the family. Genevieve met her first husband, Harvey Davis, at a dance held at the Grand Ballroom on Mackinaw Island. They married and settled in Detroit. They were only married six years, for Harvey caught tuberculosis during the 1940s. Genevieve moved her husband, and  three children, William, Harvey, and Sue to Oscoda. After Harvey's death, Genevieve worked at Sie and Gert's, a restaurant in Oscoda, where she met Kenneth.

Ken and Gen were married in 1950. All six of them, including Gayle, in 1951, lived in the log cabin, until Ken finished building their Bank street house. Gen ran the Holiday Cabins, and Ken worked at Eymer and Duchane's (ACE) Hardware. Ken built a new house on Harbor Street next to the Matthews fishery, where they all moved

in 1958. The cabins were sold, and Ken worked as a building contractor, including homes in Lakewood Shores, and the Oscoda Yacht Club, where he became the club's first Commodore. He was a volunteer fireman and served on the school board. Ken was involved in planning for the new peer of the AuSable river, the canoe and drag boat races, placing river buoys for the coast guard, and at the time of his death in 1978, was AuSable's building inspector. Gen, was a leader at St. John's Episcopal church, over 25 years. She worked in retail, and in real estate until her death in 1980.

Their children, Bill (Kathy Lockhart), Harvey (Sue Cook), Sue (Dave Sims) and Gayle (Mike), Gordon (Dorothy Spain) and Marilyn (Birdsey) Marshall survive. Only Gayle lives in Oscoda at present.

AUGUST and AUGUSTA (HOLCKART) BOROWSKI.

August Borowski was born June 4, 1831, Augusta (maiden name Holckart) was born November 6, 1823. It is believed they were born and raised in Garnsee, Graudenz, West Prussia, Germany, now a part of Poland. Graudenz is now Grudziadz. They arrived in Tawas City about 1883.

August and Augusta Borowski were the parents of four children that married and lived in Tawas. Emilie, born October 23, 1860 later married Albert Timreck on March 30, 1884 in Tawas, Augusta, born July 24, 1864 later married Julius Bucholz on November 2, 1884 in Tawas, Paulino, born March 12, 1866 in Garenseedorf, later married George Christian Anschultz on September 28, 1885 in Tawas, and Hermine, born April 13, 1871, later married Julius Robert Killian on October 28, 1888 in Tawas City. Census records show that August was a farmer.

The Borowski name is spelled quite different on the various documents. Even on their gravestone it is spelled Barowski. On the 1894 census it is shown as Burski or Borski, and frequent documents it is Borovski. Although the 1894 census indicated they lived in the United States 11 years, the exact date or the ship they arrived on is unknown.

August Borowski died on November 23, 1920 in Detroit and was living with his daughter Emilie and son-in-law Albert Timreck at 20 Rankin Avenue in Detroit at that time.

Augusta Borowski died in Tawas on July 16, 1898. Augusta, is shown as Gusta on the 1894 census. On her death certificate it shows she was the mother of 13 children, 4 of which were living! These four, previously mentioned, are the only four with record living in the Tawas Area. The other nine most likely lived and/or died in Germany. Search of records of the Latter Day Saints produced no results. Her children, except Hermine, are all buried in Tawas in either the Emanual Lutheran Church or Zion Lutheran Church cemeteries. August and Augusta are buried in the Emanual Lutheran Church section of Memorial Gardens Cemetery.

Hermine Borowski married Julius Killian and were the parents of 12 children including a stillborn son. The children, Maurice born August 1, 1889; Eugenie "Jennie" August 25, 1891; Alex born February 11, 1893; Lydia born June 11, 1894; George born October 13, 1895; Elmer born July 13, 1897; stillborn son born on December 13, 1898; Meta born February 9, 1900; Walter born February 24, 1902; Margareta born January 6, 1905; Carl born May 18, 1907; and Chester born June 2, 1909. All of the children were raised in Tawas.

Julius Killian died on January 10, 1925 in Detroit, Michigan and Hermine Killian died on March 11, 1941 in Detroit. Along with three of their children they are buried in the Evergreen Cemetery in Detroit, Michigan.

More information on Hermine can be found on the biography of Albert and Amalia Kilian, including her picture with her husband and six of their children.

KARL BUESCHEN.

Karl was born in Germany and came to the United States at the age of 15 years. He went to Toledo, Ohio to be near relatives and went to work in a meat packing shop. (butcher shop).

On April 19, 1911 he married Minnie Oehus, she was also from Germany and had moved to Ohio. Shortly after their marriage they came to Iosco County and settled in Reno Township, Section I where they purchased 280 acres in Reno Township and 640 acres in Grant Township. Trees had been cleared, but stumps had to be removed before they could build or farm. Dynamite was used and stump machines pulled by horses/oxen.

In 1914 a large barn was built and

several smaller ones, sheep shed, pig barn and tool shed. Down through the years more land was cleared and silo's built. Many cattle and sheep grazed on the pasture land.

There were many changes over the year. Roads were bad, horses were the main means of transportation. The D & M railroad came from Tawas, Emery Junction, Taft, Hale and Rose City. This line went out about 1929.

Towerline Road was the main road north to Hale and south to Reno Cemetery then west to join M-65 near the AuGres River, and south to Whittemore. There was no electricity in the area until 1935.

The Bueschens had five girls. Martha the oldest (died at a very young age), the other girls were Alma, Hilda, Ella and Wilma and they helped on the farm, milking cows, making hay and whatever needed to be done.

In 1927 the original house was jacked up to put in a basement. They had a bad storm which was thought to be a tornado. It was very frightening, but all were safe.

In August of 1945 several of the barns burned and dad decided to sell the farm and do some other kind of work The farm was sold to a Mr. Ulrich. Dad stayed on for a year, then moved to a place on M-65 by the AuGres River.

The Bueschen daughters married over the years. Alma married Arlie Sherman, Hilda married Joe Barnes, Ella married Warren Britt and Wilma married Howard Britt.

Minnie passed away in 1960 and Karl in 1967. Their daughter Alma died in the year 2000. The other three girls still live in Iosco County. *Submitted by his daughter, Hilda (Bueschen) Barnes-Soper.*

BURDETT FAMILY. Howard William Burdett and Mary Jane Green Burdett first purchased land on Lake Huron in Baldwin Township in 1966. They moved there from Rochester, New York in 1967 living in unwinterized summer cabins on the property until the completion of their first house in 1968. Howard W. Burdett descends from a family that arrived in the Virginia Colony from England in the early 1700s and migrated westward across Virginia to the Ohio River. He was born in Parkersburg, West Virginia in 1939. The Green family ancestors of Mary Jane Green Burdett were Quakers who arrived in Pennsylvania from England in 1686. This line migrated to Georgia then to Ohio and finally arrived in the Michigan Territory in 1833. Other of Mary Jane's ancestors came to Jamestown

and four were among the Pilgrims on the Mayflower. Her maternal grandmother was born in Scotland immigrating to Kalamazoo County, Michigan in 1871. Mary Jane was born in Dearborn, Michigan in 1938.

From 1968 until 1976 Howard and Mary Jane Burdett resided in their Baldwin Township home and participated in church and community activities. Howard served as a Trustee of Baldwin Township and was a member of and ultimately chaired the Iosco County Planning Commission. He also chaired the Building Committee of the Tawas United Methodist Church during the building program that resulted in the church's current building on M-55 in Tawas City. Mary Jane was elected a Commissioner of Iosco County, the first woman ever to be so elected. She served as Vice Chair and ultimately Chair of the Board of Commissioners. During her term as County Commissioner, Mary Jane gave birth to Cristina Jean Burdett and Howard William "Bill" Burdett, Jr.

In 1976 Howard's employment in the Finance Department of The Dow Chemical Company took the family to Hong Kong for four years, which necessitated the sale of their Baldwin Township home. While on home leave to Iosco County in 1977 they found a parcel of land in AuSable Township, which they purchased in 1978. The following year they began construction of a home on this site and occupied it upon their return from Hong Kong in 1980.

In the fall of 1980 Cristina Jean Burdett began kindergarten in the Oscoda Area School system. Cristina's brother, Bill Burdett, followed in 1981. Both Cristina and Bill completed all of their primary and secondary schooling in the Oscoda Area system. Cristina, graduated in 1993 as salutatorian of her class and Bill graduated in 1994 as valedictorian of his class. Both of them went on to Yale University in New Haven, Connecticut. In 1993 and again in 1994, Bill Burdett and his partner, Beau Kilmer, representing Oscoda Area High School, won the MIFA State Championship for Class B schools in policy debate.

Upon their return from Hong Kong, Howard and Mary Jane Burdett resumed their participation in church and community activities. Howard served on the Board of Trustees of the Tawas St. Joseph Hospital and was the initial chairman of the AuSable Valley Community Mental Health Foundation. Mary Jane founded and for 10 years was the president of Tawas FISH, an interdenominational church sponsored organization having the mission to help those in need in the Tawas Area.

In September 1980 Howard's parents, Delbert Foster Burdett Jr. and Margaret Elaine Keener Burdett, moved from Cincinnati, Ohio to Oscoda where they resided for the remainder of their lives. Delbert F. Burdett died in Oscoda in 1981 and Margaret Keener Burdett died in Tawas City in 1992. They are both interred in Pinecrest Cemetery in AuSable Township. Mary Jane's mother, Dorothy Taft Green, widow of Maurice Warner Green, resided with the Burdett family until her death in Tawas City in 1991. She is buried in the Green family plot in South Wayne Cemetery, Wayne Township, Cass County, Michigan.

Howard W. Burdett, Mary Jane Green Burdett, Cristina Jean Burdett, Erik William "Bill" Burdett Jr. at 1997 Wedding of Cristina and Erik in Tawas United Methodist Church, Tawas City.

Cristina Jean Burdett married Erik Michael Lien at the Tawas United Methodist Church in 1997 and has moved to St. Paul, Minnesota. Bill Burdett upon graduation from Yale attended the University of Michigan Law School and is practicing law in Detroit.

LOUISE EUGENIA BURGESON and OTTO PAUL ERNST. Louise was born on the Baldwin Township farm of her parents, on August 18, 1903. Her father, John Burgeson, born in Varberg, Sweden on December 13, 1862, had come to America alone at age 17. He worked his way west on construction crews building railroad tunnels, ultimately arriving in Oscoda, Michigan, where he worked 6 days a week as a logger. In 1886 he purchased 40 acres of timber cutover land (which became the family farm) in Baldwin Township, using a rented team of oxen on his Sunday day off to pull stumps. John roomed in AuSable Township with the Swedish immigrant family of Aaron and Johanna Alstrom (aka Ahlstrom), who had a daughter, Ida Sophia, born April 5, 1872. Ida Sophia and John were married on March 8, 1889, and lived on the farm they established until their deaths in 1943 and 1961, respectively.

The sixth of 10 children (Amelia, Ida, Emma, Carl, Edith, Louise, Nels, Edward,

Alice and Jennie), Louise walked a mile from home to attend a one-room school at the corner of Monument and Bischoff Roads (now the Baldwin Township Hall). After the 8th grade she went to the Tawas City High School, boarding with a classmate on school days during the winter months. As a senior, she was the captain of her undefeated state championship high school basketball team. She then attended Ypsilanti State Normal College for teachers, and moved to Detroit, where she taught 8th grade physical education and coached her boys basketball team to a city championship.

John and Ida Alstrom Burgeson family (Louise at far left in top row)

While in Detroit, she met Otto Paul Ernst (born in Manchester, Michigan, November 16, 1898), who was then a salesman for Swift Packing Company. Louise and Otto were married on Groundhogs Day, February 2, 1933, during the depth of the depression. While Louise continued teaching to provide a paycheck, Otto and three friends decided to go into the wholesale meat business for themselves, forming Metropolitan Restaurant and Hotel Supply Company on the Eastern Market in Detroit. Vital to the success of the enterprise was a cash loan from Louise' father, John Burgeson. Having had a premonition regarding bank security, John Burgeson had withdrawn all his savings from the local bank just days before the national "bank holiday," and was one of the few persons at that time fortunate to have available money. Louise's charm and concern for others were important factors in Otto's business success. Louise and Otto had two sons, John Richard, born May 28, 1936, and Robert Edward, born July 12, 1939, both in Detroit, Michigan.

Son Robert Edward was married on January 16, 1965, to Nancy MacDuff, of Mt. Clemens, Michigan, and they, in turn, had two sons, Robert Edward Jr., born July 8, 1968, and Gregory Bachor, born May 10, 1971. After gaining experience in the wholesale meat business working for others, Robert went into business for himself in 1966, aided by the tutelage of his father and office assistance from his mother, and

Aunt Alice and Uncle Joe Felts. Robert Jr. married Kiristin Mary Duffiney, on March 17, 2000, and they have two children, Alexandria Lynn, born November 5, 2000, and Gabrielle Alyssa, born November 22, 2002. Gregory married Nicole Marie Shankie on May 17, 1997, and they have one son, Drake Alexander, born September 5, 2000.

Son John Richard was married on September 8, 1962 to Janet Lee Mohr of Brooklyn, Michigan (born in Lake Odessa, Michigan, February 23, 1938), when J. Richard was a student at the University of Michigan Law School. J. Richard and Janet moved to Iosco County in September 1964, when Richard was the unopposed candidate for county prosecuting attorney. He was the first Iosco County District Judge, elected in 1968, and was appointed to the Circuit Court bench by Governor Milliken on October 20, 1980, where he continues to serve to the present. Richard and Janet have three children: Matthew Edward, born November 24, 1967; Julia Louise, born May 27, 1969; and Andrew Jerome, born June 18, 1971. Matthew married Ellen I. Hiotaky on October 12, 1991. They have three children: Kara Elizabeth, born September 1, 1995; John "Jack" William, born January 14, 1997; and Stephen Markus, born July 21, 1999. Andrew married Lisa Semple, of Sandusky, Ohio, on October 7, __. They have two sons, Otto Paul, born September 9, 1998, and Joseph Vinton, born October 28, 2002. Julia married Richard Henri Clement of North Bay, Ontario, on August 31, 1998, on Mackinaw Island, Michigan.

One of Louise' most cherished childhood memories was helping her mother preserve fruits and vegetables and cook and bake for the family on the old kitchen wood stove. Less fond recollections included the times spent pulling wild mustard and picking potato bugs in the fields. (She has confessed to talking the kids on the neighboring farm into giving her the bugs they collected so it would appear to her father that she had really been working.) Returning to the farm, together with several sisters, to help cook when the threshers came was an annual event; the meals served to the men on such occasions were renown throughout the county. Throughout her lifetime she remained devoted to her parents until their deaths, and to the family farm which she cared so much for, and which still remains in the family today.

LOIS CARMICHAEL (1928-). I was born in Hazel Park, Michigan. My connection to Iosco County is from my father's side of the family. His sister Edith Erle and

her husband Vern lived on this farm with their only child, Muriel. I loved visiting them there in the country. They had cattle, sheep and turkeys, apple trees and a garden. My Aunt Edith cooked on a wood-burning stove. She canned her meat, fruit and vegetables. My Uncle Vern made sure I had a swing ride out of the barn door. The rope on the swing, hung from the highest rafter in the barn. The barn has a barn hill, so I was already high up before I went flying out of the barn. I was really glad when the ride was over and my feet were on the floor. The outhouse was a little far from the house. But there was a white enameled pot with a lid on it under the bed at night.

JAMES and CATHERINE (MCDONALD) CATALINE. James (born 1822 in Canada, died 1899) married Catherine McDonald (born 1827, died 1896) of Ireland. They came to Michigan in 1858, settling first in Huron County; the day before Thanksgiving in 1893, he migrated further to Iosco County. James and Catherine had six children, five living to adulthood: James Leslie (born 1849, died 1929); Hester "Annie" (born 1852, died 1935); Thomas "Adam" (born 1856, died __); John (born 1858, died __); Adolphus (born 1860, died __); and Jennie (born 1866, died 1948). The two girls stayed in Huron County; Annie married John Murphy and Jennie married Will Scott. Adam and John married sisters, Sarah and Allice Hurford (born 1862, died 1886).

Back, l-r: Jesse Chase, Durin Cataline, Sadie Whitford Cataline, Martin Cataline, George Jackson, Frances Cataline Jackson. Middle, l-r: Almeda Cataline, Sarah Cataline Chase, James L. Cataline, Emily Williams Cataline. Ground, l-r: Adelbert Cataline, Clio Cataline, Acial Cataline, Leslie Cataline

Adam and Sarah married in 1880 and had two children, May and Alger. John and Allie had two children, Dolphas and Kattie. Allie died during childbirth and Kattie died four months later. John later married Viola Godwin. Adolphus first married Annie Campbell (born 1862, died 1897). They had three children: Shubeal, Benton and Sterling "Shod." After Annie died, Adolphus married Lucy Shepherd and had a son, Glen. James L. married Emily Williams (born 1852, died 1921) on April 25, 1871 in Newburg, Michigan. They had five children: Durin (born 1872, died 1957), Sarah (born 1873, died 1956), Martin (born 1886, died 1954), Herbie (born 1879, died 1883), and Frances "Frankie" (born 1890, died 1971).

Durin and Sarah married a sister and brother, Bertha Chase (born 1881, died 1907) and Jesse (born 1873, died 1954).

Durin and Bertha had five children, four surviving: Gertie (born 1899, died 1900), Adelbert "Delbert" (born 1904, died 1986), Almeda (born 1906, died 1997), and Leslie (born 1907, died 1995). Bertha died when Leslie was three weeks old. Delbert and Almeda went to live with Jesse and Sarah, who had no children of their own, and Leslie was taken by James and Emily.

Durin later married Minnie (Hamilton) Beadle. Minnie had two daughters from a previous marriage, and one daughter, Ulene, with Durin. Durin married Alma (Chipps) Bronson after Minnie died.

Martin married Sadie Whitford (born 1881, died 1968). They had two children: Acial (born 1905, died 1983) and Clio (born 1907, died 1988). Acial settled in Holt and had two children, Robert and Beth. Clio settled in Lansing and had three children: Jean, Dolores and Larry.

Frankie married George Jackson (born 1884, died 1960). George was born in London, England. He came to Michigan at the age of 12, leaving his parents and at least one sister. George resided with the Curtis family, Mrs. Curtis being his aunt. George and Frankie had no children of their own, but took in Leslie when Emily died. George was a schoolteacher in Whittemore for many years, also leading various scout troops and was very involved with the Masons and other local organizations.

Delbert married Chistina Wolters and had two daughters, Gertrude and Bernice. Bernice has three daughters. Almeda married Lewis VanWyck and had one daughter, Evelyn. Lew and Almeda settled in East Tawas. Leslie (born 1907, died 1995) moved to Lansing with Frankie and George and married Sarah Leach (born 1910, died 1998) in March 1926. They had four boys: James (born 1927) William (born 1932), Richard (born 1935) and Ronald (born 1937, died 1995). These four were raised in Eaton Rapids, William lives in East Tawas at this time. Ulene married Arthur Goupil and settled in the Houghton Lake area and had four sons: Gary, Dean, Arnold and Rick.

ADELBERT and ALMEDA (CREGO) CHASE.

Adelbert was born Oct. 2, 1846 in Hawkinsville, New York to Rev. Orrin W. Chase and Martha Parker. He joined the Union Army in New York and was in the 189th Volunteer Infantry, Company K. Adelbert's company was present at General Lee's surrender, soon after which, he was discharged. On June 9, 1869, Adelbert married Almeda Crego. Almeda was born in Hawkinsville October 27, 1852. Adelbert was a farmer, both in New York and in Michigan. Due to an illness contracted during the war, Adelbert was never a physically healthy person.

Adelbert and Almeda had two children, Jesse W. and Bertha May. Jesse was born August 3, 1873 in Hawkinsville, New York. He married Sarah Anna Cataline, daughter of James L. and Emily (Williams) Cataline, on May 24, 1898, in Tawas City. Jesse and Sarah never had children of their own, but did raise Adelbert and Almeda Cataline. They also lived on and worked the farm for his father.

l-r: Jesse W. Chase, Almeda Cataline, Almeda Chase, Adelbert Chase, Sarah Cataline Chase, Adelbert Cataline

Bertha was born January 26, 1881 in Hawkinsville, New York. She married Durin Cataline on July 2, 1898, in Tawas City. (Durin is Sarah's older brother.) Bertha had five children. One child lived only two days. They had Gertie May (born 1899, died 1900 before her first birthday), Adelbert James (born 1904, died 1986), Almeda Emily (born 1906, died 1997) and Leslie Wilbur (born 1907, died 1995). Bertha died August 5, 1907. When Bertha died, Leslie went to live with his Grandpa and Grandma Cataline.

Delbert married Christina Wolters and had two children, Gertrude and Bernice. Gertrude had no children, but Bernice had three daughters. Almeda married Lewis VanWyck and had one daughter, Evelyn. Evelyn had eight children. She currently resides in Lincoln Park, Michigan. Almeda and Lew were lifetime residents of East Tawas.

Leslie went to live with an aunt and uncle after his grandmother died. He moved to Lansing with them, where he married Sar-

ah Leach (born 1910, died 1998) in March of 1926. They had four sons: James (born 1927), William (born 1932), Richard (born 1935) and Ronald (born 1937, died 1995). The four boys were raised in Eaton Rapids, where two of them currently reside. William is currently residing in East Tawas

CHIRKO FAMILY.

Joseph W. Chirko (born 1915-2002), son of Joseph P. and Amelia Chirko, who emigrated from Russia, and Lucina Pagel (born 1919-2002), daughter of Benjamin S. and Una Locke Pagel, were married January 26, 1946, in Detroit Michigan. They lived in Harper Woods, Michigan, for 27 years.

Joe worked for the Detroit Edison Company for 38 years as a mechanical engineer in power plant pipe design and stress analysis and then as supervisor on the Nuclear Power Plant-Fermi 2, at Monroe, Michigan. Lucina served on the Harper Woods School Board for 16 years, the Wayne County School Board Association for 10 years, the National School Board Association Public Relations Board and the Wayne County Tax Allocation Board. Both were active in many community projects.

The Pagel cottage, built in 1929, paid for by Grandfather Locke, was deeded to my sister and me in 1949. In 1971, we bought my sister's interest and on retirement in 1975, moved to East Tawas. Our son-in-law, John A. Webb II, remodeled part of the cottage for our permanent residence.

We have four children:

1) Joseph Michael (born 1948-) graduated from Bowling Green University and earned his MA from the University of Arkansas. He was a pro caddy for Mark Haynes for three years. In 1978 Joseph married Miriam Wells (born in England and reared in Texas) in 1978 and they live in Houston, Texas.

2) Charles Pagel (Todd) (born 1949-), a U.S. Air Force Academy graduate and C-130 navigator in the Orient in the 1970s. He is now teaching at the U.S. Air Force Academy. Charles married SuTzen from Taichung, Taiwan and is now divorced. They have a son, Jason Pagel (born 1976).

3) Dianne Beth (born 1951-) graduated from Wayne State University and MA from Michigan State. She married John A. Webb II. Dianne is a supervisor for Child and Family Services serving the northeast section of lower Michigan. John teaches in the Tawas area schools and is a licensed builder. He built their beautiful home in Lakewood Shores, Oscoda, Michigan.

4) Suzanne Kay (born 1953-) graduated from University of Wisconsin-Stout, mar-

ried Ralph Hartsworm from King, Wisconsin. They live in Waterville, Ohio. Ralph is with Prudential Life Insurance and Sue with State of Ohio Social Services.

From my childhood, I have wonderful memories of summers in East Tawas, such as:

•Taking 12 hours in an old touring car, picnic lunches, flat tires and much dust to drive from Detroit on gravel roads to reach East Tawas.

•Our cottage was built in 1929. Mr. Nellem was the builder. Beams for the living room were brought in from the woods by Al Norris, manager of the Tawas Beach Association. Concrete window slabs from the old Tawas Sugar Beet Factory are still on our property.

•Nelt Sims, a hermit, and his dog Towser, lived on Lake Huron near Bay to Lake Drive. He walked to town weekly for supplies. We enjoyed his company and had picnics at his place on Lake Huron. Nelt Sims died while at the Iosco County Poor House.

•The sand roads on the plains leading to Sand Lake where we went to see the Indians who came to camp there.

•Iargo Springs before and after the CCC boys improved the area.

•Climbing to the top of the lighthouse—what a thrill.

•Going to farms with my mother - Nelkie's for churned butter and milk with cream on the top, Dimmick's for eggs and many others, for vegetables.

•Rushing to Elmer Kunze when our dog met a porcupine.

•Being stranded on Tawas Bay when the Lixey Fishing Boats came in from their nets and being towed ashore.

•The hikes in the woods, picking berries and oh, the poison ivy!

Now living in East Tawas, we love the summers, the fall with the color, the winter and the wonderful cross country skiing at Corsair and the Monument area, and the spring with all of its beauty. *Submitted by Lucina Jane Chirko.*

CHARLES and JOHANNA (GAUL) CONKLIN. Charles was born April 17, 1887 in East Tawas to Thomas and Mary Ann Conklin who came to this area from Niagara County, New York. Charles had two brothers, Ray and Fred. Thomas owned and operated the Conklin Grocery and Feed Store at the corner of Newman and West Westover Streets in East Tawas until around 1900 when Lorenz Klenow took over the business known to this day as Klenow's Market.

Charles married Johanna Gaul, daughter of Fred and Caroline Gaul of Tawas City on August 20, 1914. One daughter, Margaret Mae died at birth in 1919. In the 30s, Johanna built and operated Conklin's Greenhouse, now known as Moehring's Greenhouse, on West Westover Street in East Tawas. In 1940, Johanna's nephew, Herman Moehring entered the business which today is owned and operated by his son, John Moehring.

Charles Conklin watering plants at Conklin's Greenhouse on West Westover Street in East Tawas (around 1935)

The Conklins first lived at 304 W. Westover, where the Moehrings took up residence in 1940. Leslie Nash constructed a new brick home for the Conklins on the corner of West Westover and Locke Streets.

Charles was employed as a bookkeeper at the Detroit and Mackinaw Railway. In those days, he walked to and from work. The exact times signaled by four whistles—one at eight o'clock, noon, one o'clock, and five o'clock.

Charles was a member of the Masonic Lodge, and he and Johanna were members of the East Tawas Methodist Church.

Johanna died in 1953, and Charles in 1959. They are buried in Evergreen Cemetery, East Tawas, next to Thomas and Mary Ann Conklin.

EDWARD and VIRGINIA (RISTOW) COYLE. The family owned business of Coyle's Fish and Chips was established in 1965 by Edward and Virginia (Ristow) Coyle. In its earlier days it was a fish house and Bay Gas Station built on the property owned by John Coyle, Edward's father. The Evelyn J was the family owned boat, which caught their own perch on Tawas Bay. Gill nets were used until they were banned and then the fish had to be bought at the fishery in Bayport, Michigan in the thumb and in AuGres.

The oldest of the children, Cheryl Coyle (Schley), Tom Coyle and Mike Coyle cleaned the fish and Gayle Coyle (Smith) and Kelly Coyle (Vadnais) helped in the preparation. It was a true family owned business, from cooking to waitressing to washing dishes. People would drive for miles to stand in line to wait for an all you could eat fresh perch dinner at $1.25. Good Friday was always their busiest day of the year. Homemade fudge and candy could also be purchased which was made by Bob and Bertha Trudell of Oscoda. The main cooks in the early days were Maxine Bessey, Virginia Lacassio, Ruth Gauthier and Lou Lacy. Waitresses were JoElla (Pintkowski) Cholger, Blinda (Pintkowski) Baker, Geraldine Landry, Janet (Kasischke) Bolen, Kay (Kasischke) Price, Kathy Deering and Sal Cholger, just to name a few.

Coyle's Fish and Chips

Edward Coyle passed away in 1969 and his wife Virginia and her children continued the business. The building went through numerous remodeling projects including one to repair a kitchen grease fire in 1976. The business was sold in 1978 to Dick and Liz McKenzie. The restaurant, which was located on US-23 on Lake Huron, in Tawas City has since been torn down and is now the site of the Northbay Condominium project. Virginia and her children along with their famlies still reside in the Tawas area with Cheryl Coyle (Schley) and family residing in Madison Heights.

CHARLES MARTIN CURRY, DVM. Charles was born on the Curry farm southeast of Mason in Bunkerhill Township, Ingham County, MI on September 23, 1883, the son of Harvey Manning Curry (born 1855, died 1913) and Nancy Maria Potter (born 1856, died 1931), and grandson of the Rev. Volney Manning Curry (born 1815, died 1864) and Amy Putnam May (born 1822, died 1894). He married Lutie Irene Paulger (born 1881, died 1961) of Farmington at Detroit on June 4, 1908 at the home of her mother, Mary Eliza Ely-Paulger (born 1862, died 1924) on Vinewood Avenue. They were the parents of three children: Charles Harvey Curry (born 1909, died 1979) of Long Lake; Volney Manning Curry (born 1910, died 1976) of Lansing and Mary Elizabeth Curry (born 1912, died 1980) of Commerce, the wife of Ralph M. Keller Sr. (born 1910, died 1965). Dr. Curry received his early education at the Birney School and Dansville High School.

After graduation from the Ontario Veterinary College at Toronto, Dr. Curry practiced briefly at Leslie, Farmington, Mason, and Midland before settling in Bay City in 1910 at 509 N. Johnson, just down the street from his real estate entrepreneur brother, Volney Manning Curry (born 1881, died 1954) also DVM. In addition to his veterinary practice he owned a livery stable, later an automobile garage, in downtown Bay City just south of the noted Winona Hotel.

He and Mrs. Curry were members of First Presbyterian Church, the Masons and Eastern Star. In 1921 the Currys bought a house at Long Lake, after previously spending summer vacations at Sage Lake and Sand Lake. At the advent of World War II, Dr. and Mrs. Curry rented their home in Bay City and moved permanently to Long Lake. They participated in village activities, helping to found the Sixty Lakes Club.

Dr. Curry greatly enjoyed the outdoors, and was an avid hunter and fisherman. Mrs. Curry was skilled at "fancy" work, spending many hours working at embroidery, crocheting, and tatting: in fact, she sold her handiwork, earning $1,000 with which she purchased the five bedroom cottage at Long Lake. Both Dr. and Mrs. Curry loved to garden and to can fruits and vegetables. His specialties were garlic dill pickles and venison, and hers were peaches and apple sauce. They also greatly enjoyed playing cards: his favorite game was cribbage and hers was bridge. Having played semi-professional baseball as a young man, Charles was a lifelong fan of the Detroit Tigers.

After suffering a stroke he died at Tolfree Hospital in West Branch on March 26, 1964 and was buried next to his wife in the family cemetery at Felt Plains, Ingham County, MI near his birth place. He was survived by his three children and five grandchildren: Ralph M. Keller Jr., Susan I. Keller-Tussing, Julia E. Keller-Pipkin-Antonelli, John C. Curry, and Janet T. Curry-Brown. The house at 8612 Front Street, Long Lake is still owned by the family after 80 years.

DELOSH FAMILY. Great-great-grandfather, Isodore DeLosh, came from France and settled in Canada. He married Jane Daily and moved to Monroe, Michigan where this writer's great-grandfather, Joseph, was born April 5, 1857 and died May 1, 1940. He married Hannah Poole (born 1862, died 1884) and had three children. Joseph remarried Augusta Holmstron (born 1864, died 1924) and had eight children, one being this writer's grandfather, Claude (born in Breckenridge, Michigan November 17, 1890, died May 3, 1972). They moved to the Turner

area and in 1907 he married Rena Shotwell (born July 7, 1890, died January 28, 1957) and they had 11 children.

William (writer's father) was born Septem-

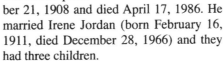

ber 21, 1908 and died April 17, 1986. He married Irene Jordan (born February 16, 1911, died December 28, 1966) and they had three children.

Flora (born May 16, 1910, died September 21, 1999) married Joseph Roberts (born September 21, 1913, died August 24, 1997). No issue.

Annie (born September 12, 1914, died May 22, 1973) married Morris Gupton and they had one child.

Herman Joseph (born September 17, 1916, died December 21, 1996) married Jean Pipesh and they had two children.

Blanche (born January 14, 1918, died October 27, 1996) married Arthur DeLoge and they had six children.

Harold (born October 20, 1920, died November 28, 1973) married Irene Rivet (born December 11, 1927, died January 2, 1981). No issue.

Dewilda Alice (born September 3, 1923) married James Franks (born October 14, 1917, died November 19, 1990) and they had seven children.

Clarence (born March 28, 1926, died October 22, 1922) married Rose Boyer and they had four children.

Maxim (born October 6, 1927, died July 18, 1994) married Betty Smith and they had four children.

Harry (born June 13, 1930, died April 27, 1951) married Earlene Riley. No issue.

Norma (born October 30, 1932) married Harold Moser and they had three children.

Claude started work at US Gypsum in Alabaster working in the quarry April 25, 1914. In 1922 he was made a master mechanic in charge of maintenance, plant's building, tranway and marine loader. He was considered an expert on the tranway which carries the gypsum rock from shore to the crib. The crib opened for the first ship in July 1929. It took 36 hours to load a ship. The operation in later years took about 10 hours. Once the traction cable broke, dumping 18 buckets from the tramway into the deepest waters. He recalled that nine became tangled in one section and each time the work crew hooked one, the weight of those attached to it prevented pulling it up.

Claude established quite a reputation as a catcher for the company baseball team, one of the best in the area for many years. He told of traveling to Gypsum, OH to meet the company team from that plant. The Alabaster team lost 3-2 while their spirits were raised on the train ride home, only to find six of the opposing players were on their way back to Detroit to resume play with the Detroit Tigers.

Claude retired having worked 50 years with US Gypsum in 1973. Newspapers state "Only two men have served as mill maintenance foreman during the past 45 years at US Gypsum, the late Claude DeLosh and his son William. Effective July 1, the latter retires, and it will be the first time in 60 years that the DeLosh name will be missing from the payroll. William completes 41 years of service. His first job, in June 1932, was a tunnel man, he then loaded a tramway buckets also working at the marine bin before becoming a mill maintenance foreman. He supervised installation of automated bucket loading equipment and rebuilding the secondary crusher. One job that Bill remembers was the time the return cable on the tramway parted and 31 buckets dropped into the Saginaw Bay, all were fished out of the water. An avid baseball player like his father, there were many fond memories of the DeLosh years in Alabaster.

JOHN and FLORENCE (GRAVES) DOOLEY. John was born May 8, 1900 to Peter Dooley and Mary (Near) Dooley in Logan Township, Ogemaw County. Florence (Graves) Dooley was born in Plainfield Township, Hale on July 20, 1901 to Elmer Graves and Maud (Soper). Florence taught school for seven

Barn

years before they were married on July 4, 1926. John worked as a carpenter while living in Birmingham before he and Florence moved to Hale. They farmed with Elmer Graves for two years until 1931 when John and Florence bought the McCory Farm which was located half a mile south of Elmer's farm on Towerline Road. John and Florence had three daughters: Ila, Alice and Wilma.

John built a barn in the Summer of 1937. He hired his uncle William Near to oversee the building of the barn (he learned this trade in Canada). Florence, with the assistance of a hired girl, Buelah (Van Wormer) Putnam, fed the crew two meals a day from her large garden.

Forms were built for the lower barn wall that would be the foundation for the entire barn.

Platforms were built along the top of the forms to walk on and work from A ramp was built to get the wheel barrels of wet cement and supplies up to the platform and then the cement would be dumped into the forms. Otto and Ross Shellenbarger were two of the men from the crew that wheeled the wet cement up the ramp. They had to start running to get up enough speed to make it up the ramp and not spill the cement. A man would stand at the top of the ramp with a hook. He would hook onto the wheel barrel to help pull it up and get it turned on the platform. After dumping the cement in the form, another man would poke the wet cement with a long pole. This was done to get out air pockets to keep the cement wall from cracking when it set. On the day of the barn raising, men came from neighboring farms to help raise the beams and rafters. Brace Shattuck walked the beams to drive wood pegs in mortise and tendons.

They had a barn dance when the barn was completed. A piano was taken up the approach to the hay floor. Many people came and the cars were parked for a mile down the road each way. I wondered as a child, how grown-ups could stay awake all night, when I was so excited and having fun and couldn't stay awake.

In the summer of 1946, Jim Wilson asked John about taking his team of horses to the Ogemaw County fairgrounds for the horse pulls. John said he had no truck to haul the horses and had a field of hay to cut. Jim told him he would have a truck the morning of the pull and be over the next day to help with the hay. The team (Fan and Bess) was purchased from Ray Parliment of West Branch, and won first place in the heavy weight pull.

John called for square dancing and enjoyed his team of horses. Florence enjoyed picking berries. Both enjoyed hunting, fishing and playing euchre. John and Florence were active in the Grange and Iosco County Fair, and were members of the Hale United Methodist Church.

JOHN RAPHAEL and PHILOMENE EUGENIE (MARTIN) DUMONT.
My grandfather, John Raphael Dumont, and my grandmother, Philomene Eugenie Martin, left Riviere-du-Loup, in Quebec (approximately 1889) and traveled to the United States looking for work. They

first stopped in Bangor, Maine and later moved on to Lowell, Massachusetts. They married on February 19, 1884.

It's believed that they had relatives in each of those areas. By 1893, the family with four living children, left

John Raphael Dumont and Philomene Eugenie Martin married Feb. 19, 1884

Lowell and traveled to the Iosco County area. Their first child born in the Oscoda area was my father Emmet Amil Dumont (born August 28, 1893). Grandpa first worked at loading ships at the docks. He later bought three 40 acre parcels of land on the banks of the Pine River. This was on the southwest corner of the river and the County Line Road. He had to clear land and build a house to live in. He earned their living selling wood products and butchering pigs and deer. He was the preferred butcher used by the Jewish families living in the area. They trusted him to observe their kosher requirements. He made many pieces of household furniture and turned out a few coonskin hats.

They had 15 children of which 12 reached adulthood. My grandmother was a tiny woman about five feet tall. She could do anything and everything a pioneer woman needed to do to feed, dress

Emmet Amil Dumont and Mary Amelia McGillis married on June 20, 1928

and care for a large family. My family is Roman Catholic and had to go to mass at Mikado by horse and buggy. Mikado is located about five miles north of the farm in Alcona County. The family had cousins living on farms nearby with the surnames of Martin and Michaud. In his late 50s, Grandpa developed cancer. He was sick for five years before he died. My Uncle Leo Dumont was 13 when his dad got sick. He was the oldest boy still at home so he quit school to help care for the family. There were two younger brothers and three sisters at home. The family moved into Oscoda about 1914. Their house is still standing facing Park St. It had two field-stone porches. My Uncle George and Aunt Frances Dumont lived next door with their three children, Ed, Art, and Ethel

Rose. My dad's sister Emma married Fred Landon. They lived in Tawas City all of their married life and reared their family there. She died in the year 2000 at the age of 91.

My parents, Amil and Amelia, married June

Jean Marion and Janice Marie Dumont married on Oct. 20, 1951

20, 1928. They had a farm in Alcona County. He also had a produce route down along Van Ettan Lake and in Oscoda. He sold eggs, butter, chickens and produce in season. It was a family affair to gather, wash, bundle and load the car each Friday morning. My dad was a widower, with a 9-year-daughter, Elaine, when he married my mother. They reared seven children on the farm: Joe, Mary, Janice, Frank, John, Jim and Martin. All of us attended Oscoda Schools and graduated from there.

My husband, Jean Marion, and I (Janice) were married on Oct. 20, 1951. We live in Rochester Hills, MI (a northern suburb of Detroit). We are the parents of eight sons: Mike, Joe, Chuck, Tom, Jim, Rob and Ron (twins), and Andy. They were all born between 1953 and 1965. Jean worked in construction . After the boys got bigger, I was an office manager for a small manufacturing firm for 20 years. We are both retired now. My father, my husband, and two of our sons (Joe and Tom) are Navy veterans. Our immediate family totals 30 now. They keep as busy. I also sing in a choir and do volunteer work at our local library. *Submitted by Janice Dumont Marion.*

JOHN WILLIAM DURANT.
John (born 1862, died 1938) and his wife Anna Elizabeth Chambers moved to Grant Township from Canada in 1899. They lived and farmed on Meadow Road with their five children: Mabel, Ethel, Elmer and Alma (twins), and Henry A.

Children of John and Anna Durant, Back l-r: Mabel, Ethel, Alma. Front: Henry and Elmer (year unknown)

All the children were married in Tawas starting with Mabel who married Lester Decker on December 26, 1902. Later they moved to West Branch.

Ethel married Walter H. Pringle on August 2, 1903 and lived in McIvor where they operated the McIvor General Store.

Alma married George McArdle on October 29, 1902 and her twin Elmer married Saima Hagland May 21, 1912.

Henry A. married Ruby M. Hall on September 15, 1909. With the exception of Mabel, they all raised their families in the Tawas area. John and Anna were laid to rest in the Memory Garden Cemetery in Tawas City.

ROBERT WILLIAM ELLIOTT JR.

Robert was born in East Tawas, Michigan on January 8, 1930. He was delivered at home as there was no hospital at that time in Tawas. He was the youngest son of Kathryn and Robert Elliott. He attended St. Joseph Catholic School for eight years and graduated from East Tawas High School in 1947. He then went to the University of Notre Dame in South Bend, Indiana and graduated in June of 1951. After a few months working with his father and brother in the Tawas Bay Insurance Agency, he was inducted into the U.S. Army. He served at various posts until he was stationed at Fort Benjamin Harrison outside of Indianapolis, Indiana. There he worked in the Finance Center where he handled Korean Combat Pay for the Army and Air Force.

Elliott Family

In August 1952 he attended a USO dance and as the song *"Some Enchanted Evening"* says "You will see a stranger across a crowded room." Aileen was dancing with another boy, but Robert cut in and that was the beginning of their romance. Aileen Marie Lipps was born in New Albany, Indiana, the daughter of Mildred and Arthur Lipps and she was an advertising-journalism graduate of Indiana University in Bloomington, Indiana in 1951. She was working as a copywriter for an advertising agency in Indianapolis. In May 1953 Robert walked her to the nearby Catholic Church and at the Blessed Virgin's Altar he gave

her a diamond ring. They were married on November 28, 1953 at St. Mary's Church in New Albany, Indiana with both families and friends in attendance.

After a honeymoon in Florida and further schooling in Philadelphia, Pennsylvania, the couple returned to East Tawas where Bob rejoined his father and brother in the agency. On January 6, 1955 their first son, Robert William III, was born. On March 19, 1956 Kevin Arthur joined the family, followed by Mark David on November 17, 1957. The only girl, Julie Ann, was born on September 28, 1959 and Charles Scott on December 28, 1986.

After graduating from college, all five children were married. Robert III married Roberta Mussato of Crystal Falls, Michigan on August 19, 1978; Mark married Susan Rybinski of Detroit, Michigan on September 27, 1980; Julie married Ronald Rybar of Mt. Clemens, Michigan on July 16, 1983; Kevin married Tina Musselman of Muskegon, Michigan on July 27, 1986; and Charles married Julie Green of West Branch, Michigan on November 2, 1991. The family has now grown to include 14 grandchildren: Jennifer Jane and Maureen Marie Elliot; Robert William IV and Anthony John Elliot; Peter Kevin, Daniel Robert and Nicholas Arthur Elliot; Matthew Elliott and Megan Marie (twins) and Macauley Keith Rybar; Benjamin Charles, Hannah Margaret, Katherine Elizabeth, and Samuel Joseph Elliott.

Bob has been very active in the insurance industry and in civic activities in the Tawas area. He was President of the Tawas St. Joseph Hospital Board, Tawas Area School Board, Lion's Club and the Independent Insurance Agents of Michigan. He has served on the Board of Commissioners, the Mental Health Board and as a Director of the Huron Community Bank. He is currently a member of the Iosco Transit Board and the Family Independent Agency Board. In the year 2000 he was inducted into the State of Michigan Insurance Hall of Fame.

Aileen was the teacher and director of the Tawas Headstart Program for 23 years. She retired in 1996 to travel with Bob and become involved in other activities. She volunteers as a Spiritual Care Giver at Tawas St. Joseph Hospital, CCW of Holy Family Church, Tawas Area Fish Program, and is an active member of the Iosco County Quota Club.

In 1982 Jack Elliott retired from the Tawas Bay Agency and moved with his wife Louise to Sun City, Arizona. At that time Mark Elliott, who had graduated from Ferris University and was employed by the Aetna Insurance Company in Grand Rapids,

returned to Tawas and joined the Agency. His brother, Kevin, who also graduated from Ferris and was working for the St. Paul Insurance Company in Houston, Texas, came to West Branch when his father purchased the Diebold Agency located in downtown West Branch. Charles, who graduated from the University of Notre Dame and was a certified public accountant in Grand Rapids, returned and joined Kevin in the Diebold Agency in 1989.

Robert Jr. retired from active participation in the Agency in 1998. He keeps busy pursuing his hobbies of hunting, gardening, walking and traveling, as well as serving on boards and taking care of his duties as the current Mayor of East Tawas, a position he has held for eight years.

ROBERT WILLIAM and KATHRYN SANDS (PLASECKI) ELLIOTT SR.

Kathryn was the youngest child of Jacob and Frances Sands (Plasecki) who immigrated to the United States from the village of Pakosc, Prussia. She was born in Tawas City, Michigan in 1895. She had two brothers, Frank and Michael, and four sisters: Mary, Frances (who became a nun and took the name of Sister Edwardine), Sophia (known as Angela), and Anna.

Kathryn completed her schooling in the Tawas Area and was employed at the Western Union Office in Alpena and as a telephone operator in northern Michigan. Through this job she met Robert William Elliott, formerly of Harrisville, who was of Irish and English descent. Robert was employed as a freight and passenger agent for the D & M Railroad.

Robert and Kathryn married on November 11, 1917. They settled in East Tawas where Robert continued to work for the D & M Railroad. Their oldest son, John Carl, was born on September 22, 1920, their daughter Kharla Rae on December 19, 1924 and their youngest son, Robert William Jr., on January 8, 1930.

With three young children to support, Robert Sr. decided to go out on his own and quit his position at the D & M. He bought a small insurance agency located in downtown East Tawas from Sarah Richards. He began small with his wife Kathryn acting as his secretary. They had the phone hooked up to ring at the house as well as the office and Kathryn took the calls when Robert was out soliciting business.

After graduating from the University of Detroit and serving in the U.S. Navy during World War II, John returned to East Tawas to join his father in the Agency that was called the Tawas Bay Insurance Agency. He was accompanied by his wife Louise Austin whom he married while he was stationed in San Francisco. After graduation from Notre Dame, Robert Jr. joined the agency in 1951. Sister Kharla Rae had married Curtis Weaver of Saginaw, Michigan in 1948 and they reared two daughters, Mary and Kathy. Kharla died on November 14, 1993.

After Robert Sr.'s retirement from the agency in 1960, he and Kathryn spent their winters in Sarasota, Florida where he loved to walk to town and visit with friends that he had made there. He died in July 1964 and Kathryn died two years later in June 1966.

RALPH FERBER FAMILY.

We Ferbers, moved to Iosco County, Oscoda in 1980, although we had bought property, cleared the land and built a cottage on Tawas Lake in 1971.

We are of German heritage, Ralph, the son of Rev. Hugo and Laura (Schmidt) Ferber, Pastor of St. Pauls Lutheran Church, Millington. Edna, the daughter of Norman and Ottilie (Petzold) Kurpsel. Two of our grandparents are directly from Germany and Austria

We both grew up in Thumb area where we were born. Ralph living in the parsonage on Millington Rd. and later moving to the town of Millington as a young lad. Edna grew up on a farm on Birch Run Rd., one of four daughters on a "working farm" totaling 400 acres, which operated as Kurpsel Bros. We each were taught the hard work way of life. Both Ralph and I had the joy and memories of going to a one-room school before consolidation in late '40s. We both graduated from Millington High School with Honors.

Ralph had different jobs, driving gas truck and milk truck route, before being called to serve his country in the U.S. Army for two years, from March 1953-55. This being during the Korean Conflict. He was stationed at Ft. Sill, Oklahoma, then sent to Pirmasens, Germany his second year.

During these two years, Edna worked at two small offices, one the Frankenmuth Brewing Company and Millington Truck Body, waiting the return of her fiancée and planning their wedding for May 15, 1955.

Our marriage was blessed with two children, Gene L. (Barbara) Ferber living in Clarkston, Michigan and Linda C. (Richard) Maurer now living in Shawnee, Kansas with our three grandchildren: Jacob, Caraleigh and Luke Maurer.

After returning to civilian life and working other jobs, Ralph joined the banking arena in 1964, starting in Millington at the Branch of Frankenmuth State Bank. He worked hard, going to Banking School,

working his way thru and up the corporation ladder. He was branch manager when offered the opportunity to move to Oscoda as President of Oscoda State Savings Bank, this happening in late 1979. As you know, we made the move from Thumb area where we had lived all our lives!

We enjoy the area. While Ralph was busy with his job and Edna tiring of emptying moving boxes, knowing something more was needed to fill her days, so in March 1980 began the career of volunteering at St. Joseph Health Systems and also for Red Cross on Wurtsmith Air Base.

Ralph was very active in Rotary and the Student Exchange Program. We hosted five students from various countries. He also was on the Tawas St. Joseph Hospital Board for nine years.

In January 1994, after a lot of hard work and more than many hands full of memories, Ralph retired from Banking then named First of America.

We have settled into retirement. We travel, but are still year-round Oscoda residents. We remain very busy, Ralph now volunteers also for the hospital driving the Courtesy Coach. He also remains busy with church-related volunteerism.

We love the area, and living on the Bayou, enjoying all the wildlife. We never know what animal we may see from deer, turkey, bobcat or fox. Our children tell us we have our own Zoo.

ALVIN and LAURA (UPTHEGROVE) FORSHEE.

Laura Upthegrove married Alvin Forshee from Twining in 1947 and in 1950 they moved from Prescott to Hale to operate the Forshee Funeral Home until 1983 at which time they retired from the business. They have three children: Lonnie, Wade and Dawn.

Lonnie married Margaret Betts and they have two sons, Shane and Chason, and one daughter, Sheena. Dawn is now Mrs. Michael Brown all of whom reside in Hale. Wade is attending school and working at Ypsilanti.

The Upthegrove farm has been kept in the family with the exception of the house and a few acres with the hopes it will remain so for the future generations. Although not operating as a farm, it is a pleasant place to enjoy nature.

Alvin passed away in 1994 and we miss him very much.

PETER ZENS GACKSTETTER.

Peter was born on January 1, 1871 in Ohio. His first wife, Daisy Pearl Draper, the mother of his children, died on November

16, 1917 during child birth. Together they had John Christian, Marie Barbara, Lewis Andrew, Louella Sophy (born Dec. 15, 1909, died March 19, 1989), Anna Louise (born February 6, 1911), Rollie Fredinend (born November 5, 1913, died November 23, 1966), and William Fredrick (born October 18, 1915).

Following the death of Daisy, Peter moved to Alabaster seeking work in February of 1923 under the sponsorship of Jack Robinson and worked on the Robinson farm. Peter later married Mary Suzor Bullock. In 1925, the family moved to Tawas City where Peter worked For Detroit and Mackinac Railroad. During 1926, he also operated a small restaurant. They moved the family to East Tawas in 1927. When Peter was laid off from the railroad, he began an ice delivery in the area.

John, Marie, and Lewis returned to Ohio while Louella, Rollie, and William remained in the Tawas area and Louise later moved to Bay City.

FREDERICK and CAROLINE ROSETTE (SCHEWE) GAUL.

Caroline Rosette Schewe, aboard the *Bremen,* arrived in New York City on December 26, 1872. She and two brothers arrived in East Tawas in January 1873. There she married Frederick Gaul, a Prussian immigrant. A baby son, Willis, died in May 1877 during the influenza epidemic, and 3-year-old Amel succumbed a few days later. The following month Caroline gave birth to Theodore. Theodore's was the first baptism recorded at the Emanuel Lutheran Church, newly organized in August 1877.

In early 1878, the Gauls purchased approximately 160 acres of farmland from Augustus Zimmett and his wife. Eighty acres of this property, at the corner of Kobs Road and M-55, remain in the family. That year Caroline's parents arrived in East Tawas with their three youngest children and Caroline's son, Hermann, age 7.

Caroline and Frederick Gaul in the 70s standing in front of their farm house which was located on the southeast corner of Hemlock and Kobs Roads in Tawas City. The year was 1915.

The Emanuel Lutheran Church baptismal registry records the births of four more children: Mary, Emma, Frederick and Johanna.

Hermann married Martha Look, and was employed the Mackinac Railway. Theodore became a teacher and administrator, dwelling in Alpena, Pickney and Muskegon. Mary married William Langworthy, and they operated a fruit orchard in Traverse City. Emma married Herman Moehring Sr. and resided in Detroit. Frederick moved to Saginaw, and Johanna married Charles Conklin, son of T.W. Conklin, who owned the grocery now known as Klenow's Market. Johanna established and operated Conklin's Greenhouse for several years

In 1940, Emma's son, Herman Moehring Jr. and his wife, Bernice (Mohn) and family moved from Detroit to East Tawas to assume the proprietorship of the greenhouse now owned and operated by youngest son, John Moehring

A large number of Schewe descendents reside in the Port Hope area.

GUSTAVE C. GRAF/GRAFF/ GROFF.
Gustave (born 1864, died 1942) immigrated in April 1882 from Bromberg, Posen, Germany with his parents, Carl Graf and Wilhemina Maik and young sister Ottilie (born 1867, died 1949) married John Wehr.

They arrived in Tawas to join his brother Michael (born 1855, died 1933) married Augusta Ebert and sister Henerritta (born 1860, died __) married Jacob Klein Augusta (born 1858, died 1940) married Julius Rohde. A brother Julius stayed in Germany.

Gustav lived in Tawas City before purchasing a 40-acre farm on Rempert Road in Tawas Township on October 11, 1887.

On September 17, 1888 he married Elizabeth M. Hosbach and continued farming with his parents until their deaths – Carl in 1895 and Wilhemina in 1910.

Bottom Row, l-r: Lydia, Augusta, Elizabeth, Emma. 2nd Row: Ella, Minnie, Olga, Ida, Louise. Back: Albert, Charles and William

Children: William (born 1889, died 1985) married Alma Blunk, Dorothy Sedal;

Charles (born 1892, died 1976) married Lillian Kohn; Ida (born 1893, died 1977) married Edward Kussro; Minnie (born 1895, died 1937) married Charles Hill; Gustave (born 1896, died 1894); Louise (born 1897, died 1984) married Herman Kussro; Olga (born 1899, died 1984) married William Look; Lydia (born 1901, died 1992) married James Lee; Ella (born 1903, died 2001) married William Hass; Albert (born 1907, died 1999) married Elizabeth Konenskie; Emma (born 1908, died 1998) married Harlan Brown, Carl Look.

He purchased an additional 80 acres. In his passing on April 21, 1942 his youngest son Albert continued working the family farm. Albert purchased an additional 80 acres to keep the tradition of farming going with the help of his wife Elizabeth Konenskie whom he married on February 26, 1930 and their children Willard, Betty, Darlene, Gerald, Carolyn (born 1948, died 2000) and James. This was the era when horses were traded for tractors.

Of this 200-acre farm 40 acres that Gustav purchased from his brother-in-law, John Hosbach, was later divided between Willard and Gerald who still reside there today.

The rest of the farm is still operated by his youngest son James and his wife, Thelma Muckenthaler, and their children, Troy, Melinda and Rebecca.

JOHN GRANZ and DONNA UPLEGER.
John and Donna had two sons and one daughter: Brad (1968) married Irene Childers and had Heather. Brian (1969) married Nicol Loveless. Julie (1970) married Chris Schwartzkopf and had Johnathon and Katie. He served in the Vietnam War (1961-1964).

John and I got married May 28, 1995. We live on a small farm in Imlay City. He worked at GM in Pontiac. He retired Jan. 1, 1998. We enjoy gardening, hunting and fishing. In 1994, John got a 5 x 6 bull elk (405 lbs.) and 255 pound bear in 2000. We both are life members in the NRA and John is a life member in the North American Hunt Club. I am also a member of Huron Shores Genealogical Sciety, NRA-ILA, Second Amendment Task Force, and life

member of Citizens Committee For The Right To Keep And Bear Arms, We study with Shepherd's Chapel.

CHARLES S. and MARY L. (KLINGER) GREENE.
Charles Greene was the second oldest of five children born to Frank and Antonia Zelinski (name was changed to Greene), who were immigrants from Poland in the early 1800s. These early years were on the home farm on Wilbur Road, then employed with Detroit and Mackinaw Railroad as a carpenter until his retirement.

Charles married Mary L. Klinger, daughter of John and Mary Klinger whose farm was located on Monument Road in Baldwin Township. Mary's father, John, as a young man emigrated from Alsace Loraine France and was employed in the local lumber mills in East Tawas. Charles and Mary had five children: Florence, Walter, Harold, Wilfred and Russell.

Florence married Carlton Merschel, son of a long-established East Tawas family who had the local hardware store in Tawas. Carlton was owner and operated Merschel Dry Cleaners in Tawas. They had two daughters, Mary Louise and Janet.

Walter worked at his own accounting firm and was a certified public accountant in Detroit. He married Loretta Kennedy and had five children: Jerry, Joseph, Kevin, Marilyn and Paul.

Harold was a photographer in East Tawas and later in Saginaw. He married Kathleen Richter and they had two sons, Harold and Michael.

Wilfred and his wife Ila (Goupil) resided in Bay City for 30 years and retired to East Tawas, 205 Wilkinson Street. Wilfred was a dry cleaner and in later years employed by General Motors Co. in Bay City. He and his wife recently celebrated 58 years of marriage with their five children: Sue Butler, Boyne City; Pamela Everett, Anchorage, Alaska; Larry of Bay City; Jeffrey of Grayling; and Ann of Traverse City.

Russel and wife Valerie (Chestler) had four children: Patsy, Diane, Tom and Gary. Russ worked for *News Press,* a local newspaper in Iosco County and was also a local photographer.

Of the five children of Charles and Mary, four sons served in World War II: Walter, staff sergeant in Army served in England and France; Harold, tech sergeant in Air Force, served in the Pacific; Wilfred, 1st lieutenant in Air Force served in Africa, Sicily and Italy (rated pilot with 57 missions); Russell, tech sergeant in Army Signal Corps served in the Pacific Theater.

All sons saw combat and returned home safe and sound.

A brain tumor claimed Charles' life at age 56. Mary his wife stayed in Whittemore for a few years while the younger children finished school, then moved to Flint to be near her son Arthur.

Lois, the eldest daughter, married Edward Urboneat, Bay City, Florida; Marion married Walter Kuzynice, Bay City, Los Angeles; Evelyn married William Cormer, Royal Oak (daughter Barbra); Ila married Wilfred Greene, Bay City, Florida and now lives in East Tawas, (children: Sue, Pam, Larry, Ann, Jeff); Arlene married Greg Murray, Flint (six children, all of Flint); Tim married Wilma - Laurie/Ted Yokey, Mary, Gregory (deceased), Allen Christopher Do wife Denise.

CHARLES WESLEY HAIGHT.

His grandfather, Charles Wesley Haight, was born in Ontario, Canada, Yarmouth Township, Elgin County in the year 1855. Grandpa told many stories about his life as a young man, but little about his family. His mother had died at his birth. He lived with his father who worked as a circus roustabout.

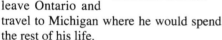

Charles Wesley Haight, Chief of Police of East Tawas, Iosco County and engineer of the East Tawas Waterworks Superintendent about 1915 with his granddaughter, Rosamond Sanderson Swanson

Grandpa had dreams of another country, another land where he would make his own life. In 1874, at age 19, he would leave Ontario and travel to Michigan where he would spend the rest of his life.

He was never to be in contact with his father in later years. Perhaps he tried, one does not know what his relationship with his father was.

Joining a traveling crew of lumbermen in northern Michigan, he quickly became part of a camp, felling great timbers and leading a rugged existence summer and winter. He traveled from one saw mill to another. He lived in barns of hay and cooked food over roaring open fires. He told of putting out pots to collect maple sap and later when it snowed, boiling the sap and throwing it onto the snow to make candy for the crew. Food was plentiful. One can imagine the great forest in the north at that time where plenty of game was available, bear, deer, rabbit, pheasant and fish. An immense area, in some places impenetrable, untouched, unspoiled by man.

Grandpa learned to use the peavey, a long, metal rod or pole that is used to guide the slippery logs down the rivers to the mills. He was well known for this art that not many risked because of the danger of the work. He told many stories about near death when the logs jammed and he, expert with his peavey, would break the jams and ride the logs down to the mills. One never tired of hearing these stories the way Grandpa told them. The giant beaver dams, the animals that the men tamed in the forest, the greatness and the vastness of this area of Michigan wilderness.

He was 29 years old when he came to the Lake Huron area and there met our grandmother, Anna Nitz. She and her older sister, Tillie (or Matilda), had come to this country from Germany on a great ship, she at 16 years of age. It was 1879 when they arrived and settled in Upper Michigan with relatives.

Grandpa met Anna (she was 21) and they quickly fell in love and were married at Ausable, Michigan on July 4, 1884.

They bought or rented a house near the lake in the Brooks Ranch area. At that time the Tawas Beach Club, the first Country Club near the lake, was established. Grandma quickly became a worker at the Club and became famous for ice-cream making in the kitchen. She had plans for a large family and Grandpa began his plan for a better house; one which would later be built on Alice Street in East Tawas.

Two children born during the first years of marriage died in infancy. The first girl, Edith, was born in 1889, followed by Harry in 1892, Eva in 1895, Earl in 1897 and Granville in 1898, Carl in 1900. Carl, the youngest son, was born in the Alice Street House, all others at Brooks Ranch.

The last child born in Alice Street was little Noble. We have often, in the long ago past, heard his name mentioned. We would visit the graves in the East Tawas Cemetery. Little Noble is interred in the same plot as Raymond Sanderson, husband of Eva, on a hill overlooking the entrance to the cemetery. A small lamb on a nearby grave marked the spot for us.

In or about 1926 Grandma was bedridden from an operation and would never walk again nor leave her bed. This did not prevent her from being very much a part of what was going on in house or with all of us. She helped run the house from her bed. She was a mover and a shaker - she always had been.

Four of her sons had been in France in military service and all had returned safely in 1918. She had had many children and she had a wonderful husband and a successful life. She was a very happy grandmother.

We judge the Alice Street house to be at least 98 years old since built. At this writing, 1995, the property has been leveled. Hopefully the great pine forested area to the rear of the site still remains. The glorious trees, tall and green, graced the lot, making a background for the house. The Grove, as it was called, was at least 20 years older than the house—the lot chosen by Grandpa who loved trees and all growing things.

Grandpa planted gardens every year, flowers of all kinds. Cold winter nights he would sit by the fire with his catalogs and write out the orders for his seeds and plants. The snow was still deep out there but the order would be placed, mailed and the packets of beautiful color would come and then we'd look forward to another planting - beginning again another year.

I will never forget the Depression years - that time when there was no Depression for our family. Grandpa would give away food to all who needed help - baskets and boxes of food and flowers from the garden. There was always more than enough for everyone who came and for us besides.

Grandpa had his jobs to do. He was Superintendent of the Water Works Plant for East Tawas and worked in the big building near the water tower. He was also chief of police for the town of East Tawas, wearing a uniform, carrying a billy-club and not a gun – for there was little crime in those days. He wore his badge proudly and he was often seen with a little girl on his arm – that would be his granddaughter who followed his very footsteps. He was a caring, loving man who later taught that little girl that fishing was fun and how not to be afraid of hard work and dedication.

And so we will never forget you, Grandpa and Grandmother Haight. We will always remember you lovingly and we thank you for all you did for all of us – for so very many. You taught us how to live and how to love and of the beauty and the opportunity that is out there for dedicated survivors.

You chose a place to make your home and raise your family to live and to grow in one of the finest states, MICHIGAN, where one could still live off the land, survive to begin again when all might be lost before. It is all out there still for those with courage and with a will.

GEORGE E. HALL.

George (1847-1919) as a young boy he and his family moved to Port Huron, Michigan from Canada. In

1874 George moved to Tawas City where he worked as a sawyer at the Hale mill and later at the Emery mill. The months that the mills were not in operation. George drove the stage between East Tawas and AuGres.

George married Ada Rath in 1881 and purchased a farm on Hemlock Road where he was a prosperous farmer. He became active in his community by serving on the Greenwood School Board and on the Grant Township Board. He and Anna had three daughters. Lottie born April 17, 1883, Ruby Mae born April 25, 1890 in Iosco County and Hazel born Sept. 16, 1892 in Grant Township, Iosco County. Lottie married Louis Pringle Feb. 17, 1902 and they raised their family in the Flint area. Ruby Mae married Henry A. Durant in a joint ceremony with her sister Hazel, who married John G. Katterman, on Sept. 15, 1909. George, Ada and Lottie and her husband, Louis are buried in Memory Gardens Cemetery in Tawas City. Hazel who died July 8, 1910 is buried in Greenwood Cemetery in East Tawas. Ruby died at the young age of 29 and her husband Henry was left to raise two boys, Alton and Hazen in Grant Township. Henry and Ruby, along with their baby boy, who was with them only 5 months, were also laid to rest in Memory Gardens Cemetery.

CLARK HAMILTON.

Clark spent his entire life in East Tawas. He was the youngest of five boys born to William and Mary (Gamble) Hamilton. He was born in 1877 likely in St. Clair County. His father and stepmother, Louise (Welton), made the move to East Tawas in 1880. At later dates his aunts, Rachel Jane and Ellen Bell (Hamilton) and her husband Christopher Creamer, moved to Iosco County. Also, it is believed his uncle John and aunt Mary Ann (Eller) Hamilton settled in Alpena.

Not much more is known about Clark except during his lifetime he made several property transactions in East Tawas and he traveled with his father downstate to visit with relatives in St. Clair County and across the St. Clair River to Watford, Ontario. He remained single throughout his life and could only put an x for his name. Upon his death in 1946, at the age of 75, he left his real estate and personal belongings to Fred and Dorothy Christian. It is not clear what the relationship was between this couple and Clark. East Tawas is his place of death. Clark's Iosco burial site is unknown.

Clark's grandparents, James and Mary (McLean) Hamilton, came from Cummertrees, Scotland to Warwick Township, Lambton County, Ontario.

ELLEN BELL HAMILTON.

Ellen was born either in Lambton County, Ontario or St. Clair County, Michigan. She was born December 20, 1858. Her parents, James and Mary (McLean) Hamilton, had migrated ca. 1845 from Cummertrees and Dumfries, Scotland to settle in the Watford area of Lambton. Ellen's middle name came from her Grandmother Rachel McLean's maiden name Bell. The McLean, Hamilton, and Bell families all settled in the same area. The exact location of her birth is unknown because her parents at times made their home on the American side of the river. Her family one time lived in Clyde Township and another time in Burtchville Township not far from Port Huron.

However, Ellen spent most of her younger days in Lambton County. Both the 1881 and 1891 census have "Nellie" at home with her parents.

She married Christopher Creamer in 1892. It is likely that he was born in Mt. Clemens, Michigan to parents, James and Diane (Stone) Creamer. Tragedy struck on October 6, 1893 with Ellen's death at Long Lake, west of East Tawas. Fire was the cause. She was 35 years old and is buried in the East Tawas Cemetery. Her niece, Helen Hamilton of Watford, thought the couple had a son. Christopher gave up some Iosco land by court order in 1909 with no additional data on his whereabouts beyond that date.

Ellen had a brother William who lived 54 years in East Tawas and a sister Rachel Jane who lived with him for a shorter period of time.

RACHEL JANE HAMILTON.

There were several Hamilton families that settled in the upper eastern part of Michigan. Rachel Jane or "Jen" was a late comer. It is believed she came to East Tawas after 1900 and it is known that she lived with her brother William until her death in 1924 or 5.

"Jen" was born on June 13, 1855 near the farming town of Watford in Lambton County, Ontario in what was called Canada West. Her parents, James and Mary (McLean) Hamilton, had migrated to Warwick Township, Lambton ca. 1845 from Cummertrees and Dumfries, Scotland.

There were 11 Hamilton children (six boys and five girls).

Sometimes the family lived in Warwick and other times they made their home in Burtchville or Clyde Townships near Port Huron, Michigan.

Rachel Jane had a most difficult youth and not of her own making. She was in the home of a Dr. John D. McLeay looking after his wife, who was expecting a child, when the doctor took advantage of her. Out of this abusive relationship, Jen had a child. She named him Ernest Hamilton (born ca. 1874). Because of this experience she and her son were at times shunned. In fact, according to her niece Helen Hamilton (born 1902, died 2000) of Watford, there was the time when Rachel and Ernest went visiting Helen's family and Ernest had to remain in the car. He could not go into the house.

While living in Warwick, Rachel Jane met an English born lad by the name of Matthew Crow. She married him on November 2, 1876 in Watford. He was 37 and she was 21. They had a daughter Sarah Ann (born ca. 1877). This too turned out to be an unhappy story after "Jen" discovered she had married a bigamist. The 1881 Lambton census has her living at the home of her parents with her two children. However, she does not appear in the Lambton census of 1891. It is not certain how many years went by before she headed for East Tawas. Even her new life there was difficult. A failed cataract operation had left her mostly blind. Ernest married Minnie Batterton in London, Ontario on August 28, 1903. In a play on names he stated that James Hamilton was his father and Jennie McLay his mother. Sarah Ann married "Len" Smith and it was said they lived in Winsor, Ontario. Len and Sarah had a daughter Florence and maybe a son as well.

Rachel Jane's niece, Helen, left the impression that in spite of all of the difficulty the family really had a very warm love for "Aunt Jen." She died ca. 1924 in East Tawas. It is not certain where her remains rest.

WILLIAM HAMILTON.

The history of Iosco County includes more than one Hamilton family as early settlers. William Hamilton's family can be counted as one of them. He lived in East Tawas for over 50 years, had a wife and five sons.

William was born Jan. 19, 1844 in southern Scotland in the small and simple village of Cummertrees. His father James came from the nearby town of Dumfries. His mother, Mary (McLean), came from Cummertrees where her family worked on the Duke of Queensberry Estate. They were Presbyterian and the village church cemetery is a genealogical treasure chest of family ancestral names including McLean, Bell, and Nicholson.

James and Mary Hamilton, with their son William, migrated to North America ca. 1845. Their destination was a small pioneer farming community of Watford, Warwick Township, Lambton County, Ontario. William had seven brothers and sisters born in Lambton, his youngest brother born in St. Clair County, Michigan and two more sisters born in either Lambton or St. Clair counties. On occasion the family criss-crossed the St. Clair River between the two counties to visit or to establish their home on either side of the border. Sometimes some of the children would live with relatives or others. Life was difficult and this eased the burden of feeding a large family.

In 1861 the family resided in Burtchville Township, five miles north of Port Huron. William, who was 18 years old, was away working on his grandmother McLean's farm near Watford.

The 1860s mark the era of the bloody American Civil War. Although William was old enough, he never served in the Union forces. He and his family were still subjects of the British Crown.

By 1864 William was back in Burtchville and now married to Mary Elizabeth Gamble. In 1868 he buys 80 acres from his in-laws for one dollar. In the 1870 census Burtchville remains their home, however, by 1880 William and his family had moved to Fort Gratiot Township also in St. Clair County. There were five sons: Joseph (born 1865, died 1922); James (born 1866, died _); Robert Thaddeus (born 1869, died 1919); William (born 1871, died 1947); John Walter (born ca. 1876, died 1953); and Clark (born ca. 1877, died 1946).

The 1880 census of Fort Gratiot reports a Louisa or Louise (Welton) as William's spouse. It is not known what happened to Mary. This may be strange because the death records of sons, John and Clark, and that of William all have the name Mary Gamble as his wife and never is there any mention of Louisa.

William may have been in Iosco County as early as 1878. By November 1880 he had bought property in East Tawas. Why he settled in Iosco County is unknown.

William may have been a jack of all trades. One story, told by his grandson Lloyd J. Hamilton of Port Huron, is that William worked on the railroad. Lloyd's brother Alvin W. thought he owned a boarding house in East Tawas. At times he was a laborer. He probably had many jobs over the years.

William became an American citizen on June 7, 1888 in the Circuit Court in East Tawas. He affirmed he had lived in Michigan for 24 years and had been a residence of Iosco for seven years. By obtaining American citizenship he had forfeited his allegiance to the Queen of Great Britain something his father James had refused to do.

The 1900 census for East Tawas lists William with Louise and Clark. Louise passes away in 1907. In the 1910 Baldwin Township census there are six people reported in the household: William, Isaac Welton, Elizabeth J., Charlotte Garden, and Clark Hamilton.

In the following years William and son Clark lived together in East Tawas. During this period William's sisters Rachel Jane (born 1855, died ca. 1924 and Ellen Bell (born 1858, died 1893) move to East Tawas. Ellen, "Nellie," married Christopher Creamer. A fire will be the tragic cause of her death. Rachel Jane or "Jen" lived with her brother.

William also had a younger brother, John Bell Hamilton (born 1849, died _), who it was thought lived in Alpena with his wife, Mary Ann (Eller) (born 1838, died _).

On Dec. 13, 1932 William died in East Tawas. He was almost 89 years old. His youngest son, Clark, died in 1946. It is not certain exactly where the two are buried in Iosco County.

There is never any mention about the whereabouts of his son James. The three other sons all made their homes in the Port Huron area where many descendants still reside.

Eldest son Joseph married Elmira Brown in October 1892 in East Tawas. They had six children: Frank, Roy, Ethel, Blanche, Joseph and Alice.

Data on second son James is lacking.

The third son, Robert Thaddeus Hamilton, married Mary Ann McAllister, aka Smith or Hauver in Port Huron in September of 1890. Their children were Vina, Lloyd John, Ilah, Joseph, Robert Emery, Alvin Wesley, Freddie, Hazel, Odelene, and Sharlet Moree. Joseph, Freddie, and Sharlet died at birth or infancy.

William married Hattie Green in August 1892 in Port Huron. They had a daughter Emily Mary Hamilton.

John Walter and Mabel M. Leaym were married in June of 1903 at Port Huron. Their children were Isabelle, Russell, Crystal, and Mildred.

Clark remained single throughout his life. His property in East Tawas went to Fred and Dorothy Christian.

RICHARD DONALD and PATRICIA RUTH (MURPHY) HERMAN.
Richard Donald Herman first fell in love with Patricia Murphy when he saw her singing *"Daisies Don't Tell"* at an East Tawas High School talent fair. They were married on June 6, 1942, and their first son was born while Don was serving in World War II in Europe. Upon Don's safe return from the war, he and Pat stood out on the Tawas dock and decided to settle in East Tawas. They moved into the house at 108 Smith Street that had been built by Don's grandparents, Richard August Herman and Amelia (Schroeder) Herman, when they came to East Tawas from Germany in 1875. Don and Pat raised seven children there: Richard, James, Carol, Susan, William, Mary, and David. Don and Patricia still live there.

Don Herman is the son of George August Herman and Nellie Rae (Stewart) Herman. George and Nellie were married in 1908 after Nellie, having taken a train trip from Detroit to visit the Holland Hotel in downtown East Tawas, spotted George playing violin in the hotel orchestra. George worked in the offices of the Detroit and Mackinaw Railroad. He and Nellie lived at 301 E. Bay Street, around the corner from George's parents, and had three children: Winifred, Dorothy, and Richard Donald "Don." Don Herman became an accomplished artist, and designed the Mackinaw Mac logo for the D & M Railroad. He worked for 40 years at the Merschel Hardware store in downtown East Tawas, which was owned by his brother-in-law, Norman Merschel.

Patricia Murphy is the daughter of Gerald Murphy and Grace Miller. Gerald and Grace had three other children: Ted, Jack, and Geraldine. Patricia's grandfather, John Murphy, was an engineer on the D & M Railroad, and died in a train wreck in Alpena on April 25, 1907, during the week he was to retire. He left behind his wife May (Boomer) Murphy and their two young sons, Gerald and Patrick. John Murphy and May Boomer had come to Tawas from Ontario. John Murphy's family had come to Ontario from Ireland. The Boomer family had moved to Ontario in the early 1800s, and was originally from colonial Massachusetts. May (Boomer) Murphy was descended from Richard Warren, who arrived in America in 1620 on the *Mayflower,* and from Deacon John Doane, a prominent early leader of Plymouth, Massachusetts.

Don and Pat Herman are an attractive, generous couple.

Their house has always been filled with family, friends, music, home-cooked food, and love. Don and Pat have twelve grandchildren, and two great-grandchildren.
Submitted by: Julie Herman, New York, New York, September 2002.

EARL LLOYD HERRIMAN. Earl, a farmer in Grant Township, was born in Ancaster, Ontario, on October 10, 1891, son of Herbert and Alberta (VanSickle) Herriman. He married Loretta Mills in November 1911. Loretta was born in Tawas City on November 3, 1893, daughter of William and Loutisha (Bessey) Mills. The Earl Herriman homestead on McIvor Road, was destroyed by fire February 1933 with no personal items being recovered. Earl bought another farm SW of McIvor and Hemlock Rds.

Loretta Mills and Earl Lloyd Herriman

Ten children were blessed to Earl and Loretta; all reared to work hard, love their neighbors, and respect their family.

1) Harold William was born November 23, 1912. At 18 years old, a car accident left him with a deformed leg; a year later Harold died from a perforated bowel.

2) Allan Herbert (born 1914, died 1983) married Vera Freel, was a farmer in this area; rearing six children: Faye, married Roger Whitford and presently residing in our area; Phyllis, Kenneth, James, Joy, and Donna.

3) Ina Lucille (born 1917, died 1918 in infancy).

4) Kenneth (born 1919, died 1998) was soldier in World War II, retired from General Motors in Detroit. He married Erma Lou Pfahl of Grant Township, and of this union were Dale, Connie (this author), and Randy.

5) Earl "Lynn" (born 1922, died 1984) moved to the Detroit area as a young man, married Irene "Germaine" and had one son Jeffery who resides in the downriver area. A second marriage was to Mavis; he lies in Memory Gardens.

6) Dorothy (born November 1924) married Jerry Whitney (born 1916, died 1971) of Bay City; they had Ina and Gayle. Dorothy resides in the Tawas area with husband Leo Curtis.

7) Olen (born September 1926) married Gertrude Smith (born 1930, died 1987) of Omer; they had Carol, Verna, and Raymond who is a Baptist pastor in Indiana. Olen resides in Florida with wife Betty (Harland).

8) Clare Victor (born September 1928) married Betty Lou Brown of East Tawas. Clare was elected Justice of the Peace in 1962 serving two years, and has served on the Tawas Area School Board 14 years; he was named Mason of the Year for his "Outstanding Service and Dedication" by the Tawas Masonic Lodge in September 2003. Clare and Betty have four children: Harold "Chris" in Arizona, Sherry in Washington, DC, Craig who served as Sheriff of Iosco County, and Harvey who is manager of Dean Arbor Chevrolet/Cadillac. Harvey married Marilyn Keasel who is a principal for the Whittemore/Prescott Schools.

9) Leland (born April 1932) married Rosalin Gackstetter (born 1934, died 1981) of this area. They had two sons, Eric and Keith, who reside in their home state of New York, and adopted Cathy, Ramona and William. Leland spends the winter months in Florida with wife Susan (Dunfey).

10) Elwood Creig (born April 1934) resides in the Flint area with wife Margaret (Whiteford) of Grand Rapids; they met at the Tawas High School and had children: Craig, Rodney and Kirk. Loretta died November 24, 1948, a woman who will live forever in her children's hearts. Earl married Edith Estella Misner in 1951 from Ontario. Earl died May 12, 1971, and lies peacefully beside his dear Loretta in Memory Gardens. *Submitted by Connie Chism.*

HERBERT HERRIMAN. Herbert, a farmer in Grant Township, was born November 18, 1866 in Ontario, the only son and third child of James Herriman and Miriam VanSickle, daughter of William and Elizabeth (Smith) VanSickle. James died of typhoid fever in 1871 leaving his young family in Norfolk County, Ontario. Sisters, Elizabeth and Martha, remained with stepfather Lewis Crandall, but Herbert lived with Miriam's sister, Phoebe, married to Deacon Sylvester Smith in Wentworth County, Ontario.

A Native American bloodline entered this Herriman family when in 1797 Indians captured young Diadamia Herriman from the shores of Lake Ontario. Craige Herriman from Brant County, Indian Lands married Levina Jane Pettit of Ancaster in 1834; they had Thomas, Elizabeth, James (our subject's father), Caroline, George, Jeptha, Squire, and Martha. Herbert married Alberta VanSickle December 24, 1890. She was born March 1, 1869 in Ancaster, daughter of Elijah Lockman and Elizabeth Ann (Drake) VanSickle.

The VanSickle family founded the Baptist Settlement in 1801, migrating from New Jersey. Herbert and Alberta had two sons born in Canada, Earl (born 1891, died 1971) and Victor (born 1897, died 1992), before they moved to Michigan looking for better opportunities. The young Herriman family shared a train boxcar with other families from Ontario, Jack Burt, Wally VanSickle, Ruben VanSickle, Ellsworth VanSickle, and Vern Papple, settling on the Hemlock Road. Herbert lived with Jack Walls the first winter while clearing his land, selling the wood to Tawas residents and building his home. His original 40 acres was purchased from Henry Watts. Later he purchased 40 acres from Bill Brown and another 40 from Henry Watts.

Herbert Herriman and Alberta VanSickle

Alberta died on February 11, 1910, leaving Earl, Victor, William (born 1899, died 1959); Clarence (born 1902, died 2000); Ada (born 1904, died 1966); and Howard (born 1910, died 1978) was born eight days before his mother's death. Alberta (VanSickle) Herriman's body was returned to Ancaster, Wentworth County, and she lies in the Stenabaugh Cemetery. Young Ada remained with her VanSickle grandparents, attended the Toronto Bible College, becoming a Nigerian missionary. Earl continued to help farm the homestead until his brothers returned to Michigan to join the family when Herbert married Augusta Watts in 1913.

Augusta opened Herriman's Store, which was the building on the NW corner of M55 and Sand Lake Rd., originally a blacksmith shop owned by Jack Watts. She willed the store to her young stepson, Howard.

Herbert's third wife was Mary Elizabeth Latham. Herbert was a successful farmer, treated his livestock well, and loved by family and friends. He was able to provide meals and pay hired farm workers during the Depression. Victor married Beatrice Ruddock of Marshall, Michigan, and lived on the Herriman homestead. Earl married Loretta Mills, daughter of William and Loutisha (Bessey) Mills. William married Bernice Smith, daughter of Rueben and Charlotte (Hyland) Smith. Clarence married Gladys Latham, daughter of Lyman Peter and Rachel (Chambers) Latham. Ada married Homer Avey and reared a family in Detroit, Michigan. Howard married Sophie Marzar. Herbert became deaf in later years, learning to read lips. Herbert died April 11, 1947, and is buried in Memory Gardens. The Herriman homestead remains in the family line. *Submitted by Connie Chism.*

SIMON and LOUISA HETCHLER.

Simon's great-grandfather, John Balthasar Hetchler (Hetzler) came to this country from Erbach, Wurttemberg, Germany in 1749 on the boat "Albany" arriving in Philadelphia, Pennsylvania. Other members of the family came over later and they settled in Lancaster County, PA. They bought land, and as with other Pennsylvania Dutch pioneers, carved a home out of the wilderness and helped develop this new country.

In time, some of the family members migrated to New York. Simon's grandparents, Nicholas and Polly (Conkle) Hetchler, moved into Wheatland, Genesee County, New York. On their 100 acres, they built a cabin made of hand-hewn logs. It was the birthplace of ten children, one of which was Peter Hetchler, father of Simon. The cabin now stands in Genesee Historic Country Village in Mumford, New York. It is considered the first permanent home in Genesee County, New York and was moved to its present location in 1966. Appropriately, it was the first building moved to the historic site.

Simon and Louisa Hetchler

There was a Hetchler family cemetery on the original family homestead in Wheatland. In the 1950s, a new high school was soon to be built on the land so all of the bodies were exhumed and put into a single grave in a nearby cemetery. There is only one original gravestone that lays flat on top of that single grave and it is barely legible. There are no records available, but Nellie, wife of Peter and mother of Simon, was one of those buried there. She was born in 1814 and died in 1842, age 28 years.

Simon was born September 28, 1839 in nearby Scottsville, New York. Simon served with Company B, 100th Regiment of New York Volunteer Infantry during the Civil War. His two older brothers also served in the war and his oldest brother, John Balthasar Hetchler, died while in the war. Records show that Simon was wounded on August 16, 1864 as the regiment engaged the enemy in a skirmish near Deep Run, Virginia.

Louisa Giesy was born in Alsace-Lorraine, Germany/France September 28, 1845, the daughter of Barbara Werely and George Giesy. She came to this country with her family about 1850. She married Simon Hetchler in Gorham, New York and they had one child, Nellie May Hetchler, born December 1871.

Simon and Louisa lived in New York and Virginia, and came to Michigan in early 1900. Their daughter Nellie and husband Elmer Streeter with their sons, Glenwood Elmer and Forrest Simon, came on the same train into Emory Junction, National City.

The Hetchlers bought a farm on Ora Lake Road that adjoined the farm bought by Elmer and Nellie Streeter. Simon and Louisa were Charter Members of the Hale Methodist Church. There is a Bible still in the family that was presented over 100 years ago to Simon from the first minister of the Hale Methodist Church, Rev. Clifton Scott.

While Louisa did not often have an opportunity to re-visit her family in New York, she maintained albums of the "postals" she received which chronicled the activities of her New York family. In fact, these "postals" enabled family historians to ultimately trace the origin and history of Louisa's family.

Louisa was an excellent seamstress and she made many quilts, especially of the "Crazy Quilt" design. The fancy stitch "featherstitching" that covered the connecting pieces of fabric was flawless.

Their daughter, Nellie Streeter, died April 25 1906 at age 34 leaving her husband Elmer and sons, Glenwood age 12 and Forrest age 10. Simon passed away in 1913.

In her later years, Louisa spent the summers in her own home on Ora Lake road, but in the winter lived with Ebner and Katie Streeter in Hale. She was very fond of the young Streeter children there. Her grandson Forrest said that Louisa would not ride in automobiles, but she loved to ride in the sidecar of his circa 1920 motorcycle.

Louisa died in 1922. Nellie, Simon and Louisa are all buried at Esmond Evergreen Cemetery in Hale, Michigan.

WILLIAM JACQUEL.

William Jacquel, Yockell, Yokell, Yockel, Yokel or Yorkell, was born November 7, 1857 in Rimouski, Quebec, Canada. He was the son of David Yokel and Octavie Charette. David was baptized March 22, 1832 in Ile Verte,

Canada. David and Octavie were married February 23, 1857. They had four known children: William (my great-grandfather) was born 1857 and died in 1942; Euphemie Louis Edouard (born 1866, died 1932); Alfred (born 1868, died 1933).

William Yockell and second wife, Regina Morin

William was a lumberman who moved to Michigan about 1871 and became naturalized in about 1888.

On June 6, 1880 William married Angeline Ouellette, daughter of Joseph Ouelette and Caroline Gagne. They were married in AuSable, Iosco, Michigan. Most of their thirteen children were born in Oscoda, Iosco, Michigan. The children's names were Victoria Dorianne (born 1880, died 1955) married Theophile Brien; William (born 1881, died 1899 in Massachusetts of a perforated bowel); Amanda Maude (born 1885, died 1939) married Henry Lanoie; Mildred Melvina (born 1886, died 1970) married Albert Henri Belisle; Meulormia Mance (born 1886) married a Lajoie; Adlord Edward (born 1889, died 1944) married Emma Cote; Marie Anne (born 1889, died young in 1891 in Michigan); Alfred "Freddy" (born 1891, died 1971) married Rose Brodeur April 17, 1914; Joseph (born 1892); Marie Anne (born 1894, died 1925) married Albert LeBlanc on the same day, April 17, 1914, as her brother.

The remainder of the children were born in Massachusetts or Rhode Island; they were Ernest J. (born 1896, died October 9, 1927 in Cleveland, Cuyahoga, Ohio; Frank (born 1898, died 1969 in Connecticut); William[1] (born 1900, died 1987) was born in North Adams, Berkshire, Massachusetts and baptized under the name Yackel; Amelia (born 1907, died 1973) was born in Central Falls, Providence, Rhode Island.

My great-great grandfather William came to Michigan during the logging boom there and stayed until at least 1894 as that is where I found them on the Michigan State Census in that year. They were living in Oscoda, Iosco, Michigan at this time.

After leaving Michigan they moved to the East into Massachusetts then into Rhode Island where he died in 1942. After my great-grandmother died in 1922 he married a woman named Regina Morin. William died in April of 1942 in Manville, Providence, Rhode Island and is buried there.

[1]This William is my grandfather who married Ora Savage daughter of Alfred Savage and Mathilda Morrisseau (Morrison). He and Ora had five children born in Central Falls, Rhode Island. They were William Joseph George (born 1923, died 1971); Amelia Melvina (born 1924, died 1980); Aurora Blanche (born 1925); Ernest Donat (born 1929, died 1996), my father; Leo Armand (born 1930, died 1996). *Submitted by Sandra Yorkell-Parker.*

MATTHIAS "MATT" JORDAN.

Matt (born 1878, died 1963) was the youngest son of Joseph Jordan and Kathryn Schneider. Joseph and Kathryn both emigrated from Germany in 1863. They were married in Detroit in 1866. They then headed West. Their daughter Gertrude was born in Wisconsin in 1867, followed by Anna in 1868. Next they settled in Nebraska where they had three sons: Joseph in 1870, John in 1872, and Henry in 1874. On October 22, 1877 they traded their farm in Nebraska for a farm in Sherman Township, Michigan—sight unseen. They set-

Matthias Jordan

tled on their 80 acre farm in Iosco County, and in 1878 Matt was born, followed by Kathryn in 1880. Matt grew up on that farm with the East Branch River running through it, and became quite a well-known hunter and trapper in the area. In January 1904 Matt married Maude Higgins and they reared their children on that farm: Henrietta (born 1904, died 1949), Aubrey Patrick (born 1905, died 1957), Matthias (born 1907, died 1962), Kathryn (born 1911) Clarence (born 1912, died 1977), Wilhelmina (born 1916, died 1981), Elizabeth (born 1913, died 1975), Micheal (born 1919), James (born 1920, died 1966).

Matt owned and operated two saw mills in Sherman Township. He worked for Henry Ford for a time. Henry Ford used to come up and hunt at the farm. Matt also worked at National Gypsum. Maude was the Sherman Township treasurer for many years. Matt and Maude were very well known for their musical talent. Matt played the fiddle and Maude played the piano. Throughout their lives they played at many dances and functions in the area. Matt loved to dance and was quite a storyteller. Maude passed away in 1944, Matt stayed on the farm with his son Michael who married Dorothy Pierson in 1954 and started raising their family. On February 27, 1963 Matt died in the woods on that farm where he was born and raised. Michael and Dorothy still live on that centennial farm at 3465 Turtle Rd. in National City, where they raised eight more Jordan children.

MR. and MRS. CHARLIE KATTERMAN.

We were married December 20, 1916. Charlie had 40 acres of land and he built a nice little home on it with a nice large living room, bedroom and a work room, which was called a pantry in those days. He also built a barn and a small building for his grain, which was called a granary at that time. He had five cows, three horses, one colt, and also chickens. But times were very bad those days, one was very lucky if one would get one dollar an hour. As a rule, one would only get one dollar a day.

The first winter of our married life, Charlie and another gentleman, by the name of Mr. Lake hauled cord wood on sleighs to Tawas. I do not know how much they got a cord for it. I do know the road was bad with steep hills and lots of snow. At times, they would have to hook one team of horses ahead of the other to haul the load through the bad places. There was a time they would not get home until 10 and 11 o'clock p.m.

The two men worked together a lot that winter, they cut and hauled popple pulp bolts 3 feet long to McIvor for Mr. Walt Pringle. He would put them on freight cars and ship them away. They always spoke of them as poverty blocks. They cut another kind of wood called tagelder. They were cut in 2 ft. lengths, they said it was used for powder. This was all in war time. The size of wood was 3 inches and smaller. Charlie was a very good man with an ax. He would lay the pole on a block of wood and one chop would cut it off.

Charlie always loved to hear sleigh bells. He always had a couple on his horses when he used a sleigh and a strap of bells when he used the cutter. Charlie bached it for a few months before we were married. It always pleased him to see a light in his house when he came home from his work and he knew his supper would be on the table. Sometimes I would go to the door and listen and could hear the sleigh bells. Then I knew he was an his way home from work. We raised a family of six children: Eleanor, Edna, Thelma, Louis, Donald and Reta. Donald was our nephew, but we loved him just as dearly as the rest.

In our early life, Charlie always kept four horses and at a busy time of the season he would drive one team on a disc and he would plow or harrow with the other team, until the boys got old enough to take over. All the children helped on the farm with what ever there was to be done.

Before we came to Tawas City we had 200 acres of land. He built a large house and barn and a tool house and a number of smaller buildings. We milked 17 cows and we bought a tractor in 1946. We always raised a lot of chickens, as we could ship them and get a good price for them. We had no luck with ducks and turkeys. We had a large garden and also had strawberries and raspberries. All the children helped take care of it.

With our children all married and becoming of an age unable to take care of it, we had an auction sale on October 14, 1961, selling all the machinery and sheep. Everything else had been sold previously in 1961. We bought a lot in Tawas City and Charlie built a home on it. We have to give our children lots of credit for what we have today. All our children were with us to help celebrate our 50th, 60th, and 65th anniversaries and a host of our grandchildren were with us too.

After we moved to Tawas City, Charlie still was very active. He took care of a small garden, and also mowed lawns for other people, until he was 90 years old. Both of us were members of the Zion Lutheran Church. Charlie was baptized and confirmed in this church, and I was confirmed in the Lutheran Faith. We had a very long and happy married life together and I will never forget the fond memories he gave me. I will cherish them as long as I live. We celebrated our 66th anniversary before Charlie passed away February 28, 1983. He was laid to rest in the Zion Lutheran Cemetery at the age of 92 years. *Submitted by Delia Katterman.*

ALBERT and AMALIA (STEINHURST) KILIAN.

Albert was born April 7, 1830 and his wife, Amalia (Steinhurst) on August 18, 1823. It is believed they were born and raised in Koslin, Butow, Pommern, Germany, now a part of Poland. Butow is now Bytow in Poland.

The Albert and Amalia Kilian family included two children, Emilie (born February 18, 1861) and Julius (born October 11, 1864).

The Kilian name was spelled Killian on many of the records after arrival in the United States.

Emilie, age 20, arrived in the United States aboard the steamship *Oder* on June 25, 1881 in New York City. (Ship manifest ID #36128). Port of Embarkation was Bremen, Germany. Destination was Tawas City,

Michigan. On October 22, 1881 Emilie married Moritz Elster in Tawas, Michigan, and had five children all born in Tawas.

Julius and Hermine (Borowski) Killian with children Alex, Maurice and Jennie in top row. George, Lydia and Elmer (bottom row) about 1898/99

Albert and Amalia along with son, Julius, arrived in the United States aboard the steamship *Lessing* on April 12, 1884 in New York City. (Ship manifest ID #37702). Port of Embarkation was Hamburg and Havre.

Tawas City was a lumber town in the 1880's and it was believed the families worked for the lumber mills in Tawas.

The Kilian family were members of the Emanual Lutheran Church in Tawas City. Moritz and Emilie Elster were members of the Zion Lutheran Church in Tawas City.

Albert died in Tawas City on May 25, 1895. Amalia died in Tawas City on August 10, 1892. They are buried in the Emanual Lutheran Church section of Memory Gardens Cemetery in Tawas City. However, neither Albert or Amalia have a headstone to identify their gravesite. On the 1894 census of Iosco County, Albert was living with son Julius.

Emilie died on January 6, 1925 in Tawas City. Moritz and Emilie (Kilian) Elster are buried in the Zion Lutheran Church Cemetery.

Julius Killian married Hermine (maiden name Borowski) on October 28, 1888 in Tawas City. They had 12 children and in approximately 1912 they moved from Tawas City to Detroit, Michigan. Julius worked in Detroit for the Burroughs Adding Machine Company as a carpenter foreman.

Julius died in Detroit on January 10, 1930 and his wife Hermine died on March 11, 1941. Both are buried in Evergreen Cemetery in Detroit, Michigan along with three of their children.

More information on the family of Julius and Hermine Killian can be found in the biography of August and Augusta Borowski.

JENNIE KILLIAN. Jennie was born in Tawas City on August 25, 1891 as Eugenie Emile Hermine Killian, Jennie was the

second child and oldest daughter of 11 children of Julius and Hermine Killian. Her youth in Tawas was devoted in helping her parents with the younger children.

Louise Elster and Jennie Killian

Her best friend was her cousin, Louise Elster. Louise, born in East Tawas on October 7, 1887, was the daughter of Moritz and Emilie Elster. Emilie Elster and Hermine Killian were sisters, daughters of August and Augusta Borowski who immigrated to Tawas from Germany in 1893 and both Borowski sisters were married in Tawas City.

Jennie and Louise grew up in Tawas and in 1907 they together left to work as maids in Ypsilanti, Michigan. Soon after, Louise met Fritz "Fred" Beyer and was married in Detroit.

Louise introduced her cousin, Jennie, to Fred's brother George and they also married in Detroit on April 1, 1911. George and Fred Beyer were born in Freiburg, Silesia, Germany and immigrated with their parents to St. Louis, Missouri in 1893. Their father, Herrmann Beyer worked for the Burroughs Adding Machine Company in St. Louis and when the company relocated to Detroit in 1904, he moved with them. His sons also took jobs with the company soon after locating in Detroit.

These two Tawas cousins became sisters-in-law and also next door neighbors on Hobart Avenue in Detroit. Their husbands, Fred and George Beyer, had less than a mile to walk to work. Jennie's father, Julius Killian, moved from Tawas to Detroit and also took work with Burroughs and also located on Hobart Avenue.

George and Jennie (Killian) Beyer had one daughter, Dorothy, born on September 12, 1913 in Detroit. Fred and Louise (Elster) Beyer had four children: the oldest daughter, Helen born in 1912 in Detroit. The daughters, Dorothy and Helen, became the best of friends as their mothers had always been. Helen was maid of honor at Dorothy Beyers marriage in 1934 to Joseph Durkin.

Jennie Killian Beyer died in Dearborn, Michigan on September 14, 1970. Louise, while visiting in Tawas City, died in 1961. George and Jennie Beyer, Fred and Louise Beyer are buried side by side in the Woodlawn Cemetery in Detroit.

Jennie's daughter, Dorothy Beyer Dur-

kin had two children, Thomas Durkin and Janet Durkin Mondro. Both are currently living in Florida and combined are the parents of seven children and 12 grandchildren. These 12 grandchildren can now trace their great-great-great-great-grandparents Albert and Amalia Kilian and August and Augusta Borowski, to Tawas City for where they both located to from Germany in the 1880s, and in which both sets of gggg-grandparents can be found buried in the Emanual Lutheran Church cemetery in Tawas City. Jennie Beyer is the great-great-grandparent and the link that originated in Tawas City for these 12 great-great-grandchildren. Additional information on Jenny's grandparents who immigrated to Tawas City can be found on biographies of Albert and Amalia Kilian and of August and Augusta Borowski.

BLAISE ALLEN and CAROL (BLACHA) KLENOW. Blaise was born on September 30, 1952 to Robert and Rosemary (Mielock) Klenow. Blaise attended East Tawas kindergarten, followed by studies at St. Joseph School through the 7th grade. He graduated from Tawas Area High School in 1970. Still a few weeks from his 18th birthday he started college at Saginaw Valley, later transferring

Blaise, Brad, Carol and Brett Klenow

to Michigan State where he received his BS degree. In 1987 he received his MBA from MSU. He works for Daimler-Chrysler where his job has taken him all over the world on various company projects and often to Stuttgart, Germany.

In July 1976 Blaise married Carol Ann Blacha at St. Valentine's in Redford Township. Carol was born January 24, 1954 in Detroit to Harry and Dorothy (Halwacks) Blaca. Blaise and Carol met in math class at MSU. Carol was a math major. Received her BS degree in 1976, master's from Oakland University and doctor of Education from Wayne State. She is employed as an ISD assistant superintendent. For several years to the present time she is President of the Utica Schools Board of Education. The whole family helped with "Dr. Mom's" election campaign.

Son Bradley Allen was born June 2, 1982 and son, Brett Allen was born July 25, 1987. Carol addressed the graduating class and gave son Brad his diploma at the Palace of Auburn Hills graduation for Eisenhower High School in 2000, and will do the same for son, Brett in 2005. Carol spends graduation day at the Dome as Utica School System has four high schools each with their own graduation ceremony.

Brad graduated from MSU in 2004 and will be continuing his post graduate work at Virginia Tech in pursuit of a marine engineering degree. Both boys are excellent students. Brad and Brett played Little League baseball where Blaise coached for several years and was president of the association. Brad and Brett also played football from junior high through high school and both boys played with their Eisenhower team at the Silver dome. Ike did not win but it was a great experience and "dad," the sports fan, was very happy. Brett is also on the IKE wrestling team.

The family has enjoyed boating for many years. Blaise and Carol recently completed a trip from Florida to Lake Huron through the inner-coastal system and in July the family including Elwood, the corgi, will be going to the North Channel for their annual boating vacation. Blaise's first boat was a flat-bottom row-boat built by grandpa Mielock when Blaise was four. They caught many perch in those days. Currently they don't fish, but with a floating house they have TV, music, food, bathroom, etc. and unlike a summer home, no grass to mow. The view from, the flying bridge is fantastic, but Capt. Blaise does give crew assignments. The ship's name is "Persnickety." Blaise worked at Jerry's Marina during high school and early college years. The family resides in Shelby Township, Michigan.

ROSEMARY (MIELOCK) KLENOW.
Rosemary, the only child of Ernest and Florence Mielock, was born on September 29, 1929 in Detroit, Michigan. She started kindergarten at age 4 at Fitzgerald School. Following kindergarten she attended St. Francis de Sales school through the 10th grade. The family then moved to East Tawas where she attended East Tawas High School graduating in 1946. She attended Northeastern School of Commerce in Bay City. Upon completing the business course she began employment with the Detroit and Mackinac Railway on April 7, 1947 where she worked continuously until retirement on August 23, 1991. For 30 years she was the local chairman of TCU, Huron Lodge; treas.-manager of the D & M Credit Union; and chairman of the GTW System Board of Trustees. During her 44 year railroad career she held a variety

of positions including clerk-steno for the assistant general manager, accountant, general accountant and the last several years payroll and insurance accountant.

Rosemary Klenow with Winston and Nigel

Married to Robert C. Klenow on October 7, 1950 in St. Joseph's Church, the newlyweds moved into their home at 825 Smith St. East Tawas, which had been designed and built by Robert. Son, Blaise Allen Klenow, was born on September 30, 1952. Robert Klenow died on May 13, 1953.

Rosemary was moving from the family home on the night of the tornado in June 1953. In 1954 Rosemary purchased a lake front lot in Baldwin Township and her parents purchased the adjoining lot. Rosemary and her dad designed a home with floor to ceiling windows taking advantage of the lake view. This home was then built by Ernest, who was a building contractor. Florence and Ernest enjoyed the lake area so much they soon built a home on the adjacent lot and in 1958 a Mielock Family reunion was held there.

Son Blaise, graduated from Tawas Area School in 1970. He graduated from MSU and accepted a position with then Chrysler Corp. He later received his MBA also from MSU. He continues to work for Daimler-Chrysler where his work has sent him all over the world including frequent trips to Stuttgart, Germany. Married To Carol Ann Blaca on July 31, 1976, they have two sons, Bradley Allen (born June 22, 1982) and Brett Allen (born July 25, 1987). Blaise and family reside in Shelby Township, Michigan.

Rosemary has spent many years volunteering for organizations holding a variety of positions and is a past president of the PTO, PTA, BPW, (Woman of the year 1985-86) OGC, Quota Club, Huron Lodge, D & M Credit Union, and currently continues as President of Iosco County Historical Society and Huron Shores Genealogical Society, other organizations include Ladies Literary, Ry. Bs. Women, D & M Historical Society, and Tawas Hospital Auxiliary.

A lifelong interest in newsletters has

led Rosemary to be editor or columnist for *The Totem Post* (high school), *The Ledger* (college) ICHS, (museum), *Quota Quips, Huron Express, The Turtle* (D & M Ry.), HSGS (genealogical).

Rosemary currently shares her home with two miniature Schnauzers, Winston and his son, Nigel; 800 collectible bears; two cabinets of Precious Moments figures; 75 turtle collectibles; 24 Seraphim angels; and oodles of family history, photos and many books. Keeping busy in retirement is no problem - keeping up is, but as the old saying goes, "it is better to wear out than to rust out."

LOREN HENRY KLENOW.
He was the son of Martin and Annette Klenow and the third of four children. In 1879, his parents brought him, his brother John (born 1872) and his sister Maggie (born 1876) to Iosco County where they settled on a homestead farm in Baldwin Township. There, another brother, Joseph, was born in 1889.

Loren (born 1877 in Germany, died in 1939) married Julia Toppa (born 1880, died 1948) of Baldwin Township in 1899. The couple was blessed with eight children: Frances, Henry, William, Ann, Russell, Richard, Beatrice and Edward.

In 1900, Loren established the L.H. Klenow Grocery in East Tawas. As his family and the town grew, he branched out into the contracting of cement products and the harvesting of ice. He also contracted to move houses upon occasion. By the early 1920's he saw a need for and established a gas and oil business. This was followed by a car dealership. In 1925 he purchased the LaBerge Shoe Store and operated it under the name of L.H. Klenow and Sons.

Four of Loren's sons remained in East Tawas to eventually take over the management of his several businesses.

Henry (born 1901, died 1953) married Bernice McMurray in 1920 and became manager of the grocery store. Seven children were born to this couple: Rita, Lawrence, Henry, Mary Jeanne, Janet, Joan and Kay. Henry served as mayor of East Tawas from 1942-1953.

William (born 1903, died 1956) married Irene Lixey and had one son Bill. William managed the gas and oil business until shortly before his death.

Richard (born 1908, died 1969) managed the family shoe store for most of his adult life. He served in the Army from 1943 to 1945 during World War II.

Edward (born 1913, died 1953) engaged in several occupations in the East Tawas area, including managing the shoe store with his brother, Dick. He married Grace Merschel. Their six children are Norma, Ruth, Tim, Lynn, Charles and Carol.

A fifth son, Russell, completed his work in dentistry at the University of Michigan and opened a practice in Bay City, Michigan in 1931. After service in World War II, he opened a dental practice in East Tawas. Dr. Klenow married Mary Piechowiak of Bay City.

Frances, the oldest daughter, managed the family shoe business for several years before her marriage to Edward Sheldon in 1937.

Ann "Dolly," the second daughter, earned her teaching certificate at Central Michigan University and taught for two years. She married James McCamley of Flint where the couple raised their three children, Ann Margaret, Edward, and Patrick.

LAIDLAW. The Laidlaw family is originally from the city of Hawick, Scotland. Descendants left Scotland for America in 1825. Members of the Laidlaw family settled in Delaware County, NY, including William and Margaret Laidlaw. This couple had 12 children, including James and Ebenezer. Ebenezer and his older brother James worked in the lumber business in their youth. After acquiring some money, Ebenezer. and James Laidlaw moved to Iosco County in 1866. They purchased more than 1,000 acres in what is now Tawas Township in May 1866. The two brothers established a shingle mill, E & J Laidlaw. In addition to great amounts of shingles, lumber was produced at the mill. As an example of the quality of the forest, one particular ten acre parcel of land produced nearly two million board feet of lumber! Plank Road, an original (toll) road to the 'Plains' country, was built of heavy plank milled at E & J Laidlaw. A small community arose around the mill, called Laidlawville. It consisted of several homes, a boarding house, a post office, general store and a one-room schoolhouse. After James Laidlaw died in 1877, Ebenezer continued the mill work. Devastating fires destroyed the mill on two occasions. In 1886, Laidlaw donated lumber used to construct the Wilber Township Methodist Church. Declining prices and depleted forests contributed to poor profitability during later years of mill operation, however. Laidlaw sold his mill in 1892, and the family moved back to the old settlement in Laidlawville and began farming.

Ebenezer Laidlaw was more than a lumber man and farmer. In 1868 he, with Henry Loud of AuSable, organized the Republican party of Iosco County. In 1888, he was elected Judge of Probate, a position he held for 12 years. Additionally, he was a supervisor of Wilbur Township.

Ebenezer and his wife, Amelia Lake Laidlaw, married in 1868 and had eight children. One of them, Walter Ellsworth, married May Culham in September 1900. They settled in the old family farm on Laidlaw Rd. The original farmhouse, constructed (approximately) in 1868, burned in 1907. A new farmhouse was constructed on the original site. Walter Ellsworth "Els" assisted his father in the lumber business in his early years, then turned to farming. For some time, Els and May operated a restaurant in Tawas City. Els, too, was active in local politics. He served Tawas Township in many capacities, including supervisor.

Walter Ellsworth and May had four children. One, Walter James, married Illa Carter in December 1933. Upon the death of Walter Ellsworth in 1949, Walter James and Illa Laidlaw returned to the old family farm with their family of five children. Walter and Illa were teachers. The children of Walter and Illa chose to enter various fields of medicine, rather than farm. The properties, including the farmhouse and barns, remain in family ownership.

The Helen Laidlaw Foundation, honoring Helen Laidlaw, daughter of Walter Ellsworth and May, provides scholarships to students from NE Michigan who enter a health care field.

ERNESTINE (LARSON) LANDGRAF. Ernestine grew up on Tawas Point. It was mostly sand and sand dunes, and the Tawas Point Lighthouse was located on the southwest tip of the land, which was owned by the U.S. Coast Guard.

The Coast Guardsmans' children enjoyed ice-skating on a pond known locally as the "Lighthouse Pond." Many people from "down state" owned or rented

Ernestine E. Larson

cottages on the Point, and many brought friends and family their for summer vacations.

The children that lived on the Point attended school in East Tawas. During her early childhood years, her mother Bess drove her

and several other children to school. Later, bus transportation was provided by Baldwin Township. Ernestine graduated from East Tawas High School in 1937, and Iosco County Normal in 1938. She currently lives in Mentor, Ohio, and has four children, ten grandchildren, and six great-grandchildren. Her children also reside

Ernest J. and Bessie P. (Trudell) Larson

in Ohio: Ronald Butterfield of Painesville, Bonnie (Butterfield) Swatowski of Mentor, Donna (Butterfield) Pollack of Painesville, and Robert Landgraf of Painesville.

Tawas Point is unique. There is no "home" quite like it. It is where she and her family have spent wonderful vacations. Tawas Point will always hold a very special place in her heart. Her father enlisted in the Life Saving Service in 1914 and served in the United States Coast Guard for 32 years.

Tawas Point is a strip of land between Tawas Bay and Lake Huron, truly the sunrise side. The beaches were beautiful in the summer, and a wonderful place for marshmallow roasts along the shore. Wild flowers were abundant. Some of the species were wild iris, trailing arbutus and wild roses. All could be found near the lighthouse and in the wooded areas of the point.

U.S. Life Saving Station - Tawas

The keepers of the lighthouse were very friendly people and considered a part of the Tawas Point families. The existing lighthouse was formally owned by the United States Coast Guard. It is presently owned by the Michigan State Park system. The lighthouse's new lighting, outside of the building can be seen across Tawas Bay. A beloved beautiful structure which has endured through the years.

Memories of Tawas Point are dear to my heart, and a new favorite place for my family to enjoy.

BERTHA AUGUSTE LANGE.

Bertha, the eighth child born to Gottlieb and Johanna Matscherodt Lange, was born January 5, 1880 in Tawas, Michigan and died June 3rd in Greenville, Michigan.

Bertha Auguste Lange

Bertha married Johannes David Adolph Dommer on November 29, 1897 in Tawas, Michigan. Johannes was born February 26, 1875 in Tawas and died in Chicago, Illinois. Bertha and Johannes had six children: Dorathea, Walter, Irma, Johannes, Colmore and Robert Dommer.

Dorathea, Emilie Ida Dommer was born March 2, 1898 in Alabaster Township and died February 17, 1979 in Greenville, Michigan. She was married to Frank Webster who was born November 2, 1911 and died November 28, 1978 in Greenville, Michigan.

Walter Carl Franz Dommer was born October 4, 1900 in Alabaster Township and was married to Hilma Gram. Hilma was born in Sweden May 15, 1905 and died March 22, 1997. Walter and Hilma had three children: Eugene, Grace and Walter Jr.

Irma Dina Emma Dommer was born March 2, 1903 in Grant Township and died April 18, 1979 in Greenville, Mississippi. She had married Emory Throwbridge.

Johannes Herman Paul Dommer was born November 7, 1905 in Emery Junction, Michigan.

Colmore Dommer was born October 22, 1917 and had five children. He died August 5, 1982.

Robert Dommer Sr. was born July 6, 1922 and died July 14, 2000. He had four children.

Bertha Lange married for the second time to Emory Throwbridge who had earlier been married to her daughter Irma.

The third marriage of Bertha was to Edward Hagen. He was born in 1882 and died in 1962. They had three children, Erma, Louis and Richard Hagen. Bertha and Edward Hagen are buried side by side in Oakwood Cemetery in Lowell, Michigan. *Submitted by Charles R. Birnbaum, great-grandson of Gottlieb and Johanna Lange.*

CHARLES CARL LANGE.

Charles, born August 18, 1872 in Wyandotte, Michigan, was the first child of Gottleib and Johanna Lange born in the United States. He married Emilie Ottilie Ziehl April 18, 1897 in Tawas City, Michigan. She was born May 9, 1875 in Germany and died December 5, 1963 in Tawas, MI. Charles and Emilie had eight children.

1) Otto Lange was born May 1, 1898 in Tawas and died May 2, 1898.

2) Fred August Lange was born June 2, 1899 in Tawas and died June 2, 1899.

3) Hildegard A. Lange was born July 26, 1901 in Tawas and died September 24, 1984.

Charles Carl Lange and Emilie Ottilie (Ziehl) Lange

She was married to Elgin Curtis Ulman November 10, 1921. He was born August 20, 1896 in Tawas and died November 5, 1934. They had three children: Ruth Evelyn Ulman (born October 5, 1925 in Tawas, died November 6, 1976) married Ervin Gauthier on October 27, 1951 and had one child Kenneth. Kenneth was born November 6, 1952 in Omer, Michigan and died March 25, 1990 in Tawas City, Michigan. Hildegard and Elgin also had two children who died before 1934.

4) Frederick Frank Otto Lange was born December 21, 1903 in Tawas and died December 18, 1925 in Alabaster Township while at work at the gypsum plant. He accidentally fell into a gypsum bin and suffocated. He married Edith Johnson November 26, 1924. She was born about 1907 to Alfred and Ella Oster Johnson.

5) Frieda E. Lange was born March 15, 1906 in Tawas and died May 17, 1996 also in Tawas. She married Carl Herman Krumm December 14, 1925 in Tawas. Carl was born November 27, 1901 and died April 27, 1982. His parents were August William and Augusta Damerau Krumm. Frieda and Carl had two children, Helen Edith Krumm (born December 13, 1925) and Marion Ellen Krumm (born March 18, 1929).

6) Elsie Frances Lange was born October 17, 1908 and died June 18, 1932 at University Hospital in Aim Arbor, Michigan.

7) Esther Laura Minna Lange was born June 28, 1912 in Tawas and died October 7, 2000. She married Oran Elwood Ulman March 2, 1935. Oran was born to John and Clara Proper Ulman on October 13, 1913 and died January 5, 1998 in Tawas. They had three children: Donald, Larry and Linda Ulman.

8) Leo Herman Emil Lange was born August 2, 1914 in Tawas and married Alma Mae Ulman August 14, 1937 in Tawas. Alma was born to John and Clara Proper Ulman. Brother and sister, Oran and Alma Ubnan married sister and brother, Esther and Leo Lange. Leo and Alma continue to reside in the Tawas area on his father's farmland on Lorenz Road. *Submitted by Charles R. Birnbaum, great-grandson of Gottleib and Johanna Lange.*

FRIEDERICKE MINNIE LANGE.

Friedericke, born April 24, 1863 in Erfurt, Germany, was the first child of Gottlieb and Johanna Matscherodt Lange. She died March 11, 1948 in Roseville, Michigan. She married Gotthilf (John) Bernard Schmalz September 21, 1879 in East Tawas, Michigan. He was born October 20, 1846 in Kosclin Province Pommern, Germany to Johann and Charlotte Schulz Schmalz. He died June 2, 1895 in Port Hope, Michigan. Gotthilf had two brothers, Rudolph Ernest Schmalz, who stayed in Iosco County, and Edward Schmalz. While checking family records some family members spell the name Schmalz and others use Schmaltz.

Friedericke and Gottliff had six children:

1) Amalia Auguste Schmatz was born February 14, 1881 in Tawas and died at age 2 months on April 14, 1881.

2) Paul B. Schmalz was born February 28, 1885 in Port Hope and died July 25, 1959. He married Hannah Kosloske around 1910.

3) Johannes George (Johnny) Ludwig Schmalz was born January 23, 1888 in Tawas Township and died in June 1906 in Millington, Michigan.

4) Ida Augusta Johanna Schmalz was born March 22, 1890 in Tawas, MI and died September 7, 1923 in Detroit, Michigan. She married Frederick Lang. Ida and Frederick had five children: Theresa Fredericka Lang, William Frederick Henry Lang, Arlene Olga Lang, Frederick Gustav Emil Lang II and Marvin Herbert Lang.

Top Row, l-r: Lillian (Young) Lesh, Anna Marie Sielaff Pritchard, Margaret Pritchard Anthony. Center, l-r: Arnold Anthony, Emma (Lange) Sielaff, Mervin Anthony. Bottom, l-r: Carol Lynn Anthony and Frederick Anthony

4) Alvina Adeline Caroline Schmalz was born November 11, 1892 in Tawas, Michigan and died July 7, 1970 in Los Angeles, California. She was married to F.H. Troike.

5) Julius Ernst Schmalz was born July 1, 1894 in Port Hope, Michigan and died April 22, 1962 in Frankenmuth, Michigan while fishing in the Cass River. He married Bertha Ruth Berndt October 27, 1920 in Port Hope, Michigan.

On July 21, 1897 Fredericke Minnie Lange Schmalz married Herman Lawsitzke. He was born March 23, 1858 and died January 3, 1916 in Port Hope, Michigan. They had one child, Herman Robert Johann Lawitzke. Herman was born December 20, 1900 and died January 3, 1980. He married Minna Amelia Ida Eggert on February 21, 1921 and had ten children.

On May 15, 1940 Friedericke married the love of her life, Herman Dommer. Herman was born in Germany on August 17, 1863 and died May 15, 1948 in Roseville, Michigan. Herman grew up in the Tawas area and was Friederickes' first love. When they went to my Great-Grandfather Gottlieb Lange to ask permission for them to marry he said no. He felt Herman couldn't take care of his daughter properly. Years later and having been a widow twice, whom should she meet but her first love. It seems they both went to the same doctor and ended up one day in the office at the same time. They lived out their lives together and died only two months apart in 1948. *Submitted by Charles R. Birnbaum, great-grandson of Gottleib and Johanna Matcherodt Lange.*

GOTTLIEB LOUIS LANGE.

Gottlieb, born in November 1835 in Germany, was the son of Steven Lange. Family records unfortunately have no information on his mother. He married Johanna Matscherodt about 1862 in Germany, she was born August 26, 1839 also in Germany.

Gottlieb and Johanna had 10 children, four born in Germany: Friedericke Minnie Lange, Emma Wilhelmine Frederike Lange, Anna Minna Lange, and Franz Ludwig Lange. The remaining six were born in the United States, Charles Carl Lange, Hermann Christian Georg Lange, Oscar August Lange, Bertha Auguste Lange, George Gotthilf Lange, and Edward Carl Lange.

Eight of the 10 children reached adulthood. George Gotthilf who was born September 15, 1882 passed away on May 11, 1889 and Edward Carl who was born July 20, 1885 passed away February 17, 1889.

Somewhere between January 1870 and August 1872 they came to the United States first living in Wyandotte for a year. They bought a wagon and horses and started out with their five children and one cow to Tawas, Michigan. They settled on land on Laidlaw Road near the corner of Rempert Road and built a home.

Gottlieb was also a blacksmith and built a blacksmith shop on the homestead. There was a schoolhouse across the road and at recess the children would run across the road to watch him sweating over the anvil pounding out horseshoes and whatever else was needed around the farm. To their delight he would spit on the hot anvil and a loud bang like a gunshot would send them scurrying, laughing all the way back to school.

Gottlieb died September 28, 1908 in Tawas and Johanna died January 2, 1924 in Saginaw, Michigan at the home of her daughter Anna Minnie Lange Birnbaum.

Anna was married to Theodore Birnbaum of Saginaw, Michigan and was the grandmother of Tawas city resident, Charles R. Birnbaum. Say's Charles, "I never met my Great-Grandfather or Great-Grandmother Lange and the only thing I remember about Grandma Anna Lange Birnbaum was her cookies. They were sooo…good!. I was only 8 years old when she passed away."

Another Tawas resident, Leo Lange and his wife Alma Ulman Lange still reside on the family farm of his father, Charles Carl Lange, on Lorenz Road.

HERMAN CHRISTIAN GEORG LANGE.

Herman, born September 25, 1874 in Tawas, Michigan to Gottleib and Johanna Matscherodt Lange and died March 8, 1911 in Tawas, Michigan. His first marriage was to Ottilie Pauline Anna Bischoff on April 11, 1898. She was born December 31, 1876 in Tawas to Adolph and Anne Hartman Bischoff. Ottilie died giving birth to their daughter, Ottilie Bertha Hermine Lange on February 11, 1899. Baby Ottilie died February 23, 1899 in Tawas, Michigan.

On October 14, 1900 Herman married his second wife Emilie Augusta Mueller in Tawas City. Emilie was born December 29, 1878 in Zandersdorf, Germany to August and Johanna Woitzer Mueller. Herman and Emilie had three children: Walter, Louise and Eleanora.

Walter George Lange was born February 25, 1902 in Tawas and married Caroline Klopf They had three children, Walter George II Caroline, and Linda Lange.

Louise Lange was born June 14, 1905 in Tawas and died June 20, 1961. She married Walter Betz and also had three children: Patricia, Shirley and Kenenth Betz.

Eleanora Alvina Lange was born February 25, 1908 in Tawas and married Anton Sparks. They lived in Saginaw most of their lives. Eleanora and Anton had two children. Norman Walter Sparks was born August 7, 1930 and married Rita Gedrovics on August 7, 1954. Edith Louise Sparks was born February 14, 1935 and married Jack Horvath December 17, 1955.

Herman Lange worked for the Detroit and Mackinaw Railway Co. His daughter Eleanora relates that while at work he knelt on a hot cinder and developed blood poisoning which took his life at the young age of 36. His wife Emilie then married Julius Musolff April 28, 1919 and had one child, Julius Musolff II born December 6, 1922 who married Janet McClain. *Submitted by Charles R. Birnbaum, great-grandson of Gottleib and Johanna Matscherodt Lange.*

Herman Lange and first wife, Ottilie Pauline Anna (Bischoff) Lange

Herman Lange and second wife, Emilie Augusta (Mueller) Lange

ANNA MINNIE LANGE.

Anna was born February 20, 1868 in Berlin, Germany to Gottlieb Louis and Johanna Matscherodt Lange. She died October 25, 1937 in Carrolton, Michigan. On November 24, 1887 she married Theodore Frederick Birnbaum in Saginaw, Michigan. He was born January 10, 1862 in Mecklenburg, Germany to Charles H. and Anna Marie Wolf Birnbaum and died June 16, 1936 in Saginaw. Anna and Theodore had five children: Frederick Charles, Anna Louise, Elsie, Charles Frederick, and Dorthea Katherine Birnbaum.

Frederick Birnbaum was born June 22, 1890 on Crow Island, Saginaw, Michigan and died December 22, 1970 in Saginaw. His first wife was Esther Kienutske who he married July 27, 1912. Frederick and Esther had four children: Ruth, Dora, Margaret, and Grace Birnbaum.

On May 22, 1930 he married Laura Zimmerman who was born May 1, 1909 in Saginaw and died January 12, 1982. They had six children: Theodore II, Barbara, Donald, Albert, Frederick, and Lila Birnbaum.

Rear, l-r: Anna Louise Birnbaum and Henry Felton, husband of Elsie Birnbaum. Sitting l-r: Dorthea Katherine Birnbaum, Charles Frederich Birnbaum, Minna Anna (Lange) Birnbaum (mother) and Elsie (Birnbaum) Felton

Anna Louise Birnbaum was born May 18, 1892 in Saginaw, Michigan and died March 9, 1954 in Sacramento, California. Anna married Guy Warren on March 20, 1912. He died November 21, 1914 in Pueblo, Colorado. They had one child in 1913 that died about 1914. On August 8, 1915 Anna married Jesse Gilbert Gimore in Pueblo, Colorado. He was born December 23, 1882 and died in December 1961 in Saginaw, Michigan. Anna and Jesse had two children, Donald and Everett.

Elsie Birnbaum was born May 9, 1895 in Saginaw and died November 3, 1918 in Pueblo, Colorado. She married Henry Felton February 27, 1915 in Saginaw. They had three children: Mildred, Frederick, and Henrietta. Henrietta disappeared while on her way to school and was never found.

Charles Frederick Birnbaum was born August 13, 1900 in Saginaw and died January 7, 1965. His first marriage was to Lucille Heindel on June 22, 1920 and they had three children: Howland "Bud" Marshall Birnbaum, Elaine and LuDonn Birnbaum. After Lucille had remarried she had her adult children legally change the name to Ferguson. On May 5, 1928 Charles married Marie Lillian Young in Saginaw and had six

Theodore Frederick Birnbaum. Car and child name not known.

children: Charles, Jacqueline, Jerry, Rita, Ardath and James Birnbaum.

Dorthea Birnbaum was born April 8, 1902 on Crow Island, Saginaw, Michigan and died December 1, 1987. Her first marriage was to Clarence James and they had one child, Ruth Eve James born May 4, 1919 and died February 9, 1920 in Saginaw. Her second marriage was to Paul J. Rempert on October 1, 1980 in Saginaw. He was born in Chicago but the Rempert Family later relocated to the Tawas area. They had four children: Maybelle, Delores, Leatrice, and Walter Rempert. Walter died in a tragic auto accident, in the Standish area, on his prom night October 19, 1950. *Submitted by Charles R. Birnbaum, grandson of Anna Lange Birnbaum.*

THEODOR OSCAR LANGE. Theodor was born to Gottlieb and Johanna Matscherodt Lange on June 2, 1877 in Tawas, Michigan and died April 16, 1956. Theodor married Emma Stuedemann on August 28, 1898 in Tawas. She was born September 4, 1872 in Saginaw, Michigan to Joseph and Sophia Cupp Stuedemann. Emma died February 15, 1932 in Tawas. Theodor and Emma had six children: Clarence, Clara, Martha, George, Louis, and one unnamed child.

Theodore Oscar and Emma (Stuedemann) Lange

Clarence was born February 11, 1901 and died about 1962 in Tawas. He was married to Katherine Truebauer. Clarence was a Detroit Police Officer with 25 years service.

Clara was born December 31, 1902 in Tawas and died December 18, 1953. She married James Styles January 7, 1926 in East Tawas. James was born May 13, 1902 in Tawas to Frank and Elizabeth Searle Styles. Clara and James had five children: Frances, James, Meredith, Caroline and a baby Donald who died 1944.

Martha Lange was born August 13, 1905 in Tawas and died April 3 1935. She married August Wojahn December 14, 1935 in Tawas. August was born February 11, 1894 in Tawas and died July 18, 1977 in Saginaw. Martha and August had five children: Grace, Esther, George, Harry and James Wojahn.

George Lange was born September 3, 1906 in Tawas. His first marriage was to Nora Styles on April 3, 1926. She was

born to Frank and Elizabeth Searle Styles. Nora died May 1, 1927 in Bay City. On May 19, 1934 George married his second wife, Josephine Adams, the daughter of Claude and Gloria Scott Adams, in South Branch, Michigan.

Louis Lange was born May 31, 1909 in Tawas and died as a result of an auto accident on February 14, 1937 in Davison, Michigan. Louis had married Beulah Springer January 13, 1934. She was born December 24, 1906 to John and Grace Stuart Springer. Beulah had a daughter, Bethel Rempert, from her first marriage to Albert Rempert and Louis and Beulah had a son Donald. Louis, Beulah, and Donald all died immediately in the auto accident and Bethel passed away two days later on February 16, 1937. Louis worked for the US Government Forest Service and he and his family had been visiting relatives in Pontiac. On their way back to Tawas during a heavy rain with low visibility and also icy roads their car turned over in a ditch. The car was righted and they pushed onward toward home. They were following another car approaching a railroad crossing and did not see the train until it was too late to stop. The icy roads make a collision unavoidable. The family is buried in Millington, Michigan.

Theodor Lange later married Jessie Cooper Becker on April 3, 1933. She was born September 8, 1877 in Evansville, Indiana to T.J. and Hannah Watts Cooper. Jessie died April 9, 1938 in Tawas. In family records it appears Theodor Lange dropped the "E" off the last name and used Lang as did most of his children. *Submitted by Charles R. Birnbaum, great-grandson of Gottlieb and Johanna Lange.*

LATHAM. Frederick W. Latham (born 1837 in Pennsylvania) migrated to Kansas as a young man. In 1862 he enlisted in the 2nd Kansas Cavalry for the duration of the Civil War. Discharged in 1865, he married Lydia Kees and settled on a farm near Parsons, Kansas. They had three children: Mary, Guy and Peter. In 1872 Lydia died of Malaria. Frustrated by the loss of his wife and the hardships of frontier life, Frederick sold his farm and moved to Iosco County, Michigan and purchased the Sand Lake House. He remarried Ellen Tambling who had one son Maurice. Frederick and Ellen had five children: Everett, Nellie, Harry, Lydia and Arthur.

At the end of the lumbering era, he purchased and cleared land to build their home. The home was located approximately seven miles west of Tawas City on what became known as the Hemlock Road, now

M-55. Frederick was active in civic affairs and served as one of the first supervisors of Grant Township. He also operated the old Edson Post Office at this location until RFD was introduced in this area.

Latham Family

The eldest child Mary married Frank Reed. They lived in California and had two children, Charles and Alice. Guy was unmarried. Peter married Rachel Chambers and they were the first couple to be married in the Hemlock Road Baptist Church. They settled on a farm in Grant Township. They had 10 children, including four sets of twins: Gladys and Doris, Frederick, Frances and Phyllis, Howard and Harold, Guy, and Mary and Louise. Peter served on the Board of Supervisors and as Director of the School Board for many years.

The eldest Gladys, married Clarence Herriman. They operated Herriman's Country Market in Grant Township. Gladys now lives in East Tawas. They had three children: Gerald of White Lake; Marion of Hale, Michigan and Florida; and Arthur of Lee Lake, Michigan.

Doris married Clare Smith. They lived in Flint and operated a retail grocery store. Their son Willard is in Grand Blanc.

Frederick was unmarried.

Frances married Raymond Warner they had six children: Marvin, Donald, Merlin, Cecil, all of the area and Shirley of Grand Blanc and Lyle in Holly.

Phyllis married Marshall Harris. They had three children: Harold of Ypsilanti, James of Florida and Joyce of Texas.

Howard married Lura Leavoy and they live in Roseville. They reared five children: Anita of Warren; Lloyd and Floreen of Rochester; Marilyn "Kay" and Carolyn of Sterling Heights.

Harold, married Evalyn Scott and moved to Tucson, Arizona. They had four children: Marlene of Wyoming; Allen of Tucson, Arizona; Alice of Payson, Arizona; and Keith of Melbourn, Australia.

Guy married Annabelle Pangman, he is now retired living in Tawas City. They had three sons. Neil of Fraser, Kenneth of Tennessee, and Fred. Guy has remar-

ried, his wife is the former Grace Long Robinson.

Mary married Clifford Hilmoe and lived in Ypsilanti. They had three children. Dick now in the UP, Delores in Ann Arbor and Kay Marie in Ypsilanti.

Louise married George Scovill. They lived in Mt. Clemens and had three children: Charlotte in East Tawas, MI, George, in Phoenix and Marcia, in Denver. Louise remarried Matt Lappinen and they had three children: Alida and John of Denver, and Matt of Massachusetts.

Maurice Tambling married Mae Kennedy and lived on a farm in Grant Township. Evertt married Mary Bamberger and devoted his life to farming in Grant Township, also serving on the Board of Supervisors for several years. They had no children. Nellie married Morrison, they lived in Detroit and had no children. Harry married Alma Ferrister and they had one daughter Evelyn.

When Alma died Harry remarried Winona Pringle. They had two children, Warren and Elaine. Evelyn married and moved to Oregon, Warren died in infancy. Elaine married John McMurray and they now live in Tawas and are in the real estate business. They had six children: Mark, Brian, Debra, Craig, Gale and Karen. Lydia died in infancy. Arthur married Genevieve Smith and settled on a homestead in Nebraska. They had three children: Lyman, Willis, and Ruth

ERNEST A. LEAF FAMILY. Ernest, his wife Pearl M. and daughter Arlene, moved from Flint to East Tawas in the spring of 1930. The Leafs owned a drugstore in Flint. Because of the Depression, the store was struggling. Mr. Leaf saw an opportunity to have a better business and life in East Tawas. He moved the drugstore into a building owned by Abraham Barkman next to Bill's Cafe. The store was later relocated where the former Perry Drugs is now. The Leafs subsequently sold their store to Harold Gould.

Leaf's Ben Franklin Store

Ernest and Pearl began the Ben Franklin Store which was purchased by Lyle

Mooney in 1944. Ernest then became a realtor with an office on Newman Street. In 1951 the Leafs set up the Oscoda Ben Franklin Store. Ernest served one term as mayor of East Tawas. He also served on the County Board of Supervisors. He was a strong supporter of tourism and took an active role in many local events, especially Silver Valley. Ernest died in June 1952.

Pearl continued to operate the store in Oscoda. In 1973 Arlene joined her mother in the Oscoda store, and the building was enlarged to 10,000 square feet. Mrs. Leaf died in 1978. Arlene sold the store in November 1980 and retired.

Arlene's husband, Beryl T. Salisbury, retired from advertising in the Detroit area in 1973 and set up a bookstore, The Booknook, in the Holland House. It was later moved to the building on the corner of Newman and Westover Streets, which had been the Kennedy Bakery and, before that, Klenow's Gas Station. Beryl sold the Booknook in 1985. It is now owned by Neil Thornton.

Beryl and Arlene have a daughter, Anne, wife of Jon A. Obermeyer. Anne and Jon have three daughters: Jessica Archer, Sarah Obermeyer and Hannah Obermeyer. *Submitted by Arlene Leaf Salisbury.*

HERSHEL F. "HERSH" LEE.
Hersh was born September 2, 1927 in Mikado Township, Mikado, Michigan, Alcona County. His mother was born Muriel Travis on May 5, 1900 in AuSable Township, Iosco County. His father was born Fred Lee on December 13, 1891, Mikado Township, Alcona County.

Hershel F. Lee

Hershel's Mother and Father met at the Indian camp meeting in the summer of 1918 and they married May 5, 1919. In the early 1920s they bought a farm on the corner of Goddard and Alvin road. It was here that Hershel grew up along with his four brothers and five sisters. He went to a one-room school at Alvin, to about the 4th grade. At this time the Alvin school system consolidated with Oscoda Schools and he was bussed to the Oscoda school system.

Hersh, as he was called all of his life, grew up on Goddard road, and felt all the pangs of the Great Depression in the 30s. He saw his father go to work for the W.P.A. He worked on U.S. 23 connecting the shore line road between Harrisville and Oscoda, and farming became a part-time business.

Dollar bills were scarce. Hersh grew up knowing each one of the family had to contribute to the family's living.

Hersh always found himself in the woods around their small farm hunting, fishing and trapping, adding to the family life to make it better.

As the 30s gave away to the 40s, Hersh's brothers went off to war. Hersh was too young to go in the draft. He was now working in the hayfields or on thrashing machines, or what ever he could find for $1.00 or $2.00 dollars a day. He would trap in the fall to have money for school and Christmas.

It was about this time in Hersh's life that he decided to quit school, knowing that in two years he would be drafted. Hersh was drafted into the army, January 1946 and got out in April 1947.

He married Betty Jane LeCuyer June 10, 1950 and they moved to the Oscoda area. They had two daughters and one son. Hersh and Betty lived most of their lives on 205 West Michigan Avenue, Oscoda.

Hersh operated the Cities Service Station in the mid-50s, opened the Gary Oil Station and sold that in the 60s. Later, Hersh and his brother Chuck operated the Western Auto Store, on Main Street into the 70s when he sold out to Chuck and joined the Q-Stick Factory and retired from there in 1992.

Hershel was president of the Chamber of Commerce in the mid-60s. He also was a volunteer firemen for 10 years. The last volunteer work which he was most proud of was the auxiliary police officer for 12 years. He also spent nine years as a trustee on the Oscoda Township Board.

Betty Jane Lee passed away November 19, 1999 at the Iosco Medical Care Facility. Hershel Lee married Norma G. Harrison on September 16, 1999. He now lives in the Greenbush area.

DOROTHY H. LEHMAN. She was born in Hale, Michigan, December 6, 1927, the youngest child of Edward and Lottie May (Webb) Putnam. There were nine

children in the family. Ida (Bernard) Webb, Elma (Guy) Alderton, Lottie (Harold) Eymer, Charles (Mary), Leon (Beulah), John (Thelma), Gertrude Putnam, Betty (Robert) Timmer. Dorothy graduated from Hale High School in 1946. On October 6, 1946 she married J.D. Lehman from Whittemore. They have five children.

1) Kay (Robert) Mitchell spent three years in the Navy. She teaches 3rd grade at Whittemore Prescott School. Robert is retired from the Ogemaw Sheriff's Department. They have four children: Tom (Penny), Troy (Terri), Kristen and Matthew Scott. They have two grandchildren and live in Prescott.

2) John lives in Clio and has been employed at General Motors for 35 years. He spent two years in the Army (14 months in Vietnam) and has four children: David, Chad, Sean and Brittany, and one grandchild Randi.

3) Richard lives in Laingsburg and has been employed at the postoffice for 28 years. He has a daughter Rosie and one grandchild Lasandra. He was in the Navy for two years and served in Guam where he was injured. He attended University of Michigan receiving a BA degree.

4) Mark lives in Mt. Pleasant and is a professor at Central Michigan University. He has three children: Mark, Bethany and Ian. He was valedictorian of his graduating class, and also ran track, being a state champion. He attended Columbia University and also University of Michigan where he received his bachelor, master and doctorate degrees.

5) Matthew lives in Concord with his wife Kathy and their three children: Alissa, Brett and Lindsey. He is athletic director and also teaches school. He graduated from Central Michigan with a BS degree, and just recently received his master's degree from Spring Arbor College. He is also varsity boys basket coach, and girls' jr. varsity basketball coach.

After Dorothy married they moved to Whittemore where she has always lived. She worked for Collins Variety Store, the telephone company, Grabow Distributors for over 25 years. She also worked for Alpena Beverage for six years, and for an oil company for six years. She is presently employed by the Whittemore Prescott Schools as a para professional. She has been city clerk for six years, and is also treasurer for the Whittemore Chamber of Commerce. She was on the Whittemore Prescott School Board for 21 years. She enjoys crocheting, playing the piano, and her family and grandchildren.

In 1974 her husband J.D. died very suddenly, and she had to rear the last two children alone.

ERNEST LARRY LIXEY. Joseph Sordelier and wife Ann Carnet were born in Cugner Franche, Comte, France. Joseph was Ernest Larry Lixey's fifth great-grandfather. Their son, Francis Sordelier (1724) married Mary Jane Gendron (May 5, 1765). Their son Francis Charles Sordelier (January 1, 1780) was born in Assumption Sandwich, Windsor, Ontario. He married Catherine Campeau (February 18, 1800) in St. Antoine, River Raisin. Their son, Alexander Soudriette (October 2, 1801) was born near the River Raisin (Monroe, MI).

The reason for the name change from Sordelier to Soudriette is unknown. About 1833, Alexander married Elizabeth Campeau, the niece of Joseph Campeau of Detroit history. Alexander had a trading post in the Saginaw Valley (now Bay City) The Indians had trouble pronouncing his name and called him "Alexi" which eventually was translated to "Lixey." This is the reason for the change of Soudriette to "Lixey."

Joseph Alex Soudriette was the first son born of Alexander and Elizabeth in Bay City, Michigan (December 1834). He married Teresa Trudell in Bay City (February 16, 1858). Teresa Trudell was the first white woman born in Bay County.

Joseph began fishing in Saginaw Bay in the late 1840s. Some years later, he moved to the mouth of the AuSable River where a fishing settlement had sprung up, and began fishing there in 1860. Their youngest son, John Alexander Lixey (September 13, 1878) married Cora Irene Mac Murray (May 25, 1905). Their fourth child was Edward Raymond Lixey (May 16, 1912). He married Kate Ellis (November 21, 1913) in East Tawas, Michigan on April 17, 1933. Ernest Larry Lixey was born (September 10, 1934) in Oscoda, Michigan. His maternal grandparents were Vincent Ellis and Myrtle (Atherton) Ellis.

Ed worked as a fisherman with his father and brothers until it was no longer profitable. He was on the East Tawas City Council in the late 1950s. Kate and Ed had three sons: Larry, Edward Ronald (September 12, 1943) and Thomas Vincent (February 8, 1953).

Larry attended St. Joseph Catholic School through 10th grade. He graduated in 1953, the last graduating class from East Tawas High School. It consolidated with Tawas in 1954. He worked at Anderson Coach in East Tawas before volunteering for the draft in 1954. He served in the U.S.

Army, U.S. Corps of Engineers, at Presidio in San Francisco, California. He was honorably discharged in October 1956.

Larry married Charlene Kay McCall (May 25, 1957) at St. Joseph Catholic Church in East Tawas, Michigan. They resided in the Detroit, Royal Oak and Madison Heights area for 40 years. Larry worked in management for the S.S. Kresge Company. He helped open the first three K-Mart stores. He later built homes until he injured his back. He worked for Sears Roebuck and Company until a medical retirement in 1989. They returned to East Tawas when Charlene retired in 1997 from Lamphere Schools. They raised five daughters: Valori Ann (October 27, 1958), Pamela Sue (December 15, 1959), Cheryl Lynn (October 18, 1961), Lisa Marie (December 15, 1963) and Beth Anne (November 9, 1965).

Valori works at GM and lives in Madison Heights, Michigan.

Pamela married Steven Gerald Kirschke (May 25, 1984) at St. Dennis Catholic Church. Their son, Karl Gustav Kirschke was born December 16, 1988. They own a welding company and live in Madison Heights, Michigan.

Cheryl married Robert Murphy Lindner (August 11, 1984) at St. Dennis in Royal Oak, Michigan. They have two children, Jonathon Robert Lindner (July 18, 1989) and Jessica Christine Lindner (November 1991). They live in Louisville, Kentucky. Cheryl is a nurse and Robert is a urologist.

Lisa married Stephen Richard Shindler (May 20, 1989) at St. Dennis. Steve is a lieutenant in the Navy. They have lived in North Carolina, Guam, Virginia and California. Their daughter, Katelyn Emma Shindler was born (April 16, 1998) in Guam. Lisa and Steve are both nurses.

Beth married Gerald Martin Paczkowski (August 1989) at St. Dennis. They divorced in September 1992. Beth married Richard Joseph Iezzi (January 22, 2000) in a Hot Air Balloon 5,000 feet over Sedona, Arizona. Rick's son, Evan, (July 22, 1996) lives with them in Macomb, Michigan. Beth and Rick both work for the U.S. Postal Service.

Larry enjoys hunting, fishing, reading, gardening and woodworking. He especially loves spending time with his family and friends.

JACOB "SHOEPAC JAKE" LOFFMAN.

Jacob (born 1847 in Kaustby, Finland, died 1925) emigrated to America in 1972, settling in AuSable where he worked hard as a foreman of a slab-piling crew in a sawmill along the AuSable River. He also worked a stint at B.F. Smith's gypsum quarry (U.S. Gypsum) in Alabaster before settling in East Tawas in 1878 as the crew foreman at Temple Emery's mill on Tawas Bay. He met Miss Greta Granholm in East Tawas, and they married in 1880 and had five children: Matthew, Sadie, Ida, Emil and Esther.

This prolific Suomalainen (Finlander) was responsible for bringing many skilled laborers from Finland to East Tawas, among them tanners and shoemakers. Although he was not a tanner or a shoemaker by trade, Jake employed his immigrant craftsmen to manufacture the Shoepac, a waterproof high boot of lightweight leather with a sturdy leather sole. This moccasin-like boot, which was created in Finland, was the only waterproof boot available. It was constructed from local cowhides that had been processed in his own tannery on East State Street and then later at his home on Wadsworth Street. The Shoepac's heavy leather soles were purchased from Alpena and fastened to the hand-sewn upper with brass nails. Although favored by local hunters, farmers and lumberman, Loffman had a strong mail order business. His Shoepac was shipped from Louisiana to Canada. Many large orders had to be turned down because his small business just couldn't fill the demand. The business eventually closed when his veteran tanner died and rubberized footwear became available. Shoepac Jake moved to Detroit in 1918 and lived there until his death in 1925. He is buried in Greenwood Cemetery in East Tawas.

Two of Jacob and Greta's five children remained in East Tawas, Matthew and Sadie. A third, Emil moved back to East Tawas with his wife Mildred (Carlson) after retiring from Ford Motor Company. Sadie married Victor Floyt, a son of Finnish immigrants from the Tawas area. Together they had two children, Victor Jr. and Evelyn, who died in her youth. They also raised a nephew, George Jacobson. Both Victor Jr. and George left East Tawas as adults.

The oldest, Matthew Loffman became a farmer after the Shoepac business was closed. He met Ellen Pontio, a Finnish immigrant who had escaped the huge AuSable fire by catching the last boat to East Tawas. She had emigrated from Himanka, Finland in 1911 on the *Lusitania* and her immigration was processed at Ellis Island. They married in 1913 and lived in the Loffman house on Wadsworth Street. Together they had six children: Cecelia, Inez, Senia, Luella (Violet), Leo, and Leona.

Celia was accidentally shot by a deer hunter when she was 12. Violet died as an infant. In 1937, Inez married Mervin Lixey. They had four children: Jean (Schriber), Kenneth, David, and Philip. David and Jean have remained in the Tawas area to raise their children. In 1938, Senia married Donald Phillips. They too had four children: Lynn, Janice, JoAnn, and Thomas. Lynn remains in the Tawas area. Leo never married and lived in the Loffman house on Wadsworth Street until his death in 1988. Leona married Edward F. Seifert, Jr. in 1946. They had four children: Edward R. (Randy), Kim, Kurt, and Liisa. Only Kim and his wife JoAnn remain in Tawas. Inez, Senia, and Leona have lived in houses on Loffman property (Wadsworth, East State St. and Alice St.) their entire lives. *Submitted by Liisa Seifert Whitman.*

JOHN A. LOVELESS.

John (born April 21, 1936) retired after 46 years as a carpenter foreman. He was the oldest son of Cecil J. Loveless (born 1911, died 1988) and Laurel Ensminger. He was born in Mikado and moved in 1951 to the house his father built in Rochester. After graduation he joined the Air Force Reserves and married Delores Butler (June 16, 1955). He was building a house in Pontiac when it burned in 1961. They moved to a farm in Metamora in 1963, where they still live.

His grandfather, John H. (born 1886, died 1963), was born in Canada. He married Mary Felker in Bad Axe and they bought a farm in Mikado. He was a carpenter and built ships for World War I. His parents, Ephraim D. (born 1842, died 1916) and Mary Babcock had a farm and he also helped his son, Charles, at Kahn's General Store in Mikado.

John and Delores had three daughters and three sons: Doris, Ken, Jeff, Elizabeth, April, Roy. Delores and Roy Woodward had Nicol.

Family Reunion 1981 (Hadly-Metamora Park) l-r: Carroll, Paul, Jason and Anne (Church) Kitchen, Norman, Charlotte Timmerman, Grant, Warren and Watson with grandchild, Cecil.

Doris (born 1956) married James L. McDowell Jr. and they had two sons, James

III and Jonathan. Ken (born 1957) married MaryAnn Wright. Jeff (born 1959) married Selena Brown. They adopted David Jamison (born December 1996) and changed his name to Jeff Jr. April (born 1965) and Brian Nelson had Daniel. April married Craig Hurd and had one son Paul. Roy (born 1966) married Sherri Loffredi and had one daughter and two sons, Amanda, Johnny, Roy Jr. Nicol (born 1971) married Brian Granz and had two sons, Brian Jr. and Nicholas.

Elizabeth (born 1961) and David Blough had two daughters and one son: Margaret, Patrick, and Melisa. She worked mostly on horse farms. She worked at Tri-County Used Cars as a manager in the clean-up department (1989-1992). She delivered the *Lapeer County Press* (1992-1994).

John Granz and Donna Upleger had two sons and one daughter: Brad (born 1968) married Irene Childers and had Heather. Brian (born 1969) married Nicol Loveless as previously stated. Julie (born 1970) married Chris Schwartzkopf and had Johnathon and Katie. He served in the Vietnam War (1961-1964).

John and I married May 28, 1995. We live on a small farm in Imlay City. He worked at GM in Pontiac and retired January 1, 1998. We enjoy gardening, hunting and fishing. In 1994, John got a 5x6 bull elk (405 lbs.) and a 255 pound bear in 2000. We both are life members in the NRA and John is a life member in the North American Hunt Club. I am also a member of Huron Shores Genealogical Society, NRA-ILA, Second Amendment Task Force, and life member of Citizens Committee For The Right To Keep And Bear Arms. We study with Shepherd's Chapel.

EDNA LUCE. During the depression my dad got a job on the P. L. & W. R.R. in Pennsylvania and so we lived there for 12 years (he had been a master mechanic at the D. & M. in Tawas). At school the high school boys carried me up the long flights of stairs. When I was younger, I was the only one who could play the piano and the high school orchestra practiced upstairs so one of the boys or the professor would come down and carry me up to play the piano for them.

There were no art classes in that school and I was always drawing behind my arithmetic books so I think the following was meant to be. I became ill with lung problems and had to be home a lot. My dad took me to a doctor who seemed to be very observing (I bless him to this day). He said to my dad, "your little girl seems to be unhappy, does she miss school?" "Not really," said my dad,

"she wants to study art and become an artist and they do not teach art at her school." The doctor said well why don't you bring some of her drawings the next time you come. The Associated Artists have classes in an attic in an old house in Beaver, however I think it is an adult class. My dad brought a book of my drawings and the doctor said, "This child has a lot of talent and they probably will put her in the adult class." Oh happy day! I was soon drawing from life, coal miners, a lady student, servant and a colored man named Holly. I still have this portrait and other models. (The teacher carried me up the stairs)

An award winning painting "Mary Manson" was selected for a tour of the United States. The New York critics were so impressed with the water colors, I was invited to show at the Le Salon Dews Nations, Paris, France, which I regret no accepting. They described my work as lyrical, poetic and representing a world of another spiritual dimension.

After my dad passed away my friends at Cocoa Beach, Florida wanted to visit so we rented a house that happened to be on a street where many people were involved with the space program. One person became a life-long friend and arranged a special NASA tour for me. I met another man at a party who had an important job with NASA. He told me he had written a book and would go home and get it. Everyone was surprised when he gave me the book. I get first day covers from every launch ad have a piece of thermal blanket from the moon.

In 1915 polio came to East Tawas and I was one of the children at age one year who became a victim of this terrible disease. I was paralyzed in both legs and could not sit up. My parents took me to a doctor in Detroit who said I would be in a wheelchair for the rest of my life unless you can give her to me for a year for treatment and operations. This was a big sacrifice for my mother but she agreed. When the year was up I did not know her and kept crying and clinging to the nurse, which broke my mother's heart.

In the years that followed my dad took me off and on to Detroit for operations by train. I was always frightened in the operating room with doctors lined up with their masks staring down at me. Doctors were there to see the surgery performed. Dr. Blodgett, my doctor, called me "little sistah."

As the years went by, I no longer wore braces, ditched the crutches and was walking with a cane. As a teenager life became quite an adventure visiting my sister in San

Francisco going to parties where I met some important and famous people. I attended the Hilton Leach art school there and often sketched at the yacht harbor until one day my sister came running saying all military families must get off the street. Japanese planes had bombed Pearl Harbor and we were at war.

In the 40's I decided to open a gift shop in a room in the house and called it "The Shore Shop" and created everything in it myself including hand-painted furniture, bags'n hats, and small paintings. Later I had a small building put up beside our house and in a few years added a larger addition and later a living quarters in the back. It was now called "Gifts that are Different" and since I did not like my name, but liked the name Samantha and took the name "Sammy," signing it with a heart, S♥mmy and it became "S♥mmy's Gift and Gallery" because now my water colors had gained national and international recognition and I was represented by a New York gallery for six years and won national competitions and awards.

My shop in East Tawas is now in its 54th year and I have been in a serious auto accident, and running the shop from a wheelchair, plus numerous medical problems including cancer but just keep going. I believe a sene of humor gets one through life's many ups and downs. I regret not going back to see Dr. Blodgett before he died. Because of his vision and talent, I was able to lead an active, interesting life and would have liked him to know.

MASTER SERGEANT JIM LUCE. He currently serves as the Recruiting Coordinator for the Michigan Youth Challenge Academy in Battle Creek, Michigan. A typical day for Sergeant Luce involves traveling throughout Michigan representing the program and searching for young men and women that are in  need of guidance. His days serving his country did not begin in Battle Creek, but in 1967 in San Diego, California while attending the Marine Corps basic training.

After completing training in San Diego, Jim was sent to serve in the Vietnam War. While in Vietnam for 29 months, Jim worked as a combat engineer, a helicopter gunner and the Vietnamese pacification program, for the U.S. Marine Corps. He received many awards and decorations, most notably, two Purple Hearts, five Air Medals and Navy Commendation with Combat Valor device. After returning to the States, Jim continued to serve his country in the Marine Corps. He was a drill instructor in San Diego, California, a Formal Schools Instructor in Camp Lejuene, North Carolina and in 1974 he joined the Marine Corps Recruiting force in Zanesville, Ohio. In 1978, Jim thought he would try civilian life, but was soon led back into the military. This time it was the Army National Guard. He worked as a recruiter in the Kalamazoo area, and after receiving the Chief's Fifty award three times for being the top recruiter in Michigan, he was selected in 1984 to head the National Guard recruiting efforts for the entire west side of the state. After officially retiring in 1995, Jim returned to private industry, until being requested to return to government service once more last year with the Michigan Youth Challenge Academy.

On a personal note, Master Sergeant Jim Luce is an active member of his church and community. Jim is a Graduate of Sacred Heart Catholic High School, United States Army Sergeants Major Academy and will obtain his bachelor's degree in business administration through Davenport College this spring. Jim resides in Plainwell, Michigan with his wife Jane and two daughters. His desire to have a positive impact in the lives of at-risk teens is what brings him here today.

JOHN A. MARK. He was born in 1857 and died in 1940. His parents came to Canada from England in the early 1800s. John was born in Oshawa, Ontario February 24, 1857 to William and Elizabeth Beckett Mark, and moved to East Jordan, Michigan in 1866, eventually becoming a naturalized citizen of the United States. For a time he was station agent at Fowler for the old Detroit and Milwaukee railroad before coming to AuSable in 1886 aboard the steamer, Arundall, where he was employed by H.M. Loud and Sons. Following an accident in the sawmill in which he lost the fingers of his right hand, he was placed in charge of the commercial steamship dock. After recovering from the accident he taught himself to write with his left hand and was transferred to the company office. Because of the successful battle with his handicap he became known as "The Roman Citizen" by his many friends and even received letters addressed only to "The Roman Citizen." He met and married Dora Surbrook in AuSable on September 22, 1890.

In 1898 he was elected clerk of Iosco County, an office he held for 18 years. It was at this time that John and Dora Mark with their young family consisting of James F. (married Emmelie Applin of East Tawas), Ferne S., John Atlee (married Grace Slocum), William Byron (married Helen Hendrickson of Alabaster) and Elizabeth J. (married T. Henry Holland) moved to Tawas City where they added two more children, Main H. (married Ebba Peterson) and Dorothea E.C. (married Marvin Hennig). In 1906 John bought the family home at 704 West Lake Street and 25 lots along the Tawas River. The house remains family owned by Betty and Jack Willett (daughter of Elizabeth), and next door the cabin built by J. Atlee Mark is owned by Margaret and Carl Diener (daughter of J. Atlee).

John Mark   *Dora Mark*

Wm. Mark Family

After retiring from the position of county clerk, John became city treasurer, a member of the Iosco County road commission, the poor commission and the Tawas City Board of Education. John and Dora Mark were well known and very popular in both AuSable and Tawas City. They were avid baseball fans and their sons, Atlee and Byron, were well known as catching and pitching stars for Tawas City teams. John's love of gardening was apparent to his many friends who received lovely blooms as gifts. Both John and Dora were active in service organizations in Tawas City including the Masonic Lodge, Eastern Star, and the Tawas City Methodist Church where, with their large family, they made up a considerable portion of the congregation. A popular saying at the time was "the Marks and the Murphys are here, so we can start!"

NELSON RALPH MARSH. The family name of Marsh is a local name found in

Sgt. Nelson Ralph Marsh – 1943

Devon, England. Legend tells us a Henry Marsh, M.D. of Dublin, Ireland was a Physician-in-Ordinary to the Queen of Ireland. A descendant, John Marsh, born in Essex, England, in 1589, came to America and settled in Braintree, Massachusetts. Descendants of this, family migrated to Iosco County, Michigan.

Nelson Ralph Marsh, son of Herbert and Blanche Carey Marsh, was born June 5, 1916, at the Old Marsh Farm on Meadow Road, Tawas City, Michigan.

He attended school in Tawas, moving to the Detroit area in 1923 or 1924. He resided in Detroit until he enlisted in the U.S. Army in 1935, serving with the 2nd Infantry Division at Fort Wayne, Michigan, until 1938. Following his discharge, he accepted a position at the Library of Congress in Washington, DC (due to the encouragement and recommendation of the late Congressman Louis Rabaut), where he worked until 1942 when he re-enlisted in the U.S. Army. He was stationed at Fort Meade, Maryland; Fort Benning, Georgia; Army War College, Washington, DC, Fort Eustis, Virginia, and Camp McCoy, Wisconsin before leaving for assignment with General Patton's Third Army in Europe. He served with the 90th Division in Scotland, England, France, Luxembourg, Belgium and Germany, participating in the Battle of the Bulge. He earned the ETO Medal with 5 Star Cluster, Army Occupation, Expert Infantryman Medal and the Purple Heart for injuries received in Luxembourg in 1944.

At the conclusion of World War II, he returned to Washington, DC and accepted a position with the Metropolitan Police Department, Traffic Division, Accident Investigation Unit, where he worked until his retirement in 1967. While with the Police Department he attended the University of Maryland, where he received his certificate from the Law Enforcement Institute.

Nelson was married January 30, 1943, to the former Frances Alexander of Waverly, Tennessee. Frances is retired from the Library of Congress in Washington, D.C.

Nelson and Frances reside in University Park, Maryland and own a cottage on Huron Hills Drive in Baldwin Township.

•*Following is in Nelson's own words:* I'm sure all of us when we were growing up, had that "Extra Special" uncle and aunt.

I was very lucky to have my father's brother and his wife, Fred and Florence Marsh, of Tawas City, Michigan as mine.

Uncle Fred and Aunt Florence lived on "The Old Marsh Farm" on Meadow Road, just outside the city limits. This is now part of "The Hughes Estate." When the leaves are off the trees one can look across the road and creek to Memory Gardens. Where both Uncle Fred and Aunt Florence are buried.

Uncle Fred and Aunt Florence annually invited me to spend the summer with them on The Marsh Farm where I had been born on June 5, 1916. My family had moved to Detroit where my Father worked, and what a special treat it was for me to spend the summer in Tawas with my beloved Uncle and Aunt.

Uncle Fred had been employed as a logger for H.M. Loud and Sons Co. and Alger Smith, and was proud of the fact that with his mother he witnessed from the Mathews Street Bridge, the last Log Drive on the Tawas River in 1887. He was 5 years old.

Uncle Fred had served in the U.S. Army in the Dakotas and was a U.S. Army Captain, 20th Engineers in France during World War I. That is when he met Aunt Florence. She was a native of Scotland and was working in Paris, France as a fashion model. After World War I ended, uncle Fred and aunt Florence were married in New York City on July 29, 1919.

The shoes Aunt Florence wore when she arrived in Michigan are in the Iosco County Museum, along with the silver purse she had with her.

They lived in Glennie, Michigan until 1927, when they returned to Paris, France to work for 18 months. When they returned to Michigan they lived on "The Old Marsh Farm" on Meadow Road. They were very active in community affairs and active members of the Tawas United Methodist Church. During World II, Uncle Fred was Commander of the Jesse C. Hoder Post American Legion 189, and Aunt Florence was President of the Auxiliary for two years.

Uncle Fred and Aunt Florence celebrated their 50th wedding anniversary in 1969, with an Open House at the Old Marsh Farm on Meadow Road.

When I enlisted in the U.S Army, following the attack on Pearl Harbor, and went to Europe with the 90th Division and served with Gen. Patton's 3rd Army in England, Scotland, France, Luxembourg, Belgium and Germany, participating in the Battle of the Bulge and winning the Purple Heart in Luxembourg, the letters Uncle Fred and Aunt Florence wrote me were inspirational and encouraging. They kept me going! They were in the terminology of today "Been there-done that" letters.

At the conclusion of World War II I returned to Washington, DC and my job at the Library of Congress. That was where I had met my wife. She is a Rebel from Tennessee and I am a Yankee. We were married 58 years on Jan. 30, 2001.

While working at the library I was offered a position at the Washington, DC Metropolitan Police Department as an accident investigator. I retired from there, and also retired from the U.S. Army Reserves, Criminal Investigation Unit.

We are proud that some of the possessions that have brought the Marsh Family so much happiness have found a home in the Iosco County Museum. After all, what good are memories if you can't share them? — Nelson Ralph Marsh

ADDENDUM: Florence Marsh died December 9, 1982 and is buried in Memory Garden Cemetery beside her devoted husband Fred Marsh. She often stood at her window in her home and looked across the creek and road when leaves were off the trees, and could see the spot where Uncle Fred was buried. Their home is now the Huges Estates.

Aunt Florence and Uncle Fred were special people and so was their nephew, Nelson R. Marsh, my husband of eight days short of 59 years. *Submitted by Frances A. Marsh.*

ROSE E. MARTIN. She was born August 20, 1894 in Germany to John and Elizabeth Bay and had one sister, Lena Bay Sheldon. John Bay was manager of the D & M Railroad office in Alabaster. Rose married Edward John Martin and lived on the farm in Alabaster, Michigan. They reared three children:  Elizabeth Martin O'Donahue, Westland, Michigan (born July 22, 1917); Edward J. Martin, San Jose, California (born January 18, 1919); and James Herbert Martin, East Tawas, Michigan (January 26, 1923).

Rose and Edward Martin sold their farm in Alabaster and purchased the Iosco Hotel in Tawas City. They rented rooms and served meals for many years. Jim remembers growing up and living at the Iosco Hotel and going to St. Joseph School in Tawas City. All three graduated from St. Joseph School in Tawas City. Jim enlisted in the service in 1942 and Edward enlisted in 1939 or 1940.

Elizabeth went to Bay City business college. When she married Adair O'Donahue, she found employment in Detroit while he was in the service. Betty and Adair have one son, William O'Donahue living in Canton, Michigan.

Edward J. Martin met and married his wife Jane while they were in the service. She was an army nurse. They have three children: Judy, Johnny and Kevin. After military service Captain Martin flew for TWA until he retired.

Jim Martin married Donna M. Moore June 12, 1948. They have two sons, Gary James Martin (born November 25, 1951) and Gregory Paul Martin (born October 31, 1954, deceased July 1984).

When Mr. and Mrs. Martin sold the Iosco Hotel in 1939, Rose purchased 250' of property on U.S. 23 in East Tawas where she built cottages known then as Huron Court.

In 1941-42 she added on several units because her son, James, was returning home from the service to join her in the business. It was then renamed Martin's Motel. She was there until her death March 20, 1972.

Her son James and wife Donna owned and operated Martin's Motel until their retirement in 1985. They still reside in East Tawas. Their son, Gary Martin, graduated from Tawas Area High School in 1969 and Michigan State University in 1974 with a master's degree in education.

CHARLENE KAY MCCALL. Charlene was born in Detroit, Michigan November 21, 1936 to Elwyn "Red" Loyd McCall and Emma Martha Reinhardt McCall. Red was born in Gratiot, Michigan August 11, 1902. His parents were Daniel Walter McCall and Minnie Gertrude McGreaham. Emma was born March 17, 1900 in West Branch, Michigan. Her parents were August Reinhardt and Martha DeLena Rentschler.

Red and Emma were married December 1, 1930 in Lucas County, Ohio. Red was a Detroit Policeman and had many stories to tell about the notorious "Purple Gang." Emma was a beautician and taught marcelling at Kern's department store in Detroit. She owned her own beauty shop in Detroit and one of her many clients was Mayor Cavanaugh's mother.

Red resigned from the police force after 17 years, and they bought a resort on Lake Huron in East Tawas, Michigan before the end of World War II. They named it "McCall's Resort" but later changed it to "Avalon Beach Resort." The resort was comprised of seven cottages plus their home. "Red" delivered house trailers for Anderson Coach Company while Emma managed the resort. Many renters remember the fresh baked blueberry pies she made for them and the beautiful 250-foot sandy beach.

Emma was the Worthy Matron of the Eastern Star October 1954-October 1955. She joined the Rebekah Lodge December 7, 1949. She held the following elective offices: Vice Grand (1951), Noble Grand (1953) and Past Noble Grand (1954). She was a delegate to the Rebekah Assembly of Michigan in 1955 and 1956 and the financial secretary in 1957. She served in many appointed chairs.

Back row l-r: Steve Kirschke, Pam (Lixey) Kirschke, Rick Iezzi, Beth (Lixey) Iezzi, Charlene (McCall) Lixey, Larry Lixey, Jonathon Lindner; front row: Lisa (Lixey) Shindler, Karl Kirschke, Valori Lixey, Jessica Lindner, Cheryl (Lixey) Lindner, Robert Lindner; lower left is Katelyn Emma Shindler. Missing from picture: Steve Shindler and Evan Iezzi.

Charlene was in the third grade when her parents and sister, Patricia Ann McCall (born September 11, 1931), moved to East Tawas. Charlene's graduating class (1954) was the first class to graduate from Tawas Area High School. She worked for American Airlines as a ticket agent in Detroit for seven years. She married Ernest "Larry" Lixey on May 25, 1957 in St. Joseph Catholic Church in East Tawas. Larry and Charlene have five daughters: Valori Ann (born October 27, 1958), Pamela Sue (born December 22, 1959), Cheryl Lynn (born October 18, 1961), Lisa Marie (born December 15, 1963), and Beth Anne (born November 9, 1965). Please see Ernest Larry Lixey for further information on their children.

Charlene returned to work as a secretary in the Religious Education Office at St. Dennis Catholic Church in Royal Oak, Michigan (1975-1982). She worked for The Lamphere Schools (1982-1997) in Madison Heights as a secretary to the principal of Lessenger Elementary School. Larry and Charlene moved back to East Tawas when Charlene retired. Charlene is active in the Tawas Bay Garden Club, the Iosco County

Historical Museum and Holy Family Parish. Her hobbies are quilting, genealogy and gardening. She established a chapter of the Red Hat Society in 2002 in the Tawas area known as the Huron Red Hatties. She is referred to as "The Queen Mum" as part of the tradition of starting a chapter. Her favorite thing is spending time with her family and friends.

WILLIAM HENRY MCCREADY.
Iosco County Probate and Juvenile Court Judge from 1965 to 1995, William was born in Twining on July 4, 1927 to James Archibald and Lillian Mosher McCready. His father was many years Arenac County Drain Commissioner. His mother was sister to Pearl (Mrs. Guy) Spencer and Maud (Mrs. Harlan) Randall of East Tawas.

Judge McCready graduated from Standish High School in 1945 and entered the U.S. Army. During service in the South Pacific he transferred to the Army Air Corps, and was honorably discharged as a corporal in May 1947. While planning a career in the State Police, he suffered a gunshot wound which left him totally blind. He then attended Michigan State College for a BA in pre-law and University of Michigan Law School for his LLB degree. He was admitted to the Bar in March 1959 by Judge Herman Dehnke. He opened a private practice in Tawas City and later that year his political career began when six people wrote his name in on the ballot for Justice of the Peace! He was elected Iosco County Prosecuting Attorney in the fall of 1960, and was prosecutor for four years, until he was elected to the Bench.

Rae and Bill McCready

Judge McCready was married August 26, 1954 to Rachel Sue Rerick of Sturgis, Michigan, who was one of the students assigned to read to him at Michigan State. She had graduated from State in 1953 and spent the following year in Wales on a Rotary Foundation Fellowship. They were married on "Bride and Groom," NBC TV, in New York City, on her return to the U.S. She attained her MA in elementary teach-

ing at the University of Michigan while Bill was in Law School and she was teaching in Ann Arbor.

They moved into their home on First Street in Tawas City in October 1958, and daughter Linda

William H. McCready and leader dog, Zeke

was born November 12th. Second semester in 4th grade in East Tawas and one year in 5th grade at the school in Alabaster which was used for 5th and 6th grades that year, completed Rachel's teaching career. Daughter Lois was born December 27, 1960. Sons Keith and Ken were later additions, as well as a series of leader dogs: Storm, Patrick, Max, Josh and Zeke.

Rae, active in Girl Scouts, church, bowling league, was Tawas City City Clerk from 1976-1981, Regent of DAR Chapter, treasurer of U of M Club and Republican Women's Club for years, played French horn in Community Band from its beginning, and on Iosco County Board of Canvassers. Bill was active in Boy Scouts, church, Lions (District Governor 1963-64), Youth Services program at Wurtsmith AFB, and Iosco County Commission on Aging.

Linda Beth, forensic chemist, Indianapolis City/Marion County, Indiana.

Lois Jean, dental assistant, married Ron Schneemann, Ft. Wayne, Indiana, children, Heidi and Samuel.

Keith Howard, Lt. Col. USAF, graduate Air Force Academy 1984, Commander, 56th Rescue Squadron, Keflavik Naval Air Station, Iceland, married to Susan Horvath.

Kenneth Allan, computer sales, Loda, Illinois.

MALCOLM J. MCFARLANE.
In 1866, Malcolm came to AuSable, Michigan in 1866 from Glencoe, Ontario, Canada with his wife, Jennett, and six children: son Daniel and daughters: Margaret, Catherine, Mary Jane, Christy and Annie. Malcom was born in Inverness, Scotland, and came to Canada with his parents when he was a year old.

He was a builder by trade and upon arrival in AuSable, he helped build the first mill for Loud, Priest and Shepherd. Malcolm operated the Lee House in AuSable until it burned in 1882; then he built and owned the McFarlane House, located on the corner of River Street (now Harbor Drive) and O'Toole Avenue. He was one of the first settlers in AuSable, active in the founding of the Presbyterian Church, and also one of the oldest Masons in the Village. A paragraph in the booklet, *Homecoming Week On The Sable,* (July 29 to August 4, 1906) printed as the Homecoming Week Edition of the Press, the Historical Sketch prepared by Harry R. Solomon, reads:

"In 1857 the Township of Sable was organized, but was changed to AuSable by an Act of the Legislature in 1877. It was incorporated as a village in 1872 with Nelson Lipscomb as its first president, the succeeding ones being Cornelius Dietz, A.S. Backus, John W. Glennie, Justus Rogers, James E. Forrest, A.F. McDonald, C.R. Henry, Hugh Colwell, Malcolm McFarlane and W.A. Tomlinson, the latter serving as its executive until the village became a city."

Malcolm McFarlane also served as Trustee and Justice of the Peace from 1878 to 1883. He became ill in 1889 and died October 7, 1891 in the McFarlane House. His only son, Daniel McFarlane, had married Emma Jane Watson on November 27, 1888, and had become the proprietor of the hotel during Malcolm's long illness.

After Malcolm's death the McFarlane House was sold and torn down in 1894, and son Daniel moved to Austin, Pennsylvania with his wife, Emma Jane and two daughters, Anna and Janet (both born in the McFarlane House). A few years later, the family moved to Munising, Michigan where Daniel worked in Loud's Shingle Mill. He was killed by a boiler explosion in the mill on January 26, 1899, leaving his widow, Emma Jane, and four small children: Anna, Janet, Malcolm Joseph and Robert Thomas.

Malcolm J. McFarlane, his wife Jennett, son Daniel, daughter Margaret, and several grandchildren are buried in the family gravesite in Pinecrest Cemetery, Oscoda, Michigan.

Recently a "dig" at the McFarlane House site by prospectors Smith and Argentati produced a hand-blown bottle, which was given to Malcolm McFarlane's great-granddaughter, Lorraine Howitson.

CARLTON OTTO and FLORENCE LOUISE (GREENE) MERSCHEL.

Carlton (born 1911, died 1986) was one of eight children: Margaret, Norman, Carlton, Dorothy, Ruth, Grace, Helen and James, of Andrew James and Elsie Ruhnke Merschel. He was born at home above Merschel Hardware, the business operated by his father in East Tawas.

He enlisted in the Army but was honorably discharged after basic training because foot problems interfered with his ability to participate in extended marches.

Carlton's boyhood home at 415 E. Lincoln Street later became his own family home when he married Florence Greene. Their two daughters, Mary Lou and Janet, were also reared there. After Florence's death Carlton married Ruth Hess.

Florence Louise (Green) and Carlton Otto Merschel

Carlton owned and operated Merschel Dry Cleaners for 30 years. He also sold real estate, insurance, mutual funds, owned a restaurant, taught Dale Carnegie classes in leadership and sales, and served on the Iosco County Board of Commissioners for many years. He was instrumental in making the Iosco County Historical Museum a reality. He was a member of the Masonic Lodge, Businessmen's Association, Lions Club, and served on various civic boards. He enjoyed traveling and reading about everything under the sun. He was ahead of his time as far as knowledge about health and nutrition, even though he didn't always practice what he preached.

Florence, daughter of Charles and Mary Klinger Greene, lived most of her life in East Tawas except for a brief time in Detroit (to attend business school) and Florida with Carlton and the girls to try living in the warmer weather. They were building a house in St. Petersburg when Florence was diagnosed with cancer and died the following year.

As a young girl Florence enjoyed making music with her younger brothers, Walter, Harold, Wilfred, and Russell, and friends at their home at 317 Church Street. She played the piano for Women's Club minstrel shows—all kinds of music but her specialty was ragtime. Neighbors would stop what they were doing to listen to her play her piano through the open windows during the warm months. She was a wonderful seamstress and made most of her daughters' clothing.

The back yard at 415 E. Lincoln was a summer gathering place for relatives of both the Greene and Merschel families. Everyone brought their favorite dishes and played games and swapped stories. Carlton and Florence were full of love for their families and created some wonderful memories. *Submitted by Mary Lou (Merschel) Peters.*

MELBOURNE AUSSIE METCALF.

Aussie was born in 1922 in Bradford, Illinois to Frank and Annie Metcalf. He is the youngest of six children. Aussie's parents were born and raised in Australia. His father was an itinerant minister and missionary in New South Wales, Australia. His parents met in church in Cudgee, Australia

Melbourne Aussie Metcalf

and were married in 1909. They originally traveled to America in 1911, arriving at Ellis Island. Frank attended Louisville Baptist Seminary to receive his Doctorate in Divinity and accepted his first pastorate at First Baptist Church of Bradford, Illinois.

In 1915, Frank and Annie, along with their two children, Jean and Elizabeth "Bess," returned to Australia to attend to Frank's ill mother. Two more daughters, Lucille and Anne were born in Australia. In 1919, after the death of Frank's mother, the Metcalf's returned to the United States and the little church in Bradford, Illinois. Aussie and his older brother Tom were born in Bradford. Aussie was named after the city of Melbourne and the Australian people.

In 1927, when Aussie was 5 years old, George Prescott invited Rev. Metcalf and his family to visit Tawas City. Frank fell in love with the town on the bay and accepted the pastorate at the First Baptist Church of Tawas City. Aussie attended Ward School, a one-room school house in Tawas City from Grades 1-3, and attended Tawas High School from Grades 4-12. He continues to be in contact with his home economics teacher, Mrs. Ruth Benedict Coon, who now lives in Lansing, Michigan.

In the eighth grade, Aussie received his first job as a paperboy for the *Bay City Times.* He developed it into one of the largest paper routes north of Bay City at that time. From the paper route money and the money obtained from odd jobs, Aussie bought a used 1930 Model A Ford for $75 to drive his dad to conduct Sunday services, funerals and weddings at First Baptist Church of Tawas City, Hemlock Road Baptist Church and Reno Baptist Church. Aussie graduated from Tawas High School on June 3, 1942, the same day of his father's funeral. The funeral was in the afternoon and graduation was in the evening.

Later in 1942, Aussie was called to service in World War II as a machine gun operator. He fought in the Battle of the Bulge, and in 1944 was wounded near Strasbourg, France. Aussie was awarded several medals for his World War II service. After the war, he returned to Tawas City and worked as a milkman for Nelkie Dairy in Tawas City for 18 years. In 1956, he met Bernice Dewald of Turner, Michigan. Bernice was a lineotype operator at the *Iosco County News*. Aussie and Bernice were married on September 14, 1957.

In 1965, Aussie started working at Tawas Industries and retired from there in 1987. Aussie and Bernice have three children: Sheryl, Rick and Janet. Sheryl resides in Grand Rapids; Rick and his wife Susan live in Okemos, Michigan with their two children Sarah and Ryan; and Janet and her husband Dan Greenwood live in Auburn, Michigan with their three children: Jeremy, Joshua and Jeffrey. Aussie and his sister Anne of Costa Mesa, California are the only surviving children of Frank and Annie Metcalf.

EDWARD MICHAEL MIELOCK.

He was born September 1, 1896, at Alabaster, Michigan, the third of seven children reared by Jacob and Angela Budzynski Mielock. The parents and grandparents came from an area of the central European plain that was alternately dominated by Prussia, Austria and Russia.

Edward's childhood and early adulthood were spent near the family farm at Alabaster. During this period he developed a talent for carpentry and became an excellent outdoorsman in the surrounding woods. Although he first registered for service in World War I, a subsequent hunting injury denied him the opportunity of serving. A father before him, and older and younger brothers had all been in the army.

In the early 1920s he migrated to Detroit and initially obtained work as a railroad carpenter, but subsequently was self-employed in residential and commercial construction. He returned to the Tawas area to court a bride, Anna Marcella Sands. Anna was born in Tawas on May 1, 1892, the daughter of Jacob Sands and Frances Melcarek.

Her parents and grandparents also came from e same area of central Europe. They were married at East Tawas in 1924 before returning to the Detroit home and business he was building. This marriage produced three children: Frances, Edward Jr. and Anne Marie.

Frances, the oldest of his three children, is married to William White, an architect, and now resides in El Paso, Texas. In addition to being a homemaker and mother of three children: Christie, Cotter and Bruce, she also manages family rental property.

Edward Jr., the second child, is an engi-neer-educator, married Kathleen Clark, who upon raising Denny, Karen, Patrice, Mike, Maureen, Eddie, John, Jean, and Kathy, is employed as a social worker. Edward Jr. has retired from the county and joined the staff of Lawrence Tech. Although their children are scattered, Edward Jr. and Kathleen reside in Birmingham, Michigan.

Anne Marie, the third child, met Jay Brashear, a newsman, while teaching in Arizona. Married, and the mother of Jay Jr. and Jolie, she has been able to combine the career of homemaker and independent counselor. Somehow she has found additional time to continue her education. Their family resides in Scottsdale, Arizona.

When Edward Michael's contracting business floundered during the depression, employment was sought elsewhere. Although maintaining the homestead in Detroit, Edward sought work in the Tawas-Oscoda area. Here he was self-employed throughout the construction season, and trapped during the winter months. He enjoyed the winters and was successful when he returned to his earlier skills. Inasmuch as the price paid for pelts had not substantially declined, he was able to continue the maintenance of his family in Detroit.

With an upturn of construction in the Detroit area, his contracting business was resumed. The business proved successful until a shortage of materials during World War II restricted its operation. At this time Edward sought employment as a maintenance superintendent at Vickers. During the postwar period residential construction was briefly resumed although stiff competition was encountered. This competition, but most probably because of the salary and benefits enjoyed with Vickers, influenced Edward to return when requested. Edward retired from Vickers at the age of 65, which allowed him additional time for visiting family members, enjoying the outdoors, and learning new skills in woodworking and candle making.

Throughout his life Edward continued to own property in the Tawas area which provided an excuse to return to the woods he loved. He left a legacy in wood and other materials. However, his son and grandsons will probably best remember him because of his knowledge and instruction in the outdoor skills.

ERNEST and FLORENCE MIELOCK.

Ernest Mielock, eldest son of Jacob and Angela (Budzynska) Mielock was born January 25, 1893 on the family farm in Alabaster located on a road later named "Mielock Road." Ernest helped on the farm and attended Alabaster School through the 8th grade.

He worked as a short order cook while attending Bliss Alger College in Saginaw and graduated in 1912 in banking. Ernest worked for the U.S. Gypsum Company for a time and then was called to serve in World War I with the Polar Bear Division in Russia. His family was notified he was missing and they were worried until news came he was safe and recovering from influenza. Returning from the war, Ernest turned to a building career working for a time with his brother-in-law, Joseph Lubaway. Later he was a general contractor in Detroit.

Ernest Mielock, Rosemary Klenow, Florence Mielock

On January 29, 1927, Ernest married Florence Kulazeski, daughter of John and Victoria (Walters) Kulazeski of Tawas City. Prior to her marriage Florence taught school in Flat Rock. She graduated from Iosco County Normal in 1919 and Detroit Teacher's College in 1926. Her first position in a rural school included an extra $5.00 per month for filling the coal scuttle.

Following their wedding at Holy Trinity Church, Detroit, a wedding breakfast was held at their Dutch colonial style home designed and built by Ernest and furnished by Florence. The bride wore a platinum silver gown designed and made by her mother and carried pink roses. Florence's sister Dora and Ernest's brother John were their attendants.

Their only child, Rosemary, was born September 29, 1929. Florence's father died in 1930 after suffering with asthma for many years.

During the depression Florence returned to school teaching and Grandma Kulazeski came to look after Rosemary. Ernest worked for the Ford Motor Company at River Rouge. He became a tool and diemaker and continued as a defense worker during World War II. He lost an eye in an industrial accident on December 7, 1942.

In 1944, the family moved to East Tawas where Ernest and brother John went into business as Mielock Brothers Construction. Florence taught school at East Tawas and St. Joseph School. Fourth grade was her favorite class.

Ernest designed and built all of the family homes. One in Detroit, three in East Tawas, including the first ranch with cottage roof in the county and the final home on Iris Drive in Baldwin Township.

Daughter, Rosemary, graduated from E.T. High in 1946, attended Northeastern S.C. and later CMU. She worked for the D & M Railway. For 44 years, retiring in 1991. Rosemary married Robert Klenow, son of Ralph and Vera (Harwod) Klenow, on October 7, 1950. Bob worked for the Mielock Bros. until his death in May 1953. Rosemary and Robert had one son, Blaise, born September 30, 1952.

Ernest died in November 1962 and Florence in March 1970. Rosemary lives in the family home in Baldwin Township built by her father. Ernest built many homes and business buildings in Iosco County and Detroit. Florence pursued her career by building the minds of the many children she helped educate.

JACOB MIELOCK. Jacob followed a married sister Katherine in emigrating to America in 1884. Katherine and family lived in Tawas briefly before a final move to their Wisconsin farm.

Upon arrival, Jacobs first employment was in lumbering near Hancock. As the trees became depleted in the U.P., Jacob continued lumbering in the Lincoln area. On one of Jacobs weekend visits to East Tawas he met his future wife Angela, who was working as a pastry chef at the Holland or another hotel. Angela had also emigrated from Europe.

Mielock Family

Soon after marriage in 1890, Jacob was employed at the Alabaster quarry, before purchasing 40 acres of undeveloped land from his employer. Jacob and Angela settled into farming and raising a family. Their children, in birth order, were Stella, Ernest, Edward, John, Mary, James and Angela.

Jacob was instrumental in bringing other family members to the Iosco County area.

The Mielock family worked at developing the Alabaster farm by draining land and removing trees and stumps, while adding to their farm buildings. Eventually the farm grew to 160 acres, located on both sides of Mielock Road, just south of the Alabaster quarry. When the farm was sold in 1928, Jacob and family moved to East Tawas. Developed acreage was purchased that bordered the Tawas River. Later, with declining health, the Mielocks moved to smaller properties, close to the business district.

Of the Mielock children, Stella settled in the Detroit area after marriage and raised a family. Ernest also moved to Detroit after marriage and was employed at Ford while also continuing in construction on a part-time basis. Ernie and his family returned to the Tawas area with construction continuing on a full-time basis.

Edward also moved to Detroit after marriage and worked in construction. For a brief period during World War II, when construction materials were very scarce, Ed was employed by Vickers in property maintenance. Throughout his life Ed maintained various vacation homes in Iosco County.

John, after marriage, settled in East Tawas. John was self employed in merchandizing and later in construction. Some of the beautiful stone masonry around Tawas has been constructed by Ernest or John, or possibly jointly by both.

Mary began her career, teaching briefly in the Tawas area, before being employed as an executive secretary for MGM in Detroit. After marriage Mary and her husband owned a small move theatre in Detroit.

James also began his career as a teacher at a local school. Jim's next employment was as works manager at Alabaster. Jim also farmed on a part time basis while working at Alabaster. Later Jim and family left the quarry and farmed near Whittemore. He also served as a state legislator in this period. In retirement, Jim and his wife returned to East Tawas.

Angela also started as a teacher in the Tawas area. Soon after marriage, Angela and her family moved to her husband's place of employment in Gaylord. Angela's Gaylord home also provided a final home for Jacob and his wife Angela.

CHARLES C. MILLER. Sheriff Miller (born 1895, died 1934) was the oldest child of John A. Miller and Elizabeth Beesinger. Although he was born in AuSable, the family returned to the family farm in Tawas Township soon thereafter. The farm has been designated as a Centennial Farm and is

at the corner of Miller and McArdle Roads. Charles resided his entire life in Iosco after service in World War I in France. He and Earl St. Martin were the first to enlist from Iosco and their departure was accompanied with considerable fanfare. This was the "war to end all wars." After service in the motor unit, he was "over there" when the Armistice was declared on November 11, his 23rd birthday! On return, he married Grace Carpenter, of

Charles C. Miller

a pioneer family. After working for W.A. Evans Furniture, he operated Miller Tire and Electric - the "first vulcanizing and radio shop in the county.

In 1930, he was elected Sheriff and served until he was killed in the line of duty July 1, 1934, attempting a solo capture of a four time murderer. Grace was appointed sheriff to fulfill his term and the voters showed their compassion by electing her county treasurer for the next 32 years. The young widow was left with three sons: Allan, Charles and Kenneth.

The family tradition of public service, which had begun with great-grand father Oren A. Carpenter's term as justice of the peace and town clerk in 1877, was further continued when the eldest son, Allan, was elected circuit judge in 1959, a position he presently holds. Charles married Mary Stang, an old-time Tawas family, and they have four sons and four daughters: Charles, Mary Ellen Sankovich, Amy, Beth, Paul, Mark, Matthew and Estella. Kenneth married Del Burzyk of Saginaw and they have two daughters, Jane and Jill.

Judge Miller married Betty Gill and had five children: Alan Charles, Chris, Clifford, Van and Liz. Clifford owns Millers Shoes in East Tawas.

WILLIAM "BILLY" MILLS. A farmer in Tawas Township, Billy entered Iosco County with a pocketful of dreams in 1865. He was known as Billy, the fifth child of William and Mary Jane (McLaughlin) Mills. William was born 1796 in England, died 1854 in Beckwith, Lanark County, Canada West. Mary is the daughter of Laughlin and Catherine (McLean) McLaughlin who arrived Quebec City from Scotland on the ship *Neptune* in 1816. Laughlin was a ship builder and moved his young family to Perth, Lanark County, Ontario. Billy's siblings include Samuel, Mary, Sarah,

Laughlin, John, Peter, Thomas, Susan, Samuel and Marianne.

Our subject was born March 11, 1837 in Drummond Township, Lanark County, a member of 10 children reared in an ambitious and determined environment. Billy began his Michigan career in the lumber business having made a great many of the shingles that cover some of the oldest buildings in Iosco County. He invested his money in land, selecting a prime Townline lot consisting of 120 acres to start his farming business. In 1892 Billy married a young neighbor girl, Loutisha Bessey, daughter of George and Elizabeth (Frank) Bessey. George was the grandson of Jacob and Elizabeth (Slough) Bessey, a Loyalist of Butler's Rangers in Revolutionary War who was granted 300 acres land in the Canadian Niagara region.

Loutisha was born March 9, 1875 in Welland, Ontario, the oldest child in her family that includes Eugene (born 1878, died 1962); Andrew (born 1879, died 1971); Naaman, George Jr. and Samuel. Her family migrated to Iosco County in 1883 to join in the lumbering. William "Billy" and Loutisha Mills had four daughters: Loretta (born 1893, died 1948); Mary Myrtle (born 1896, died 1977), Cecilia Elizabeth (born 1902, died 1992), Willamimine (born 1907, died 1995). Billy was known for always lending a helping hand where ever he could and to whom ever he could. In the 1900s, he served on the School Board for Townline Public Schools.

When his oldest daughter, Loretta Mills, graduated from school, Billy sent her to Wingham, Ontario, to complete her education. She lived with her aunt and uncle, Mary Jane (Hele) and Thomas Allan Mills. Loretta returned to Tawas, married Earl Lloyd Herriman in November 1911, and had 10 children.

Myrtle moved to Columbus, Ohio, and married 1) Oscar Koeppel, and 2) Nobel Schenck; she had no children.

Cecilia married William Fowler and had children: Clarence, Harlan, Marion, Wanda.

Willaminine married George Biggs, naming their firstborn Billy Mills. Other Biggs children are Wayne George, Ervin Leon, Joanne and Thelma Loutisha; one child died in infancy.

William "Billy" Mills died in December 1914 as one of the oldest and highly respected pioneers in the area. His funeral was attended by the largest crowds that have ever assembled in a church in Iosco County.

Loutisha Mills married Tilden Winchell in 1920; she passed away in 1952 and is buried in the Mills family plot at Memory Gardens. *Submitted by Connie Chism.*

RICHARD MISENER. Richard was of German Ancestry and emigrated to New Jersey, from Holland in 1720. Four generations later (Adam, Peter, William, and Anthony Misener) Henry Gilmore Misener (born 1845, died 1932) was born to Anthony and Catherine Petrie Misener in Ancaster Township, Ontario, Canada. Henry Gilmore married Fedora Ann Beemer (born 1853, died 1935).

In 1879 the family settled in Kings Crossing, Michigan, and shortly moved to Whittemore. Henry moved his family to East Tawas, Michigan in 1880, where he owned and operated a shingle mill.

Henry Gilmore Misener and family, top row l-r: Joseph R. Misener, Oren Misener, Wyatt Misener; bottom row l-r: Alva E. Misener, Henry Gilmore Misener (father), Fedora Ann (Beemer) Misener (mother), Edson Misener - picture taken ca. 1903

Eight children were born to this couple, three died in infancy. The five surviving sons, "The Misener Boys," attended school in East Tawas and learned the building trade from their father, who was an expert in his line of work. The young men, married young women of the vicinity and made their homes in East Tawas.

Oren in the Life Saving Service (Coast Guard) was stationed at points in Michigan. Leaving the service he worked at the Mackinac Railroad in Alpena as a carpenter, then returned to East Tawas to retire. Alva and Wyatt were employees of the Detroit and Mackinac Railway. Edson, an excellent electrician and carpenter, aided by his brothers installed the first telephone system in the area. They obtained six hand cranked telephone sets, cut and set a mile of poles and put up the lines to the homes of their parents and their own homes.

Joseph made carpentry his lifetime occupation. He constructed homes, commercial buildings and churches in the area. He helped to build all of the original buildings at Tawas Beach Club when the association was organized in 1897. He also built and remodeled many of the cottages in the Tawas Beach Association. The home of Joseph in East Tawas is still owned by family and is one of the older homes in the area.

Oren Misener (born 1873, died 1951) married Mabel Falls of Wilber; children: Everett, Joy Misener Smith, Walter, Roger and Isabelle.

Joseph Misener (born 1875, died 1960) married Penelope Stanton (See Stanton Family); children: Ivan William and Fedora Misener Nelem (See Nelem Family).

Alva E. Misener (born 1878, died 1964) married Emma Brandt; children, Carl H., Milton B. and Helen Misener Cook.

Wyatt Misener (born 1878, died 1959) married Minnie Marie Elster of East Tawas. The couple had three children: Frederick, Arlene Misener Carpenter (See Carpenter History) and Stanley.

Edson (born 1882, died 1918) married Muriel Framm; children: Margaret Misener-Weed Gregg and Jane Misener-Weed Leech. Edward died in the flu epidemic in December of 1918. Muriel later married Dr. Weed, whose practice was in East Tawas, and he adopted both girls. Margaret lives in North Carolina and Jane resides in Florida.

A Misener reunion has been held on the third Saturday in August each year for 99 consecutive years. August 2003, they will celebrate their 100th Reunion. For more Misener family information, contact Secretary Patricia Baker, 2037 Mountain Grove Ave., Burlington, Ontario, Canada L7P 2H8.

Family records are available in the Archives Library of the Wilfred Laurier University at Waterloo, Ontario, Canada and also from Donna Kemp (Records) R.R. #6, Brantford, Ontario, Canada N3T 5L8. A website with 6,000 Misener names: http://freepages.genealogy.rootsweb.com/~grannyapple/MISNER/MISNERdata. html *Submitted by Marilouise (Nelem) Pershon.*

MOEHRING FAMILY. In 1940, Herman and Bernice Moehring and children, Elaine and David, came to East Tawas from Detroit to join Herman's aunt, Johanna Conklin, in her floral business. That was the beginning of Moehring's Greenhouse.

Herman Moehring was born March 9, 1908 in Detroit. Bernice Mohn Moehring was born May 16, 1908 in Detroit. They were both graduates of Eastern High School in Detroit, and, in 1933, were married in that city at Bethany Lutheran Church.

Four more children were born after the move to East Tawas: Christine (born 1943) in East Tawas, Richard (born 1945) in Omer, JoAnn (born 1946) in Standish and John (born 1950) in Standish.

Herman and Bernice Moehring Family

David practices and teaches orthopedic surgery at the University of California at Davis. He and his wife Virginia have two children, Kurt and Mary. Elaine, a retired teacher, makes her home in Minneapolis with her husband, Robert Granquist. Christine, also a retired teacher, resides in East Tawas with her husband, Carl Huebner. Richard, a packaging engineer, lives in Houston with his wife, Jacqueline. They have two children, Christopher and Kathryn. JoAnn, a teacher, and her husband William Pinkerton live in Roanoke, Virginia. They are parents of four daughters: Amy, Sarah, Carolyn and Betsy, and grandparents of two boys. John, owner and operator of Moehring's Greenhouse, lives in East Tawas.

Herman and Bernice Moehring were members of Grace Evangelist Lutheran Church in East Tawas. Herman was also a member of the East Tawas Volunteer Fire Department, and the East Tawas Men's Club. Bernice was a member of the Ladies' Literary Club of East Tawas for over 60 years.

Herman died in 1983 and Bernice in 2001. Both are buried in Greenwood Cemetery in East Tawas. Grandson, Robert Moehring is also buried there.

Family remembrances: the D & M's 8 o'clock whistle—time to get up; fishflies covering the sidewalks in summertime when we'd spend all day at the beach; and band concerts on the lawn in front of the old Community Building. The wailing fire whistle summoned Dad to leave the shop and run down to the fire barn, loose change jingling in his pockets. We can't forget the mournful foghorn or blinking lighthouse across the bay; swimming at the Point; or when the Gamble's Store burned down and later on, Harbor Lights. Other remem-

brances: the long walk to Sunday School at the old Grace Lutheran church on the edge of the woods, the tornado of 1953, and huckleberry picking.

The East Tawas School holds many memories: windows opened with a long, hooked pole; red geraniums brightening the windowsills on winter days, Mr. Creaser's office, and Mrs. Clark rapping on her basement classroom window to scold noisy children on the playground. We remember the dark, mysterious cloakrooms; mittens and snowpants steaming on the radiators; presidents' pictures on the wall; and the big Valentine box full of laboriously homemade Valentines. Filling the halls, upstairs and down, to sing Christmas carols, and dedicated teachers who opened up the world for us - wonderful memories all.

FRANK H. and ETHEL M. MOORE.

Frank was born August 2, 1891, son of Thomas and Attie Moore, and Ethel was born April 15, 1897, daughter of Joseph and Dora Colburn, all lifetime residents of Tawas City.

Frank and Ethel Moore were married September 21, 1915 in East Tawas. Three daughters were born to

Frank and Ethel Moore

this union: twins, Nyda Bronson (Elwood); Lyda Nelkie (Thomas); and Donna Martin (James); all Tawas residents.

Frank was employed by the Detroit and Mackinac Railway as Parts Department Manager, until his retirement in 1951. His department records showed his flair for perfect penmanship, which was admired by all. From a small shop in his garage, he painted signs and scenes upon request. His love of music was known throughout the area, playing several instruments. His TAWAS BAY ORCHESTRA was well known for dancing and made up of Tawas residents. A musical family, all three daughters joined the orchestra.

Their three girls were their pride and joy. Ethel told of it taking her an entire afternoon to take the twins, Nyda and Lyda, in the baby carriage to do the shopping - everyone wanted to "see the twins." All three girls graduated from Tawas High School and were active in music and sports. In later years, during the Silver Valley festivities, Donna was crowned Queen, and during the Perchville Festival, Lyda was crowned Queen.

An active family, Donna was employed at Barkman Outfitting Company until her marriage to James Martin. Together, they owned and operated Martin's Motel, East Tawas. They had two sons: Gary, a teacher for 30 years in the Brighton Schools, and Gregory (deceased).

Lyda married Thomas Nelkie of Tawas and has three children: James (Kathy), Janet Coyer of Tawas and Kathy Winters of Washington.

Nyda married Elwood Bronson, and owned and operated Tawas Inn Cabins, East Tawas, and Bronson Furniture in Oscoda. Elwood also operated a barber shop in the Holland Hotel, East Tawas. Nyda was employed by the Detroit and Mackinac Railway Company as the first switch-board operator and typist, then 18 years for the Social Services Dept., Iosco County, and as executive secretary for the Rebekah Assembly of Michigan from 1969 to 1999. Upon retirement received title of Secretary Emeritus.

Frank and Ethel Moore were members of the Tawas United Methodist Church. Frank was also a member of Baldwin Oddfellow Lodge #397, and Ethel a member of Irene Rebekah Lodge #137 and Tawas Bay Chapter #71, Order of Eastern Star, and enjoyed playing Bridge and Bingo.

NELEM FAMILY. William Charles Nelem was born to George and Sarah Ann Nelem in Ontario, Canada in July 1866. As a child, William Charles moved with his parents, his younger brother George Nelem, a half brother and two half sisters to the thumb area of Michigan.

When settled there, they became friends and neighbors of the Robert Sly family and

William Charles Nelem and Effie Cornelia (Sly) Nelem - wedding photo in 1887

their children: Catherine, Effie Cornelia, Margaret Etta and Ida (twins), Emma, Frank and Alex.

In 1887, William Charles was married to Effie Cornelia in Sanilac County. In 1891 they moved to Tawas City, Michigan. In 1902 William Charles, brother George and his wife, Margaret Etta (Effie Cornelia's sister) also moved to the Tawases, where they remained to make their homes. In the years to follow, Effie Cornelia's siblings, Catherine Sly Van Zant, Ida Sly McClure and Frank also made their homes in the area.

Effie Cornelia Sly Nelem's history goes back to the 1500s and she was an 8th great-granddaughter and a direct descendant of William (Elder) Brewster who came from England on the ship *The Mayflower.*

George and Margaret Etta had no children. William Charles and Effie Cornelia (Sly) Nelem were residents of the area for more than 50 years. From their first home in Tawas City, they moved to the farm that William Charles built on the Hemlock Road (M-55).

William Charles Nelem was a building contractor and built and helped to build many buildings and homes in the area. He taught his sons and grandsons the skills at which he made his living.

Cornelia, known to friends and family as "Neal," was a fine seamstress and had a millinery shop in Tawas City. The farm on the Hemlock was a fine farm of 640 acres. They were capable farmers and much of the produce and products were sold to the people of the area.

They opened their home to many a youngster who did not have one, and many of these youngsters remained with them for some years.

The couple had eight children, four died in infancy. Their surviving children were George Merle Nelem (born 1890, died 1927) married Ida Hoeft, was a carpenter and also worked at U.S. Gypsum at Alabaster while residing in East Tawas. He lost his life in an auto accident near Glennie, while on a fishing trip with Ernest Schreiber. The couple had no children.

Charles Dudley Nelem (born 1894, died 1962) married Mina Hoeft and resided in East Tawas. In 1940 they moved to Texas. They returned to East Tawas in 1952. Children: Dudley John "Jack" Nelem, Lois Nelem Hogaboam, Ida Mae Nelem Birkenback and Robert Nelem

John Franklin Nelem Sr. (born 1897, died 1952) married Fedora E. Misener (see Misener family). Children: John Franklin "Jack", Donald, Marilouise Nelem Pershon (see Pershon family) and William Nelem. John Franklin Sr. was a building contractor and built many homes and commercial buildings in the area. He served in the U.S. Navy during World War II. He was a pioneer in radio and built one of the first "crystal" radio sets in the area.

Rose Nelem (born 1906, died 1978) married Howard MacDonald. Children: Merle MacDonald, Dorothy MacDonald Henrich and Helen MacDonald Musser.

Helen Nelem married John Surprenant. The couple had no children. *Submitted by Marilouise (Nelem) Pershon.*

RUSSELL NELKIE CENTENNIAL FARM. For many generations and over 100 years, the Nelkie family has had a strong commitment to agriculture.

Paul Nelke, later spelled Nelkie, was born in 1839 in Osterivik, Prussia. He came to America from Bremen, Prussia. The ship that brought him to the United States was the *Hermann.* He arrived in New York on April 13, 1870. Paul married Regina Benke or Binkia on March 10, 1883, at the Justice of Peace in East Tawas. Paul and Regina had three children: Frank A., Elizabeth and Edith. There were also two stepsons from Regina's previous marriage to John H. Schriber. Their names were Andrew and John.

Back row, l-r: Jeff Nelkie, Russell J. Nelkie, Jane Nelkie, Russell P. Nelkie holding Michael Nelkie, Mark Nelkie; middle row: Grace Nelkie, Jennifer Nelkie, Jessica Nelkie holding son Kyle, Joseph Nelkie; front row: Christina Nelkie, Stephanie Nelkie, Sandy Nelkie holding son Timmy

In December of 1900, Bernard and Sophia Blust purchased property in Tawas City, on M-55, formerly called Hemlock Road. In 1911 they sold the property to their daughter Mary and her husband Frank A. Nelkie. They owned and operated the dairy and farm while raising nine children. Their names are Francis, Bernard, Russell J., Edward, Thomas, Anthony, Leo, Cecil, and a daughter Regina. In 1937, their sons, Russell J. and Edward, took over the family farm in a partnership.

On November 6, 1943 Russell J. married Grace Brussel and continued to operate the dairy operation,. They raised six children: Russell P., Joyce, Lloyd, Emily, Shirley, and Charles. They all had their daily chores on the farm, before and after school and helped at planting and harvest times.

While brother Edward went into the home delivery of milk and other dairy products to schools, businesses, homes; who ever was interested in home delivery, he was there. Ed married Irene Klass on May 1, 1937 and they had two children, Judy and Gary.

In 1973, Russell J. and wife sold the dairy farm to their eldest son Russell P.

and wife Jane Trudell. Russell P. and wife planned on continuing the family tradition. They have seven children: Mark, Christina, Joseph, Jeffrey, John, Kenneth and Jennifer. The kids also had daily chores before and after school.

Today, Russell P. and wife Jane still work on the family farm. They along with their two eldest sons, Mark and Joseph, have formed the farm into a limited liability company. The farm has grown to 565 acres of owned land, 340 acres of leased property, and over 300 head of cattle. Currently, the farm houses and supports four generations of the Nelkie family.

Russell P. and wife Jane's son Mark is married to Jessica Verlac, and have a son Kyle.

Their son Joseph is married to Saundra Schonschack and they have two sons, Timothy and Andrew.

Their son Jeff is a full time employee of the dairy operation. He is married to Stephanie VanWormer.

Daughter Christina is a single mother with a son Michael. She works for a local business in Tawas City.

They may leave the farm for a while, but its still in their blood and they still return.

Son Kenneth is an employee of the city of Tawas City and helps out on the farm during busy times of the spring and fall or whenever needed. Ken is married to Tara Twarog.

Son John is an employee of ACI, a subcontractor of Charter Communications. He is married to Lisa Hamel. They have two daughters, Alivia and Joslyn.

Daughter Jennifer Lynn works for a local business in Tawas City. She married Albert Anschuetz, son of Charles and Sue Anschuetz, on August 3, 2002.

Long before anyone ever heard of the automobile, farms were leading the nation in raising all kinds of foods and the milk we drink. It takes a lot of hard work, commitment, and innovation of farm families to make it work. Farmers do feed the world.

GERALDINE M. (VAN ETTEN) NEVILLE. The second oldest of five children of Cleo B. Van Etten and Vera M. (Peterson) Van Etten, Geraldine was born in Flint, Michigan in 1929. She married Eugene H. Neville and raised three children. Together they owned and operated Neville's Waste Collection in Grand Blanc, Michigan. She left there and moved back to the Hale area in 1975. Since then she has owned several businesses and is now retired and enjoying painting, sewing, and garage sales.

Geraldine's father, Cleo, was born in 1911 in Manton, Michigan and died in 1974. His ancestors were Dutch and Scandinavian. He worked for General Motors, reading and repairing barometers. His father Ora Van Etten and his father were lumbermen in northeast Michigan.

Ora Van Etter and Fleta Bell Stickler on wedding day in 1901

Ora married Be11 Stickler and they had two sons, Victor and Cleo (father of Geraldine). Ora died shortly after Cleo was born. Bell then married Charles Hodges and had four more children: Nettie, Thelma, George and Betty.

Geraldine's mother, Vera, was born in Flint, Michigan in 1915 and died in 1991. Her ancestors were from England and Norway. The Petersons were lumbermen in northeast Michigan also.

Geraldine's siblings are Donald B. Van Etten who lives in Ohio with his wife Evelyn Nichols; John H. "Jack" lives in Tennessee; and William A. "Bill" Van Etten and Nancy (Van Etten) Totten live in Grand Blanc, Michigan.

Geraldine's children: Angela K. Neville Wallace, Clifford R. Neville and Julia J. Neville Sanford, all live in the Grand Blanc area.

She lived in the Grand Blanc area for 25 years and traveled to Londo Lake in Iosco County on weekends and vacation time. She has donated many hours to the Red Feather, Red Cross, Cystic Fibrosis March of Dimes and Wheelock Memorial Hospital where she was vice president of the auxiliary.

She went to several one-room schools, grade 1-8. They would walk two miles to and from school in all kinds of weather. They played ball, rode bicycles, ice skated on Londo Lake and walked around the lake many times. They lived there from 1945 to 1948.

AARO ARTHUR NICANDER. He
was born September 18, 1917 at the farm of his parents, Julius and Alma Maria (Alta) Nikander on Turtle Road in Alabaster Township, the only surviving son with three sisters. He attended Alabaster School, graduating in 1936. While growing up he also went by the name "Otto." He joined the Civilian Conservation Corps (CCC) July 7, 1934 at Camp Cusino, Shingleton, Michigan, being discharged the same year in September to return to school.

After graduation he went to work for the Ford Motor Company in Detroit; Fletcher's gas station in Tawas City; The D & M in Tawas City where he became a boilermaker; G.M. Truck and Coach in Pontiac where he became a pipefitter/ steamfitter; G.M. Plant in Bay City; National Gypsum in National City; U.S. Gypsum in Alabaster; the Peterson Farm in Arenac County; Northern Heating and Plumbing in East Tawas; G.M. Chevrolet plant in Saginaw; and G.M Fisher Body #1 Plant in Flint.

Marion (Spencer) and Aaro Arthur Nicander - 50th wedding anniversary in 1987

He married Marion Spencer (born February 23, 1919), daughter of John Howard and Mable "Irene" (Tremain) Spencer) of AuSable on May 8, 1937 in Pontiac. He served in World War II in the U.S. Navy C.B. Corps as a pipefitter. They reared six children: Vivian G. (Clary) born 1938; Arthur H. born 1940; Sharon A. (Trout, Young) born 1942; Julius E. 1944; Aaro O. born 1949 and John J. born 1951.

Upon retirement Aaro and Marion moved to the family property in Alabaster Township in 1986. Marion died at home October 23, 1991 and Aaro followed three months later on January 17, 1992. Both are buried in Alabaster Township Cemetery. *Submitted by son Arthur H. Nicander.*

JULIUS N. NIKANDER. He was born
in Parkano, Finland on April 14, 1877 to Nestor and Anna (Koski) Nikander. He immigrated to the United States in 1902, worked as a Quarryman for the U.S. Gypsum Company in Alabaster and later as a blacksmith. He worked to help bring his four brothers: John, Oscar, Victor and Arthur, to this country.

In the latter part of 1906 he sent for Alma Maria Alta (born July 27, 1877), daughter of Jno Alta and Sophia (Lammi) Alta, from Parkano, Finland. They were married in Tawas City on February 2, 1907. They leased 40 acres to farm on Turtle Road across the road from the Alabaster High School, there they also ran a boarding house for workers from the U.S.G. quarry for a few years before the children were born. They had nine children of which four survived to adulthood: Alma Lillian "Ludy" (Albert, Maki) born 1909; Lina (Sperbeck, Lake) born 1910; Lempi "Leah" (Kemp) born 1915 and Aaro Arthur Nicander born 1917.

The deceased children were buried in the Alabaster Township Cemetery on Benson Road. His four children attended and graduated from Alabaster High School.

Julius retired from the U.S. Gypsum Company in the 1940s then spending his time farming. His wife Alma passed away on June 16, 1950 at the Legget Road Alabaster Township home of her son Aaro. Julius died May 9, 1951 due to an automobile accident while residing at the Holly Township home of his daughter Alma Lillian "Ludy." Both Alma and Julius are buried in the Alabaster Township Cemetery. *Submitted by their grandson, Arthur H. Nicander.*

ISAAC BROCK NUNN. As an ordained
Baptist minister, Isaac accepted a call to Hale, Michigan, in 1890 to organize and build a church there. He was Hale's first minister.

The congregation was inter-denominational and their donations plus contributions from lumbermen in the township supplied the funds. Stacy B. Yawger, an expert carpenter, designed and built the church. It was dedicated in 1895.

Isaac B. Nunn was born in Brantford, Ontario, Canada, June 23, 1837. His parents were Jonathan Nunn (born June 30, 1811) and Charlotte Taylor (born June 30, 1816). Both were born in Brantford, Canada, of English descent.

Mr. Nunn attended the Theological Seminary in Carroll County, Missouri, and graduated from the University of Missouri. He married Rachael Adaline Rankins on October 28, 1858. Their child, Mary Elizabeth, was born September 11, 1859. Rachael died of complications of child birth on September 15, 1859, and the infant died a month later.

Mr. Nunn preached in Carroll County, Missouri, until the Civil War broke out in 1861. His wife's family was loyal to the Confederacy and her brothers enlisted in the Confederate Army. Isaac did not believe in slavery and at that time made the difficult decision to enlist as a chaplain in the Union forces. He served with the Medical Corps until 1862 when he was taken prisoner and sent to Andersonville Prison in Georgia. In 1863, he was exchanged and returned to Canada.

Isaac Nunn then preached in Waterford, Canada, and while there met and married Mary Ann Hanstead on January 29, 1864. Mary Ann Hanstead was born in Harefield, England, near Windsor, November 19, 1841. Her parents were Henry Hanstead and Charlotte Brown Hanstead. The family moved to Canada from England in 1851.

There were seven children born to Isaac B. Nunn and Mary Ann.

1) Ida Naomi was born in Aylemer, Ontario, November 19, 1864. She married Edwin Denton in 1882 and they had five children: Lloyd, Winnifred, Morris, Stanley and Marian. Ida died November 15, 1942.

2) (Henry) Eugene was born in Aylemer, Canada, July 11, 1866. Eugene joined his parents at Hale in 1892 and married Maud Esmond. They had three children: Ainsley, Ashley (Jack), and Morley. Morley. Morley died in infancy and his mother died in January 1903.

H.E. Nunn married Victoria Sauve in 1904 and three children were born to them: Carvil, Mina and Wallace (Mike).

Eugene established a hardware business in Hale in 1895 which he operated until his death in 1922.

Two sons, Ashley and Wallace, also engaged in the hardware business.

3) Isaac Llewllyn, known as Lewis, was born in Aylemer, Canada, February 16, 1868. He came to Hale in 1901 to engage in the carpenter trade. He also served as Plainfield Township supervisor for 18 years. He married Edith Smith in January 1905 and they had five children: Ronald, Lewis, Winnifred, Charles, and Henry. Winnifred married Paul Labian in 1927 and still survives. Henry Nunn now lives in Flushing, Michigan. Lewis Nunn died July 27, 1943.

4) William Brock Nunn was born in Aylemer, Canada, May 31, 1870. He died July 4, 1953. He married Eliza Peters in Argyle, Michigan in April 1892. They had nine children: Hulda, William Glenn, Perry, Erma, Opal, Donald, Constance, Geraldine and Vere. Three of the children survive. Erma Zielter of Clearwater, Florida; Constance Dake now living in Ontario; and Vere Nunn of North Street, Michigan.

5) Edwin C. Nunn was born in Flint, Michigan, October 11, 1871 and died May 7, 1949. He married Ellen Carroll January 27, 1897. They had five children: Zella, Thomas, Alta, Geneva, and James. Geneva married Cecil Westervelt July 6, 1931, and is now living in Flint.

6) Nellie May Nunn was born in Oakley, Michigan, September 4, 1875. She died January 8, 1954. She married Fred Jennings July 27, 1898, and they had three children: Clayton, Rex and Marian. Marian now lives in Alabaster Township.

7) Albert Hanstead was born in Argyle, Michigan, January 1, 1883. He died March 1, 1943. He was known as a pianist and accompanist.

Seven grandchildren of Isaac B. Nunn still survive. His name is carried on by several great-grandsons and their sons, some of whom live in Iosco County.

WALLLACE D. "MIKE" NUNN.

Wallace D. Nunn

Mike was born in Hale, Michigan, attended Bay City Central High School, Ohio State and Michigan State Universities. From 1931 to 1941, he was employed by the Michigan Department of Conservation as a towerman, a law enforcement officer and later as assistant district supervisor at Roscommon.

He left the Department to establish a hardware store at East Tawas and operated it until his retirement. During this time, he served in many civic capacities, as a member of the County Road Commission from 1950 to 1965 and as chairman several times. Nunn Road from Bridge Street in East Tawas to M-55 was named in his honor.

He was an organizer of Silver Valley, Michigan's original family Winter Sports Park, and also Perchville, USA. He served on the Tawas Harbor Commission and was a member of the Iosco Republican Party. He was a charter member of Kiwanis, a member of Lions, and chairman of the Grace Lutheran Church Building Committee until the new structure was dedicated in 1956.

During his service on the County Road Commission, he was a director of the Michigan Good Roads Federation and President of the County Road Association of Michigan in 1961. In 1964, he was appointed by Governor George Romney to the four man Department of State Highways Officials and the Upper Great Lakes Regional Commission on Tourism and Recreation. In 1967, he was chosen by the Michigan Retail Hardware Association to receive the Governor's Minuteman Award for outstanding effort and achievement in promoting Michigan.

In June 1972, the Department of State Highways dedicated the Mackinac City Travel Information Center in his name. He served twice as Hospitality Day Chairman for Michigan Week Observance, three terms as president of the local Chamber of Commerce, and was executive director at the time of his death in 1976. The billboard at the Chamber of Commerce Office was dedicated in Mr. Nunn's memory in June 1977.

Mr. Nunn married Edna Ostling of Roscommon in 1938. Their children are Shirley Nunn Parkinson of Cadillac and Michael E. Nunn of Tawas City. Their grandchildren are Matthew and Michael Parkinson; Michael G., Mark K. and Matthew S. Nunn.

Edna Nunn has served this community as a volunteer in several organizations. She has worked as a docent at the I.C. Historical Museum for many years. She was financial secretary for 21 years at Grace Lutheran Church, served in the choir, women's groups and Sunday Schools.

Edna Nunn

She was also a volunteer for Fish, Inc. for 20 years, serving as historian. Edna continues to serve at the museum and Grace Lutheran Church. Edna was one of the original volunteers when Tawas St. Joseph Hospital was being built. The hospital celebrated its 50th anniversary in June 2003.

OCHA FAMILY.

The history of the Ocha family of Baldwin and Wilber Township begins in Canada, where Anthony Ocha with one son Joseph, lost his wife in a cholera epidemic. He met and married Esther Eleanor Heal Stanton, a widow with three small children who had lost her husband to the same epidemic. (See Stanton history.)

Anthony Ocha and Esther Eleanor (Heal Stanton) Ocha. Picture taken ca. 1885

They married and moved with their four children to Port Hope in the Thumb area of Michigan. The children were Joseph Ocha (born 1840), Sarah Stanton (born 1845), William Samuel Stanton III (born 1846) and Anna Stanton (born 1848).

The family moved and settled in Baldwin Township where they kept a halfway house for the Stage Coaches that ran between AuSable and East Tawas before the Green Railroad was in operation.

Anthony and Esther had five additional Ocha children: twins born in 1853, Benjamin and Richard (Richard died at birth), Benjamin resided in and is buried in Wilbur

Township; Franklin (born 1859) was captain in the Life Saving Service (Coast Guard) and was stationed at Points in Michigan. He disappeared from the Harbor at East Tawas in October 1896 while stationed at Tawas Point (see the book *"Sawdust Days"* book by Edna Otis for details); Laura (born 1861) married a Totten and lived in Wilber Township; Albert H. (born 1862) was also captain in the Life Saving Service. He had one daughter by a first marriage when he married Georgiana Fontaine who had three children. The couple than had 11 Ocha children.

Captains Frank and Albert Ocha of the Coast Guard are part of history on the Great Lakes of Michigan. Captain Albert for his heroic rescues on Lake Superior, of the crews of the Robert Wallace and consort ship *David Wallace*. Frank was appointed to Tawas Point Life Saving Station as captain in December of 1888. *The Iosco County Gazette* article of the issue of December 13, 1888 stated: "Frank Ocha who has gained considerable fame as a "Marine Life Saver" has been appointed as captain of the Life Saving Station at Tawas Point in place of Captain Cleary."

When Albert Ocha died at Eagle Harbor in the Upper Peninsula of Michigan in 1912, he left seven surviving children. The oldest girl was 14 and the oldest boy 11. At the time, the Townsend Bill was being brought before Congress for consideration and would, if passed, provide care for wife and families of the Life Saving Branch of Government Service.

For more stories on Albert Ocha, see books written by Frederick Stonehouse of Flint, Michigan. For more detailed records on the Ocha Family, contact Patricia Hamp, 8461 West Monroe Road, Elwell, MI 48832. Or at the website hamp@Voyager.net *Submitted by Marilouise (Nelem) Pershon.*

IVAN O'FARRELL FAMILY. The people on his mother's side of the family came from Scotland and England to Canada some time after the War of 1812. The people on his great-grandmother's side settled in Woodstock, Canada. His great-grandfather, Alexander Campbell, moved to Buffalo, New York, and when the Civil War started, he enlisted in the New York Volunteers and was wounded at the Battle of the Wilderness in Virginia, was in the hospital about a year and got a medical discharge.

After the war, the family settled in Ubly, Michigan and while there, his grandmother, Johanna Campbell, married Fred Mills of Ubly. She was born in 1856 in Woodstock, Canada.

After the big fire in Huron County, they moved to Burleigh Township in Iosco County, about the year of 1884-5 and settled on a 140-acre farm in Section 15. They raised a family of five children: Etta, Alexander, Gene, Belle, and Winifred. They are all deceased. Ivan's mother's uncle, John Campbell, was County School Commissioner in Iosco County for a number of years.

On his father's side of the family his great-grandfather, John O'Farrell, came to Canada from County Cork, Ireland, during the potato famine in Ireland in the late 1840s. They settled in Barnsville, a town near London, Canada, where his grandfather Michael was born in the year of 1854.

About the year of 1880, his grandfather, Michael O'Farrell, and two other Irishmen, Patrick Corrigan and Patrick Dunnigan, decided to go to Michigan and look for work. They went to what was then upper Saginaw, now, Bay City.

The D & M Railroad was hiring men to help build railroad lines to such places as Alger and Rose City from this county. The railroad had sent passenger coaches to Bay City looking for workers, and they were hired. Later, his grandfather secured farmland west of Whittemore in Section 4 in Burleigh Township in 1883 or 84, and he married Mary Kartus. Her parents were from Sarnia, Canada. They were married in St. Helen, Michigan and had seven children: John, Michael, George, William, Nell, Marguerite and Mable.

John O'Farrell, born December 30, 1886, married Belle Mills in Whittemore in 1908. They settled on a farm south of Whittemore on M-65 in Section 15, Burleigh Township. From this marriage, there were five children: Ivan, Elgin, Oramel, Verna and Donald.

Oramel and Elgin are deceased; Verna and Donald live in Whittemore; and Ivan was married to Doria Marsan of Prescott. They were married in 1930 and lived in Section 4 of Burleigh Township. They have two sons, Dale of Oscoda and David of Tawas City. Ivan spent 24 years as Iosco County Sheriff and retired in the year of 1972. *Submitted by Ivan O'Farrell.*

MAJOR GENERAL EARL T. O'LOUGHLIN. He is the deputy chief of staff for maintenance, Air Force Logistics Command, Wright-Patterson Air Force Base, Ohio, retired.

General O'Loughlin was born August 2, 1930, in Bay City, Michigan, and graduated from high school in East Tawas, Michigan, in June 1948. He graduated from Bay City Junior College in February 1951.

Later he received his bachelor's degree from Park College, Kansas City, Missouri. General O'Loughlin is also a graduate of the Air Command and Staff College and the Army War College.

His military career began as an enlisted airman in February 1951. He became an aviation cadet

Major General Earl T. O'Loughlin

and upon graduation from pilot training in June 1952 was commissioned as a second lieutenant in the United States Air Force.

He completed B-29 combat crew training at Randolph Air Force Base, Texas, and Forbes Air Force Base, Kansas, in January 1953. General O'Loughlin was then assigned to the 98th Bombardment Wing at Yokota Air Base, Japan. From there he flew combat missions in B-29s over North Korea. He returned to the United States in August 1953.

General O'Loughlin was then assigned to the 26th Strategic Reconnaissance Wing at Lockbourne Air Force Base, Ohio, where he became qualified to fly the RB-47E. From 1953 to 1963, he served as an aircraft commander, instructor pilot, standardization evaluator and squadron operations officer for RB-47E aircraft. In September 1963, he entered the Air Command and Staff College at Maxwell Air Force Base, Alabama, graduating in June 1964.

His next assignment was as an aircraft commander and instructor pilot for B-52 aircraft with the 379th Bombardment Wing at Wurtsmith Air Force Base, Oscoda, Michigan. From 1965 to 1968 he was chief of the Programs and Scheduling Branch for the 379th Bombardment Wing. General O'Loughlin was assigned in January 1968 as Arc Light Operations officer with the U.S. Military Assistance Command, Vietnam, J-3, Republic of Vietnam. In January 1969, he returned to Wurtsmith Air Force Base where he commanded the 379th Organizational Maintenance Squadron. From January 1970 to October 1971, he served as assistant deputy commander for maintenance and then deputy commander for maintenance with the 379th Bombardment Wing.

General O'Loughlin was assigned to Headquarters Strategic Air Command, Offutt Air Force Base, Nebraska, in November 1971. He served as chief, Maintenance Management Division, until July 1972. He then entered the U.S. Army War College. After graduation in June 1973, he became vice commander of the 97th Bombardment Wing, Blytheville Air Force Base, Arkansas. Later he was commander of the KC-135 equipped 310th Provisional Wing at U-Tapao Royal Thai Air Force Base, Thailand.

He returned to the United States in April 1974 to command the 380th Bombardment Wing at Plattsburgh Air Force Base, New York. During his assignment the FB-111/KC-135 wing received the Fairchild Trophy as the best bombardment wing in the annual bombing and navigation competition.

General O'Loughlin was deputy for maintenance, engineering and supply in the Office of the Deputy Chief of Staff for Systems and Logistics at Headquarters U.S. Air Force, from July 1975 to June 1977. In June 1977 he became vice commander of the Oklahoma Air Logistics Center at Tinker Air Force Base, Oklahoma.

General O'Loughlin became deputy chief of staff for contracting and manufacturing at Headquarters Air Force Logistics Command in December 1978. He assumed his present position in June 1979.

He is a command pilot with more than 6,000 flying hours. His military decorations and awards include the Legion of Merit, Distinguished Flying Cross, Bronze Star Medal, Meritorious Service Medal, Air Medal and the Air Force Commendation Medal w/4 Oak Leaf Clusters.

He was promoted to major general August 1, 1979, with date of rank December 1, 1979.

General O'Loughlin was married to the former Shirlee Benninghaus of East Tawas, Michigan. They have four children: Kimberly, Kevin, Kelly and Kristin.

Son of Terrence M. and Lutie E. BeMent O'Loughlin. Mr. O'Loughlin, deceased.

The family moved to East Tawas, Michigan, in August 1935. Mr. O'Loughlin was employed as appliance maintenance service man for Consumers Power Company.

Two sisters, Mrs. Thomas (Lutie) McLaughlan of Birmingham, Michigan, and Mrs. John (Terriece) Edwards of Costa Mesa, California.

In 1960 General O'Loughlin bought a parcel (80 acres) of land in Wilber Township. On the property was a hunting camp. He used this camp for recreational hunting.

In 1979 the original hunting camp was torn down and a more modern and livable year-round home was built. This area is a part-time home on his retirement from the United States Air Force.

Major General O'Loughlin is the only man in Iosco County to have attained this rank in the Air Force.

MICHAEL and EMILY O'REILLY.
They have always loved the northern lower peninsula and the feel of being "up north" away from the city, with lots of water around.

Emily's parents were raised in Benzie County, but had moved to Royal Oak in 1920. Summers were spent at their cottage on Crystal Lake at Frankfort. Mike, a Detroit native, spent summer vacations with relatives in their cottage on Lake Michigan at Harbor Springs.

Over the years they've had several houses on or near small Oakland County lakes. Water and its ever changing patterns were always so serene and relaxing.

Time for retirement in 1987 - where would they like to be? Up north, near water and Em's twin sister, Lou or where their son lives in California; but they didn't really want to live there, so they visited Lou and her husband, Pete Stoll, who live in East Tawas in his family's home on Tawas Bay.

They loved the area, and the chance to be near Lou and Pete. A big bonus was that Lou and Pete's four children and their families all live in Michigan.

Talk about luck! Three weeks after their visit in East Tawas, Lou's neighbor died. Michael and Emily bought the house right next door to her twin sister. What good times their families have had over the 15 years they've been there, and they are looking forward to many more!

They enjoy the Tawas area with its small town feeling and friendly people. It seemed like home right away, especially with all the friends of Lou and Pete.

The Tawas area is beautiful through every season. It is a lot more peaceful than the Lake Michigan side with all that traffic and busy resort area. Here there are lots of winding country roads to drive along, plenty of scenic places to enjoy, and a variety of organizations to join and support. There is always something to do.

Living in East Tawas was a great idea!

EDNA M. OTIS.
She was the author of *"Sawdust Days-When the Tawas Area Was Young,"* and died in 1974. In that book she included a brief biography which follows:

Edna M. Otis, author of *"Sawdust Days-When the Tawas Area Was Young,"* is a newspaper woman of years of experience.

She was born in Baldwin Township, Iosco County, the daughter of Helon N. and Sarah Johnson Otis, pioneer residents, who came to the country in the late 1860s, from New York state. Thus, from early childhood, stories of pioneers' days were heard

Edna Otis

as frequently as were discussions about the weather.

Following graduation from the East Tawas public schools, Miss Otis was employed in the office of the *Iosco County Gazetter,* in East Tawas. Later, she taught two years in the district schools of Iosco County, then returned to newspaper work.

In 1916, Miss Otis became editor of the *Gazette.* During the 30 years that followed, she had access to old newspaper files, also county, township, and city records, and has interviewed scores of pioneers on the subject of early days in Iosco County. Coupled with the memories that every individual files in memory's notebook, this wealth of information (much of it which was available to no one but herself) could be easily written into a compilation of historical facts and homespun incidents.

A pupil in the East Tawas schools, and later serving on its Board of Education; an attendant of the Methodist Church since childhood; publishing a Republican newspaper, and serving on the county committee and the State Central Committee of the Republican party-these facts may change some of the incidents, but they make them more understandable to the average reader.

Sawdust Days—When the Tawas Area Was Young, was suggested to the author by numerous friends who had read and appreciated *Their Yesterdays—AuSable and Oscoda.* Historical facts and incidents of this lumbering town in the northern part of Iosco County, were compiled and published by Miss Otis in 1948.

MARLENE T. PELLERITO.
She was born in 1931 in Berlin, Germany and grew up there. She received her art education at the "University für Bildende Künste." In 1954 she emigrated to the United States and came to the Tawas area in Michigan, where she met her husband. They left the Tawases in 1948 and went to Atlanta, Michigan for one year, then to Saginaw, Michigan for four

years, finally settling in Bay City, Michigan in 1983.

While living in the Tawases she occupied herself with painting and participating in the "Tawas Bay Art Fair," starting with the very first one, for 18 years. She also taught oil and acrylic painting classes for "Tawas Area Community Education from 1969-81 and 1983-86.

From 1973-75, she taught painting classes for the Tawas Bay Arts Council and from 1977-78 at the Art and Craft Hobby Shop at the Wurtsmith Air Force Base.

In 1973 she took some community education classes in pottery and continued with beginning and advanced ceramic classes at Delta College, Michigan. From 1983-2001 she taught ceramic classes at Saginaw Valley State University, Michigan and from 1985-98 at Arts Midland Galleries and School, Midland, Michigan.

She has participated in numerous juried, and invitational exhibitions and her work is represented in corporate and private collections in the U.S. and Europe. Since retiring from teaching in 2001, she has continued to sculpt, paint and exhibit.

PERSHON FAMILY. The Pershon family originates in Alsace Lorraine, in Northeastern France, consisting of former provinces of Alsace and Lorraine. The provinces were governed by Germany and France thru the years, but regained by France in 1944 after German occupation. Residing in this area were Martin Pershon and his wife Mariae (Chrzan) Pershon and their children.

Martin and Mariae's son, Joseph Pershon, left the region and made his way to the United States with his family. Joseph's son, John Julius (born 1882) was 6 years of age in 1888 when his family entered the United States and settled in Detroit, Michigan. John Julius Pershon was married to Anna (Karsney) in 1903, and the couple had nine children.

Of these nine children, the first born, John Victor Pershon (born 1904), was married to Agatha Pelzer in 1926. The couple resided in Detroit, Michigan and had five children. The eldest son, Raymond Victor Pershon, was born in 1929 and married Marilouise Nelem (born 1927) in 1949 (see Nelem history).

They resided in Detroit, but East Tawas was a large part of their lives. In 1972, they purchased a family home in East Tawas and divided their time between Detroit and East Tawas until retirement in 1986. Raymond died in 1987. Their children are as follows:

1) Kathleen Ann (Pershon) Cole (born 1950) married Stephen Philip Cole (born 1949) in 1972 and had one daughter, Sarah Jane Cole (born 1975). Sarah married Phillip Childers in 1992. Sarah and Phillip have one son, Devin Reed Childers (born 1993).

Stephen and Kathleen (Pershon) Cole

2) William Thomas Pershon (born 1954) married Melissa E. Millard in 1981. The couple had two children, Aaron Thomas Pershon (born 1982) and Kallie Victoria Pershon (born 1983). William Thomas and Melissa were divorced in 1993. William married Melissa Kail in 1996.

William and Melissa (Kail) Pershon

3) John Franklin Nelem (born 1958) married Rebecca Joyce Shoup (born 1960). The couple has two sons, Brad Michael Pershon (born 1981) and Christopher Raymond Pershon (born 1983).

Raymond made import and export his lifetime work. He began his career in 1946 with National Carloading Company, later at Judson Sheldon Corp., the international subsidiary of that company. He joined F.X. Coughlin in 1962 and in 1962-63 introduced railcarloading operations from Detroit. He was President

John and Rebecca (Shoup) Pershon

of F.X. Coughlin and Coughlin Services until his retirement in 1986. He was an active member of the board of directors of that organization until his death.

He was a member of Detroit Customs Brokers Association, one of only 11 Customs House Brokers in the early 1960s in the Detroit area. He was instrumental in helping to develop the Port of Detroit, and is a retired president of the World Trade Club. Raymond was a member of St. Constance Church, Holy Family Church and the Knights of Columbus, Council #4872.

Raymond and Marilouise Pershon

Marilouise was born in East Tawas, graduated from East Tawas High School in 1945. She then moved to Houston, Texas where she was employed by National Carloading Company. Then moved to Detroit in 1948, where she transferred to the same company. After her marriage to Raymond, she worked at National Bank of Detroit for many years. In 1975 she pursued her interest in Real Estate obtaining her associates and broker's licenses, working with Century 21 before retiring. *Submitted by Marilouise (Nelem) Pershon.*

RUDOLPH PFAHL, farmer, Tawas Township, sailed on the *"Vandalia"* in 1882 to begin his life in America. He was born December 21, 1859 in Village of Wiewiorken, Marienwerder, West Prussia, Germany, son of Michael and Caroline (Engle) Pfahl. For a short time Rudolph lived with Pfahl family members in New York. A sister remained in Germany. On a train bound for Michigan, Rudolf arrived in Iosco County where he married Augusta Zuhldorf by a Lutheran minister on December 23, 1888 in a little house on the corner of 5th Avenue and 2nd Street in Tawas City (still standing).

Augusta and Rudolph Pfahl in front of historical home on corner of 7th Ave. and 2nd Street in Tawas City

Augusta was born December 25, 1866 in the city of Landeck, same province as Rudolph, daughter of Fredk and Wilhekimina

Zueldorf. When both of her parents died, Augusta left Germany to join her sister in Michigan, Bertha Zuhldorf. Bertha married Henry Grabow of Wilbur Township, and had three children: Frederick Henry in 1892, Selma Augusta in 1891, and Minnie Anna.

Rudolph and Augusta engaged in farming on Miller Rd., where their seven children were born. In 1921 Rudolph and Augusta moved into Tawas City, currently on the list of historical homes (corner of 7th Ave. and 2nd Street). Rudolph suffered from a badly dislocated shoulder from his work in lumbering; never given proper treatment, he lived with the pain and a large hump on his shoulder. Twice a week Rudolph bought fresh fish from the Trudell fish boats coming into Tawas.

Frederick Charles Pfahl (born 1889, died 1980) was labeled "the kid" of the lumber camps. He served as a private in U.S. Army during World War I. In April 1921, Fred married Mary Eleanor Smith, daughter of Reuben and Charlotte (Hyland) Smith. They farmed 80 acres on the corner of M-55 and Sand Lake Rd. Fred and Mary had five children: Erma Lou married Kenneth Herriman of Grant Township, resided in Allen Park, Michigan; Rhea Elaine married Addison "Bud" Featheringill, resided in Belleville, Michigan; Marilyn Louise married Donald Webb, resided in Garden City and presently living in National City; Leslie Frederick married Rose Mary Kaake, resided in Bowling Green, Kentucky; Richard Lloyd married Judy Freel, resided in Hale, Michigan.

Rudolph and Augusta's other children were: Emma Bertha Katherina Pfahl (born 1891, died 1926) never married, worked for the Netherlands Counsel in Grand Rapids, Michigan; Wilhelm August Pfahl (born 1892, died 1977), worked at the D&M in Tawas City in his early years and later in a Jackson factory, he was married for only a very short time; Martha Anna Lina Pfahl (born 1895, died 1983) married 1st Emil Buch and had two children: Robert Gerald (died in infancy) and Dorothy Louise who married Harold Bublitz, resided in Tawas City and Florida. Martha married 2nd Karl Bublitz in 1942 who had two children, Harold and Donna; Louisa Ettalie Pfahl (born 1896, died 1983) married Arthur Linholm of Wyoming; they lived in Jackson, Michigan, no children; Otto Rudolph Pfahl (born 1899, died 1983) never married, worked as a machine operator in a Detroit factory. He had an outstanding memory, although he was legally blind, lived his life alone; Emil Gustav Hugo Pfahl (born 1901, died 1984),

married Bessie Bott, an accomplished vocalist. They lived in Jackson, Michigan, no children. *Submitted by Connie Chism.*

MARY ROSALIE PROPER and BOBBY DON LAW.

Mary Rosalie was born October, 29, 1931 in Alabaster Township, Iosco County. Her parents were William "Bill" and Stella Proper. She went to Tawas Area Schools and graduated in 1950. From high school, she attended Business School in Bay City, Michigan. From there, she enlisted in the U.S. Air Force in 1952. She was stationed in San Antonio, Texas at Kelly Air Force Base. Her training was at Scott Air Force Base in Illinois. She was also transferred to New Foundland at Stevensville Air Force Base in November 1953. While in the Air Force she met her husband, Bobby Don Law, and was married in September 1953.

After the Air Force, she went to Central Missouri State University at Warrensburg, Missouri, graduated with a BS degree in business, majoring in accounting, in 1960. Mary and Bobby raised three children together: Bill (born 1954), Sue (born 1961) and Kathy (born 1964).

Mary worked for 28 years as an accounting manager with Panhandle Eastern Pipeline Company before retiring in 1989. Mary and Bob still reside in Missouri along with their children and their families. Mary tries to come home to the Tawas area every two years to see old friends and family.

WILLIAM H. "UNCLE BILL" PROPER.

Bill was born in Tawas Township on May 11, 1898, the son of William and Susan (Slingerland) Proper. He had two brothers, Orval and Clyde, and five sisters: Jenny Smith, Clara Ulman, Anna Weatherwax, Gertrude Mills and Belle Wesenborn. His grandparents were Benjamin and Elizabeth Slingerland, who were one of the first family settlers in Alabaster Township.

William H. Proper – summer of 1977.

He was raised and worked in the Tawas area. He worked at U.S. Gypsum for many years until he was hurt in 1960.

In 1929, he married Stella Mae Grove in Tawas City. Together they had 10 children: Arthur Gilbert (born 1930) resides in Mulberry, Florida; Mary Rosalie (born 1931) resides in Gladstone, Missouri; James Clyde (born 1933) resides in Spokane,

Washington; Edward Herbert "Herb" (born 1935, died 1987); Dale (born and died in 1937); Nancy Sue (born 1939) resides in Bartow, Florida; Ruth Ann (born 1941) resides in Mulberry, Florida; David Andrew (born 1943) resides in Tawas City; Dora Mae (born 1944) resides in Whittemore; and Sally (born and died in 1945). They chose to raise their children in Iosco County.

Bill was a very likeable person and would help anyone in need. Around town he became known as "Uncle Bill" because he was a good-natured person. In 1973, his wife Stella of 44 years went to be with the Lord. In July 1978 Bill went to join his wife Stella in heaven. He is greatly missed by all.

LEON F. PUTNAM FAMILY.

I was born July 18, 1920, Hale, Michigan, on the family farm one mile west and one-half south of Hale on Putnam Road. This road was named after my father, Edward Orlin Putnam.

Leon F. Putnam

My dad and mother were married November 8, 1905 at Hale, Michigan. My mother was the former Lottie May Webb, daughter of Frink and Rebecca Webb. My father's parents were Frank and Mary Putnam. My Grandmother Putnam was a half-blooded Indian. My dad had two brothers, William and Fred, and one sister, Blanche. My mother was the only girl in her family of seven. Her brothers were Merton, Victor, Charles, Leo, George and John.

In my family there were nine children (six girls and three boys):

1) Ida, the oldest, married Bernard Webb and they had five children: Ruth, George, Leon, Janice and Mary Jean. My sister Ida was my first school teacher. She taught in Londo School located one mile south and three miles west of Hale. The building is still standing.

2) Elma married Guy Alderton and they had eight children: James, Lila, Cecilia Alys, Carl, Robert, Donald and Carol.

3) Lottie married Harold Eymer and they had three boys: Harold William, Richard and Larry.

4) Gertrude never married.

5) Charles married Mary Ann and had two children, Mark and Jody.

6) Leon (me) married Beulah Van Wormer on October 8, 1939 and we had

three boys: Lauren Dale (born May 1940, died July 1943); Lynn Gail (born January 1942, died three months later) and Michael Lee (born September 7, 1946). Michael graduated from Tawas High School in 1965. He married Carol Marsch and went into the Air Force for four years. Their daughter Tina was born in Japan while Michael was stationed there. They have a son Christopher (born October 1973) and now live at Holly, Michigan.

7) John married Thelma Dorston on May 25, 1946 at Dayton, Ohio and they have eight children: Patricia, Janelle, James, John, Jeanne, Connie, David and Thomas.

8) Elizabeth married Robert Timmer February 10, 1944 and they have six children: Lance, Suzette, Robert, Monique, Terrie and Michelle.

9) Dorothy married J.D. Lehman October 6, 1946 and they had five children: Kay Ann, John David, Richard, Mark and Mathew.

My dad was Plainfield Township supervisor for 12 years and was a member of the school board for many years. Both my father and mother were very active in Grange and the Gleaners for many years and they both were active in the M.E. Church. I was a school bus driver when the buses were red, white and blue. Then in 1943 I was appointed deputy sheriff under Sheriff John F. Moran where I remained until Ivan O'Farrell was elected in 1949. I was then appointed undersheriff and remained in that position until 1973. At that time I was elected Iosco County Register of Deeds and was there until retired in 1985. During the years I was undersheriff we wrote Drivers Licenses and I sat on the Concealed Weapons Board. I really enjoyed the Sherriff Department.

In 1943 when I started with the department, I was paid 35 cents per hour and 5 cents per mile for my car. I was paid four times per year and only paid when the board of supervisors met to approve the bill. Things have changed considerably since 1943. *Submitted by Leon Putnam.*

CHARLES and PEARL QUICK.

Charles Quick was born in 1884 near Glennie to Albert H. and Alice Quick. Albert was from New York and Alice came from AuSable. Her father was Louis Courser although she was raised by her mother Rebecca (Smith) and step-father Augustus Stall.

Charlie and his family lived in Thompson Township. In 1890, when Charlie was just 5 he had to walk into Glennie to report his father's death. Charlie's mother remarried (John Pilkey-Peltier) and the family

moved to Mt. Clemens in the mid-1890s.

In 1907 Charlie returned to Iosco County where he found work at the Prescott Lumber Camp. Eva Hunter and her daughter Pearl were cooking for the camp,

Charles and Pearl Quick

and on March 27, 1907 Charlie and Pearl were married.

Charlie was a carpenter by trade, working on many projects around Tawas including doing much work for the Leslie's at their Ford garage. Charlie built his family a home near 9th Avenue and 4th Street and also built a hunting camp, in Wilbur Township, which remains in the family today.

Charlie and Pearl had three children: Basil, Albert and Mildred. Basil (born 1907) owned a jewelry store on Newman Street and in 1929 he married Ruth Morrell. They had three children: Nancy, Nola and Daniel. During the war Basil worked at a war plant in Detroit and later moved to and opened a jewelry store in the Detroit area.

Albert (born 1916, died 1992) played baseball for Tawas City High School and, as quoted from the *Iosco County News Herald* December 30, 1992, "Lefty" Quick gained local distinction as an outstanding amateur baseball player, being a member of an independent team, winning two Northeastern Michigan championships in the late 30s." "Lefty" was a pitcher. Albert got his start in the jewelry business working in his brother's store learning watch repair and after a tour of duty in the Pacific during World War II he opened his own watch making and jewelry store in Saginaw. He and Patricia Frances (Noey) had four children: Diane, Robert, Sally and Joan.

Mildred (born 1918, died 1997) worked as a secretary for Barkman Lumber while in high school and until her marriage to Ard Richardson Jr. In the late 30s Millie was a Perch Festival Queen and during the war served her country in the Motor Corps. She and Ard had three children: Susy, Charles (Hal), and Ard III (Richie). Family members were often seen participating in sailboat races on Tawas Bay.

Charlie died in 1949. After his death Pearl moved to the little white house with the picket fence at the intersection of US-23 and M-55. Anyone looking for Pearl would often find her working in the many flowerbeds, surrounding her home. Her grandchildren spent many July 4th's

watching the fireworks from the "best seat in the "house." Pearl was a member of the Tawas Bay Chapter of the Eastern Star and an active and well loved member of the 1st Baptist Church of Tawas City, where until the time of her death she was its oldest member.

Pearl lived in Tawas until she was 95 at which time she went to live with Millie and Ard in San Antonio, Texas. She died peacefully in her sleep in 1991 at the age of 101. She and Charlie are buried with other family members in Memory Gardens.

PAUL JOHN and DORIS (BIRNBAUM) REMPERT.

Paul was born in Chicago, Illinois on May 15, 1891 to Rudolf and Amelia (Krueger) Rempert. While still a young boy he moved with his family to a farm in Tawas, Michigan. His siblings were William (who died early in life), Otto, Frederick, Helen, Margaret, Edward, Albert, Elizabeth and Emma. Paul was honorably discharged from the U.S. Army after World War I.

On October 1, 1921 Paul married Dorthea "Doris" Katherine Birnbaum (born April 8, 1902 on Crow Island, Saginaw, Michigan), daughter of Anna Minnie Lange and Theodore Frederick Birnbaum. The couple moved to Saginaw, Michigan and had four children: Maybelle Amelia, Delores Elaine, Leatrice Joy and Walter Marvin.

Paul and Doris visited Tawas often over the years, especially while his father, sister Emma and her husband Tom Jones lived on the farm. Paul worked at Wickes Boiler Company in Saginaw as a tube bender until his retirement.

Doris was a friendly and caring person who, besides taking care of her family, did cleaning and ironing for others. Her children remember how she took in boarders from Tawas who came to Saginaw looking for employment.

Maybelle Amelia Rempert (born December 14, 1921 in Saginaw, Michigan) married Frank C. Block on September 20, 1946. Frank (born September 12, 1923, died April 43, 1988) is buried in Roselawn Cemetery in Saginaw, Michigan. They had six children: Janis Ann, Diane Lee, James Frank, Carol Lynn, Michelle Susan and Lori Kay.

Delores Elaine Rempert (born July 18, 1926) married John VanElsacker in 1947 in Saginaw, Michigan. John died in 1972 and is buried in Sterling, Michigan. They had four children: Sandra Lee, Susan Marie, Kathy Jo and Terry John. Delores was divorced from John and later married Foster Findlay in March 1970.

Leatrice Joy Rempert was born on November 4, 1929 and married George A. Grindahl on February 5, 1955 in Saginaw, Michigan. They made their home in Midland, Michigan. George was born on December 24, 1929 in Saginaw, Michigan. They had three children: Karen Sue, Linda Kay and Julie Ann.

Walter Marvin Rempert was born on April 1, 1932 in Saginaw, Michigan and died on October 19, 1950 as the result of an automobile accident while returning to Saginaw from Tawas. He is buried in Forest Lawn Cemetery in Saginaw, Michigan next to his parents.

Paul died on February 23, 1980 in Saginaw after living for two years in Martin Luther Home in Saginaw. He is buried in Forest Lawn Cemetery with his wife and son. Doris lived in the family home during that time and later moved to South Colony Place, a senior citizen's apartment on Gratiot Street in Saginaw.

Doris died at St. Luke's Hospital in Saginaw on December 1, 1987 following surgery to repair an aortic aneurysm. She is buried in Forest Lawn Cemetery in Saginaw, Michigan next to her husband, Paul, and her son, Walter.

PAUL C. ROPERT. Paul (born March 9, 1910 in Halle, Germany, died 1986) was three months old when he, along with his parents, R. Paul and Bertha, his grandfather, Karl Prinz, and his older brother, Erich left Germany for the United States. After landing at Ellis Island they moved to the Tawas area and followed Freda, Bertha's sister, who immigrated to the area two years earlier and married George Kindell. A few years later they moved to a house on Wilkinson Street in East Tawas where his parents lived until their death in 1956. The family had four more children: George Julius (died at age 6 years old), Arthur, Elizabeth and Emma.

Paul joined his father at the D&M Railroad but didn't stay long. The lure of adventure pulled him into signing up as a deck hand on an Iron Ore Boat and he sailed for six years. On one of the trips to Superior, Wisconsin he met his future wife Angelique "Angie" Danielson. They married and lived in Superior for a few years. Paul moved back to the Tawas area with his wife and their oldest son George. In 1941 the twins,

Mary Ellen and Marvin Allen, were born in a small house on West Washington Street.

Paul went to work for Bay City Hardware in Bay City in late 1943 and a little over a year later he again moved back to East Tawas and built a house on East Washington Street. He would stay in East Tawas until he died in 1976.

When Paul moved back to East Tawas the last time in 1945, he went to work for Mike Nunn at Nunn's Hardware on Newman Street and after eight years he went to work at Tempco Furnace Company. After about a year he was hired as the Assistant Superintendent of Public Works for the city of East Tawas. Within a few years his boss, Mr. Art Dillon, retired and he became the Superintendent of Public Works. During the 20 years he worked for the city, he saw the building of a new City Hall, a new water treatment plant and a new waste water treatment plant. He was the operator of both the water and waste water treatment plants.

Paul was an active member of St. Joseph Church and a member of Knights of Columbus, serving a term as Grand Knight and later helped to find the 4th degree Post of the Knights of Columbus in the Tawas area serving as its first Faithful Navigator.

Paul was an avid bowler serving as the secretary to the Wednesday Night League for over 25 years.

RICHARD M. SAMSON. He was born 1903 on a farm in Akron, Michigan and died in 1994. His parents were William and Nancy (Dowker) Samson and he had four brothers and two sisters. Richard attended Akron School and after graduating from high school there, he went to Flint to find work. His first job was working on the Inter-Urban

Inspector Richard M. Samson

Railroad. He also worked in Canada for a year on the Hydro Electric. On July 1936 he was hired on the Flint Police Department where he remained until retirement.

He married Essel Edwards on October 19, 1925 in Saginaw. A daughter, Donna Colleen, and son, Gerald, were born. She was a nurse and took care of her brother-in-law until his death. She also nursed family members when needed. She died July 23, 1938.

On August 16, 1941, Richard married Vlasti "Val" Pesick in Flint, Michigan. She enjoys volunteering, especially 4-H, church

activities, election board and the Iosco County Fair. They had two sons, Richard W. and Dale.

In the summer of 1952 the family built a cabin (with some difficulty as there was no electricity) on a lot at Bass Lake, Hale, where they spent their summers.

In April 1953 he attended Southern Police Institute in Louisville, Kentucky and graduated June 26, 1953. In November 1957 they purchased a farm from Fred and Iva Latter located in Reno Township. The family spent many weekends and summers there until he retired July 1, 1965 when they moved there permanently.

The adult children were also employed. Donna West taught school in Montrose and East Tawas; Gerald was in the Navy Air Force and later was a math professor at Lake Superior State University; Richard W., after serving in Vietnam, was a meat inspector; Dale, also served in Vietnam then was employed with Consumers Energy.

After Richard M. retired he enjoyed raising Herefords and unusual birds, ducks, geese and fowl. Many school children enjoyed the trip to the farm. He was also involved in the Farm Bureau, Iosco County Sheriff's Posse, Lion's Club and the Iosco County Agricultural Society, of which he was elected manager in July 1965 and served until the annual meeting in 1984. *Submitted by Vlasti Samson.*

SCHERRET FAMILY. Albert Ferdinand Scherret and Justine Marquardt came to the United States from Germany with their respective families. They settled at Port Hope, Michigan, where they were married at St. John's Lutheran Church on November 30, 1880. In approximately 1893 they moved their family of eight children,

Justine and Albert Scherret

Frances Justine "Gusty," Amil, Ernest, Arthur, Wilhelm, Emma, Herman "Pete," and Martha, by boat to Tawas City and settled on a farm in Sherman Township. Their farm was next to that of Justine's sister Gottlieben and her husband Willem Draeger. Their last three children: Caroline, Maria, and Lydia, were born in Sherman Township.

It was a constant struggle to provide for such a large family on their small farm. As soon as the children were old enough they left home and went to work. This greatly relieved the financial strain on the family.

The boys went to work as lumberjacks and when the lumber industry petered out, they moved to Detroit to work in the automobile factories.

There was a terrible accident at the lumber camp involving a son of Albert and Justine. Wilhelm was only 16 years old when it happened. He was walking or standing next to a train piled high with huge logs. One of the chains holding the logs in place broke and the logs rolled off the train and onto Wilhelm, killing him instantly.

When Emma was 9 years old she went to Tawas City and lived with the minister and his wife while she attended school and also took catechism. She earned her keep by caring for the children and doing some housework. Emma finished the eighth grade and was confirmed at Zion Lutheran Church when she was 13. She then traveled to Grand Rapids to take a position as a domestic.

Emma told of the time when there was smallpox at the family farm and the baby, Lydia, was ill with the disease. She said that her father would carry Lydia around on a pillow trying to soothe her. He used the pillow because he was afraid of touching her and making scars.

Albert died on August 26, 1914 from stomach cancer. He had been an active member of the community and had been liked and respected by everybody as indicated in the obituary and in the resolution written by the members of Sherman Grange No. 1119, both of which appeared in the Tawas City newspaper. His funeral was held at his residence with the Rev. Asal of Reese officiating. Justine died on March 22, 1922 in Detroit where she had been living with her son, Art. Both Albert and Justine are buried in the Tawas City Cemetery.

Maria (Marie) Scherret Gillespie, later Marie Bellon, lived in Whittemore, later moving to Tawas City. Lydia Scherret Galliker lived in Detroit; later moving to Whittemore and finally settling in Tawas City.

ANDREW STEPHEN SMITH. He was born April 4, 1862, near Burford in Brant County, Onatrio, the son of Aurilla Tenney and Joseph Smith. When he was 3 years old the family settled in Tawas Township. On April 17, 1887, he married Emma Brintnell in Reese. They made their home in Tawas Township until February 22, 1906, when they moved to Grant Township where they remained until Andrew's death December 5, 1934. Andrew became a naturalized citizen on February 20, 1905. He was a respected member of the Iosco County farming community and of the RLDS Church. After his death his land was farmed jointly by his son

Earl and a son-in-law, Gerald Bellen, until it was sold by his widow.

Andrew and Emma had eleven children, two of whom died in infancy. The remaining nine grew up in Iosco County.

1) Olive (born April 1, 1889, died May 30, 1969 in Waukegan, Illinois) married Loren Davison and had one daughter Dorothy (born June 4, 1915 in Iosco County).

2) Edith (born December 1, 1891, died March 28, 1949 in Fort Lauderdale, Florida) married Benjamin Bitting December 17, 1919. They had five children: Leslie, Bond, Avis, Bruce and Doris.

3) Jenny (born November 9, 1894, died July 10, 1968, in Bethesda, Maryland) married first, Arthur Latham. They had three children: Willis, Lyman and Ruth. Jenny married second, Loy Woods April 6, 1945.

4) Joseph Earl (born June 16, 1897, died October 26, 1963, in East Tawas) married Olive Jenkins July 2, 1918. They had four children: (1) Margaret (born April 7, 1919, died June 2, 1990 in East Tawas) married Robert Richter June 20, 1953. They had three children: Marsha Herrick still resides in East Tawas. (2) Otis (born September 16, 1921) married Barbara Hamacher May 8, 1954 and had six children. (3) James (born February 19, 1924, d. June 18, 1986 in Bay City) married Ella Mae Weeks April 26, 1947 and had three children. (4) Joye (born May 31, 1930) married Philip Giroux December 15, 1951 and had two children. Margaret, Otis and Jim all worked at Nick Pappas's restaurant in East Tawas. Margaret remained in the area, working as a bookkeeper at Look's Garage and later as a real estate broker.

5) James Erven (born November 9, 1901, died March 1, 1976, in Dearborn) married Vera McDougald March 20, 1921 and had seven children: Donald, Norma, Ronald, Royce, Myrna, Marilyn, Larry and Janet.

6) Elizabeth "Beth" (born September 21, 1904, died April 17, 1951 in Flint) married Minor Watkins August 6, 1923 and had one daughter, Donna.

7) Beryl (born June 12, 1907, died November 1969 in Whittemore) married Charles Ward September 2, 1927 and had three children: Jack, Aileen and Jane.

8) Joy (born September 1, 1910, died July 10, 1992 in West Branch) married Gerald Bellen November 1, 1928. They had four children: OnaLee, Geraldine, Ardith and Carol.

9) Muriel (born February 17, 1913, died July 2, 1959 in Clare) married Hiram Grimason April 17, 1938. They had three

children: Mary, Sharon and David. *Submitted by Joye S. Giroux.*

FRANK SOLOMON SMITH. Frank was born June 3, 1881 in Bay City, Michigan to Solomon and Bertha (Close) Smith. He married Mary Loretta Barron Feb. 24, 1903. One son, Fred J. Smith was born December 21, 1903. Sometime around 1905-1907 Frank came to Washington State and worked as a log scaler for Pt. Blakely Logging Company. Mary and Fred followed at a later

Frank S. and Mary (Barron) Smith with son Fred J. Smith

date. They eventually settled in Puyallup, Washington. Frank was assistant postmaster at one time, a partner in a car dealership and also a county clerk. At one point he and Mary owned a store at No. Puyallup that is still standing. While they were in No. Puyallup Fred married Margaret Sheviand from nearby Edgewood. Son John (aka Fred) was born in 1923 and Margaret in 1925.

Sometime around 1927 or 1928 Frank and Mary moved to McCleary and Frank worked at the McCleary company store. At that time they lived at the top of the hill on the street that runs along side the McCleary Hotel. Later they ran a small store and gas station just across the bridge going out of town towards Elma. They had living quarters in the back of the store. At one time the store had been part of a recreational facility that had rental cabins for travelers, a swimming pool with dressing cubicles, a skating rink/ dance hall and a small park behind the rink. John learned to skate there and he and his sister Margaret played in the empty pool.

Around 1932 or 1933 Frank and Mary moved to 40 acres in Garden City. The date Frank started his real estate and insurance business in Elma is uncertain, but they moved there sometime before 1939. They bought a house across from the American Legion Hall. Frank's office was between the Legion Hall and the Post Office. In March of 1939 Frank, along with his then partner W.W. Wilson, had the opportunity to buy the town of Malone from the Mason Co. Logging Company. They resold some of the houses and rented out others.

In 1942 the McCleary Mill was sold to Simpson Logging Company. They only wanted the mill and not the company houses and business buildings, so Frank purchased the houses and other buildings in September

1942 for the sum of $26,000. He resold some of the buildings and homes and rented out others. A copy of this purchase contract along with legal descriptions is available at the McCleary Museum.

In about 1944 or 1945 John was discharged from the Army on a medical and went into partnership with his grandfather. In 1949 Frank retired and sold the business to John, now known as Fred. He later sold the business to Laurence Lucke and moved to Pt. Angeles.

In 1951 Frank had a stroke which left him partially paralyzed. At that time there wasn't much done for stroke victims and he became bedridden until his death December 21, 1954. Mary died in Lacey, Washington November 17, 1967.

This writer thinks her grandfather was a bit of a rogue but he was a wonderful grandfather and she loved him dearly. *Submitted by Margaret (Smith) Lentz.*

JOSEPH SMITH. He was one of the pioneers of Iosco County and began farming in 1867 on Meadows Road in Tawas Township. Joseph Smith was born March 28, 1810, in County Tyrone, Ireland. He immigrated with his family to Quebec in 1839/1840 where his wife and newborn daughter died a few days later.

Joseph Smith (1810-1898)

This left him alone with young son, James, until he married Aurilla Tenney in the mid-1850s. Joseph and Aurilla produced eight children in Canada: Solomon, Mary Jane, Elizabeth "Libby," Charles, Eleanor, Reuben, Andrew and Thaddeus. James and Solomon worked in Michigan lumber camps prior to the family moving to the Tawas area.

James Smith (born 1836, died 1912) married Catherine Millard in Canada and moved to the Bay City area.

Solomon Simon Smith (born 1849, died 1907) also moved to Bay City after marrying Bertha Close in Canada.

Mary Jane Smith (born 1850, died 1922) married 1st) Eli Chilson, 2nd) Orren Bennett 3rd) William Wood, died in Genesee County.

Elizabeth Mary "Libby" Smith (born 1850, died 1921) married 1st) George Stark, 2nd) Julius Rankin. Libby and George both buried in Memory Gardens.

Charles Tenney Smith (born 1853, died 1922) moved around Michigan and married Hannah Carrie Hess in Tuscola County, later he married twice more and eventually settled in Genesee County.

Eleanor "Ellen" Smith (born 1856, died 1944) married George A. Webster in Tawas City.

Reuben Smith (born 1858, died 1930) recorded as a Grant Township Pioneer by the *"Tawas Herald"* will be described below.

Andrew Stephen Smith (born 1862, died 1934) married Aramantha Emeline 'Emma' Brintnell; together they raised 11 children in Grant Township.

Thaddeus Lincoln Smith (born 1864, died 1940) married Sarah Matilda Burtch.

Joseph Smith died May 17, 1898, one year after the death of his dear Aurilla, they are buried in Memory Gardens. *Submitted by Connie Chism.*

REUBEN SMITH. He was born June 19, 1858, in Oxford, Ontario. In 1881, he married Charlotte Hyland of Tawas Township. She is the daughter of Henry and Bridgett (Hughes) Hyland who migrated to Iosco County from Rolvenden, England. Their family consisted of Jennie Hyland (born 1859, died 1950) married to John Barnett, resided in the state of Washington; Fannie Hyland (born 1861, died 1933) married George Hastings; and Charlotte (born 1862, died 1936).

Reuben and Charlotte Smith farmed in Grant Township where they raised 12 children: Fannie, Henry, Minnie, Grace, Fred, Roy, Mary, Mabel, Chester, Bernice, Clare and Celia.

1) Fannie (born 1881, died 1949) married John Burt whose family came to Iosco from Canada.

2) Henry (born 1884, died 1973) married Teressia (Barr) Bamberger, no issue.

3) Minnie (born 1886, died 1954) married Gordon Culham, moved to Saskatchewan.

4) Grace (born 1889, died 1920) married Claude Irish.

5) Fred (born 1891, died 1976) married Ethel McCullum.

6) Roy (born 1893, died 1978) married 1st) Ethel McDougall and 2nd) Dorothy Anderson.

7) Mary (born 1896, died 1977) married Fred Pfahl (Pfahl family history listed elsewhere), were active members of Hemlock Road Baptist Church and Ladies Aid; prior to this marriage, Mary worked at Buick Motor Company in Flint to provide money to build a home for her parents (Reuben and Charlotte Smith) on the NE corner of Sand Lake and M-55.

8) Mabel (born 1899, died 1969) married John VanWagnen.

9) Chester (born 1901, died 1976) married Dorothy Latter.

10) Bernice (born 1903, died 1991) married William Herriman, resuming the farm previously owned by Reuben and Charlotte Smith in Grant Township.

11) Clare (born 1905, died 1960) married Doris Latham.

12) Celia (born 1910, died 2000) married Marshall Warren. *Submitted by Connie Chism*

MICHAEL AUBURN SOMMER-FIELD. Michael was the pastor for over 35 years of the Reorganized Church of Jesus Christ of Latter Day Saints in Tawas City. He was born April 25, 1868 in Buena Vista Township in Saginaw County, Michigan. His father John Sommerfield was born in 1840 and died in 1880. His mother was Christina Munseh who was born in Prussia in August 1832 and died September 5, 1910. His parents were farmers in Saginaw.

Michael had six brothers and sisters. They were August (born December 3, 1860); John (born May 31, 1864); Andrew (born 1866); Caroline (born July 23, 1853); Anna (born 1857); and Christina (born April 5, 1862).

Michael was taken out of school in the spring to help plant crops and again in the fall to harvest the same crops. His formal education amounted to approximately the fifth grade. From his early childhood he was a Bible student and was interested in church history and history of pre-historic people in America. He was also active in many phases of civic activities, including Supervisor of the First Ward of Tawas City, and other local civic boards and commissions.

His means of transportation was always the horse and buggy and walking. In winter by sleigh or cutter. Heavy blankets of wool or buffalo hide were used to keep the riders and driver warm while traveling in the winter. A brick or stone was heated and wrapped in cloth and placed at their feet while traveling. He never did own or drive a car.

He was very active in church work. For six years he had charge of the Whittemore Branch of the Reorganized Church of Jesus Christ of Latter Day Saints along with the Tawas branch on Townline Road. In 1918 he drafted a resolution presented to the district Conference to organize a branch in Tawas City. This was unanimously approved and so the Branch was organized and a church building purchased on Mathews Street in Tawas City.

The structure was originally a Congregational Church then Presbyterian. It is believed to be the oldest structure of its kind in Tawas City. He was pastor of the Tawas City Church for over 25 years. He said as Paul of old did say, "He fought the good fight, he kept the faith." His only regret as he grew older was that he could not do more for the Lord.

Michael A. and Anna Augusta Sommerfield

He and his wife Anna Augusta raised 10 children: Clara (born April 2, 1889 d. 1970); Anna (born July 7, 1890, died 1920); George (born March 1, 1895, died 1969); Michael (born August 30, 1896, died 1964); Christine (born March 2, 1897, died 1959); Caroline (born November 27, 1899, died 1918); Florence (born February 28, 1903, died 1994); Grace (born November 27, 1905, died__); Irene (born November 12, 1907, died 1949); Myrna (born November 11, 1911, died __).

Michael worked first as a farmer then as a blacksmith for the D&M Railway and was the first to retire from there under the Compensation Act.

On Sunday afternoons he walked many miles visiting members who were incapacitated in Tawas City and E. Tawas. He visited and took communion to them. He also visited the Indian Village near Oscoda, preaching many funeral sermons for them. He never charged them. One of his daughters tells the story of being left to get the meals when her mother and the rest of the family went to Saginaw to visit relatives. The daughter was 9 years old. She was going to fix her father his favorite pie. She remembered her mother making a crust and pouring the custard filling over it and baking it. She did not remember that her mother had baked the crust first for a few minutes. She baked the pie and the crust floated to the top. She was so worried about how the pie looked that she hid it. Her kind father smelled it and asked to see it. He ate it with relish and declared it delicious. She always remembers how gracious he was about it and how understanding of her feelings. *Written by Grace M. Sommerfield Smith.*

SOUCIE. John Baptise Soucie Sr. A pioneer resident of Oscoda, (born 1850, died 1913), he migrated to Oscoda from Quebec, Canada. His wife, Lavina Lane (born 1863,

died 1935), came from Caseville, Michigan. She was considered the "Florence Nightingale," of the community. Out of 11 children, nine survived.

I) John Baptise Soucie Jr. was the eldest (born 1884, died 1960) married Ada M. Alton from Glennie, Michigan. He was known as the last of the "Lumber Jack Cooks," which started him on his life-time career of (in his words) "cookin." He was the chief cook at the dams built on the AuSable River in Oscoda. His own first restaurant was destroyed by the famous fire of 1911. He cooked for the newly formed YMCA at Van Ettan Lake, the famous Van Ettan Lake Lodge, the Greenbush Inn, and was chief cook in charge of a crew at the well known Lost Lake Woods Lodge in Lincoln, Michigan. He had two restaurants before he opened his largest and well known restaurant called, "The Rendezvous" in the Jerry Marks building on Oscoda's main street. It is still there today as a gift and clothing store. He became known throughout the area and adjoining states for his good home "cookin" and especially for his lake trout and white fish dinners, French green pea soup, and his variety of home made pies. "Stop at John's place", became the by word of tourists. John and Ada had five children:

1. Ellen Marie Soucie graduated from the University of Michigan School of Nursing, and was Director of Nurses for Pontiac State Hospital. In retirement she obtained a degree from Oakland University and also received the Distinguished Alumni Award from the University. She married Peter Gormley in 1940 and they reside in Jackson, Michigan. They have one son, Michael, married to Connie and they also reside in Jackson.

2. Lloyd F. Soucie graduated from Central Michigan University, in Mt. Pleasant. He married Helen Webb from Hale. They both taught school. After his wife's death, he remarried and he and his wife, Mary, retired to Roswell, New Mexico.

3. John E "Jack" Soucie married Jean Le Van of Oscoda and they moved to Fort Myers, Florida. Jack was assistant superintendent of maintenance, for the Dade County Schools, in Fort Myers, Florida. They retired to Franklin, North Carolina. Two children, Terry and Carol, both live in the Miami area in Florida.

4. Vera E. Soucie after two years of college had a 33 year career in banking, including being assistant cashier for the Oscoda State Saving Bank. She married Cyril Phelps Kennedy, now deceased. They had two children, Randy married to Dana and

now living in Dayton, Tennessee and Danya Kennedy of Lincoln Park. A later marriage was to Roger A. Olver from Wayne, Michigan, and Oscoda.

5. Clyde L. Soucie after serving in the U.S. Army married Faith Husted of Pontiac, and was an assistant fire inspector for the city of Pontiac. They both are retired and now residing in Oscoda, where he is a County Commissioner. They have two children: Wayne (married to Deborah) and Elizabeth (married to David), both live in Pontiac.

II) George Soucie (born 1885, died 1928) resided and died in Oscoda.

III) Ellen Soucie (born 1888, died 1912) married Joseph Gjorling and lived in Pontiac, Michigan.

IV) William J. Soucie (born 1889, died 1968) spent most of his life in Minnesota and died in Superior, Wisconsin.

V) Lawrence Soucie (born 1892, died 1935) married Susan Tremain of AuSable. He died in Royal Oak after an injury at the Alabaster Gypsum Plant. There were six children: Helen, Ann, George, Elaine, Edna and Lawrence Jr. All resided in the Royal Oak Area.

VI) Lloyd Soucie (born 1896, died 1961) married Kathleen Auener from Detroit. He was superintendent of Oscoda Water Works. There are three daughters.

1. Gloria Soucie graduated from Central University of Mt. Pleasant. She married Robert Alschimer from Detroit. She taught in the Detroit Schools. In retirement they moved to California. Their two children, Robert and Carol both live in California.

2. Joan Soucie graduated from Central University of Mt. Pleasant and married William Ryan of Ypsilanti. They resided in New Baltimore and she retired from a teaching career there. In retirement, they returned to Oscoda. There were two sons, Patrick, now deceased, and Timothy married to Kelly and living in Washington, DC.

3. Deanna Soucie married Bobbie Ruckman from Oklahoma. He was an officer in the Air Force. They have four children: Lori Ann of Texas, Karen, Stephen of Washington DC and Christopher of Oscoda.

VII) Mary Soucie (born 1900, died 1933) married Harry England of Jackson, who became a well known local barber. Their one daughter, Doris Johnson Favre lived in Oscoda until the time of her death. She has three children: Jon and Mary of Grand Rapids and Harry of Glennie.

VIII) Ann Soucie (born 1905-) married Thomas Jones, who was in the Air Force. After his death she resided until her death with a son in Hampton, Virginia. There were two sons, Tom, the eldest, was killed in Alaska and Richard living in Virginia.

IX) Loretta "Babe" Soucie (born 1909, died 1980) was the youngest and after marriage to Floyd Strong lived in Bay City until the time of her death.

A history of John's "Cookin" career is being complied by his daughters. His business ventures in Oscoda were:

Camp 8 #1. Destroyed by the fire of 1911.

Camp 8 #2. Was located on lot next to IGA Store.

The Tivioli #3. A rustic log restaurant on site of the Best Gas Station Corner of Michigan Avenue.

The Rendezvous #4. Located on Main Street and now a store called The Three Wishes.

Tourist Café #5. A family home style cooking, which is now the Thrift Shop.

Camp 8 #6. Last venture before his retirement. Home made pies, soups, sandwiches and his famous hamburgers, was located next to the former Ardra's Restaurant.

In his retirement, John continued to cook for private hunting camps and the well known Kennedy's camp. He was also the chief cook for the youth camps in the area, returning to the YMCA and the Volunteers of America. Cooking was his life time career. He was going to work the summer for the YMCA but his time had run out. He died a day before his 73rd birthday in June 1960. *Complied by Ellen Marie Gormley.*

JAMES SPENCER FAMILY. James

"Jim" Spencer was born in AuSable on March 21, 1889 to Justus Spencer and Jane Goodfellow Spencer. His brothers and sisters were: Thomas Robert (born December 27, 1884, died January 20, 1967); Ellen Grace (Colbath) (born March 28, 1887, died January 9, 1968); Agnes Ann (Sharon) (born August 23, 1891, died May 9, 1969) and John Howard (born May 6, 1896, died May 16, 1979).

Jim's father, Justus, was the son of Thomas Spencer and Ann Severn Spencer who came to this country from Kirby, near Nottingham, England about 1854. After several years in Michigan, they homesteaded the land known as Fish Point that is located between Tawas and Oscoda by Spencer Lake. Jim's mother, Jane Goodfellow, was the daughter of John Goodfellow and Agnes Clelland. While the rest of the Goodfellow family came to the Curran, Michigan area by train, John and his son Robert came by driving a team of horses and wagon from

New York. John was born in Valcartier, Quebec, Canada and his parents came from Roxburghshire, Scotland.

Jim Spencer married Dorothy Couture, daughter of Peter and Clara Beaulieu Couture. Dorothy died October 11, 1918 as a result of the flu epidemic. They had one son, James Edward "Jimmy" who was born June 23, 1915 in AuSable. Jimmy married Mary Colbath and they had two sons: Lt. James Spencer died piloting a helicopter in the Vietnam War and is buried in Arlington National Cemetery in Washington, DC, and Edward Spencer lives with his wife Cindy and two children, Jeremy and Stephanie, in Salina, Kansas.

Florence (Brooks) and James Spencer

Jim married Florence Brooks who was the daughter of Palmer Brooks and Margaret Flynn Brooks. Palmer Brooks was the son of William and Eliza Brooks who came from Canada in the 1860s. Margaret Flynn was the daughter of William Flynn whose father came from Ireland and Mary McDonald who came from Pennsylvania.

Jim and Florence had three children: (1) Virginia married Howard Smith, a Michigan State Police officer. They have two children, Charlene and Randall. Her son and granddaughter Candy live with her in Battle Creek, Michigan. (2) Eugene died at the age of 2 and is buried in the Oscoda Cemetery. (3) Ralph married Shirley Streeter from Hale. They have a son, Robin, and two daughters, Lani and Leslie. Ralph and Shirley live in Mill Creek, Washington near their daughter, Lani.

In his early youth, Jim Spencer worked on fishing boats with his father Justus in the summer and worked lumbering for the mills in the winter. He saved to become the proud owner of his own successful fishery business and captain of the many fishing boats he owned ranging from his first sailboat to the first diesel powered boat in the AuSable fishery. He knew every detail of the underwater terrain of Lake Huron reachable from the port of AuSable, where the logs and debris were located, and where the lake trout preferred to be at different times of the year. He was forced to close

his business because of failing health and the introduction of the lamprey eel into the Great Lakes that destroyed the commercial fishing industry in the area.

Florence was well known for her exquisite knit and crochet fancywork and beautiful hand sewn patterned quilts. She was also an excellent cook with a special knack for baking a delicious variety of breads, cakes, pies, cookies, etc.

Jim died September 20, 1949, saddened by the loss of his business, his failing health that left him in nearly constant pain, and most importantly, the pending death of his wife Florence from terminal cancer. Florence died April 30, 1950. They are both buried in the Oscoda Cemetery.

JOHN HOWARD SPENCER. John

was born May 6, 1896, AuSable Township, the youngest son of Justus Howard and Jane (Goodfellow) Spencer. Grandparents, Thomas and Ann (Severn) Spencer, came from the Midlands of England circa 1854 and resided in various cities in Michigan where Thomas taught music before permanently settling at Fish Point, AuSable, Michigan. Spencer Lake

John Howard and Irene Spencer in about 1917

in that area was named for the family. Maternal grandparents came to Michigan via Canada and engaged in farming and lumbering.

John Howard attended classes at the AuSable High School and at a young age started a career of commercial fishing with his father. When the July 11, 1911 fire destroyed most of AuSable and Oscoda, he was a lad of 15. He fled with his family on his father's fishing boat down the AuSable River into Lake Huron. Their home and all possessions on Second Street in AuSable, along with their fishing buildings on the banks of the river were consumed by the fire. After the fire they settled on a 212 acre farm they owned at the mouth of the Dead AuSable. The "Old AuSable Beach Resort" is located in some of that area today. Father and son continued commercial fishing from that location until they could rebuild in AuSable.

His daughters can recall stories he would tell them of how their grandfather had first started his fishing ventures relying on wind and sails; of trying to forecast weather conditions by studying signs of nature; and of working in lumber camps during winters.

In November 1917, John Howard married Irene Tremaine. Her father worked for the Loud Lumber Company and they had suffered from the ravages of the great fire of 1911. Her grandparents were farmers and came to Michigan via Canada from County Cornwall, England. The young couple raised six daughters while John Howard continued fishing in partnership with his father. At his father's death in 1927, he continued the fishing business under his own management until 1941 when he sold all equipment and moved to Royal Oak, Michigan to work for the Chrysler Corporation.

Upon retirement in 1962, he and his wife purchased a home at Tawas Lake, East Tawas, Michigan, where he died at the age of 83 in May 1979. The family can recall the anxiety they felt while waiting for their father's boat, *The Lady Grace,* the last one to return safely to shore during a gale of snow and ice that suddenly descended on Lake Huron while the boats were at their fishing grounds in December 1934. They remember that he enjoyed duck, rabbit and deer hunting, but only enjoyed rod and reel fishing after his retirement. *Submitted by grandson, Arthur H. Nicander.*

SHIRLEY and RALPH SPENCER FAMILY.

Ralph Selwyn Spencer is the son of Florence and James Spencer born March 14, 1927 in AuSable, Michigan. He spent his youth in Oscoda enjoying a carefree life of playing on the beach, swimming at the old dock and in the river during the summer, skating, and sledding onto the bayou in the winter. He graduated from Oscoda High School and served in World War II as a Seabee on Samar, Philippine Islands. He graduated from Cleary College in Ypsilanti and was manager of vendor auditing for Kaiser Motors Corporation and was manager of corporate staff operational auditing for Chrysler Corporation.

Ralph married Shirley Jeanne Streeter, October 20, 1946 at Hale, Michigan. Shirley was born June 8, 1925 to Pearle Rahl Streeter and Forrest Streeter in Hale, Michigan. She spent her youth in Hale enjoying with her friends the winter and summer outdoor activities, church activities and dancing to big bands of the time. She attended school in Hale, Whittemore and graduated from Oscoda High School. Shirley was accepted at the Henry Ford Hospital School of Nursing, but choose instead to work at the Cadillac Tank Plant in Detroit for one year. She then worked at the post office in Oscoda before and while Ralph was in the service.

Shirley and Ralph Spencer with children: Lani, Robin and Leslie.

After marriage, Shirley worked in the marketing office of Kaiser Motors Corporation in Ypsilanti while Ralph attended school and until it was time to start a family. She then applied her abilities to nurturing and guiding their three children to very successful careers.

Robin (born May 13, 1952 in Ypsilanti Michigan) graduated from the University of Michigan in Ann Arbor with a BSChem Degree Honors with High Distinction, and from Wayne State University School of Medicine. He did his residency in family medicine at Toledo Hospital and currently directs 32 primary care physicians in northern Illinois for Sisters of the 3rd Order of St. Francis. Robin married Shelley Godwin at Toledo, Ohio in September 1980. She is an RN, has a BS from the University of Wisconsin, and an MS in counseling. She is currently a child welfare coordinator for Catholic charities. Robin and Shelley live in Roscoe, Illinois and have three children: Elise Ariadne (born September 6, 1981), a senior at the University of Illinois and is on the College and National Deans List; Lauren Brooke (born January 19, 1984) will be a freshman in the College of Business at Southern Illinois University; and Jeffrey Lane (born April 19, 1986) will be a junior in high school.

Lani (born July 30, 1958 in Ypsilanti, Michigan) graduated from Mercy College in Detroit with a BS in nursing, and from the University of Detroit with an MS in health administration. She has worked as a RN and Director of Nursing in the Detroit area; and as director of patient care and rehabilitation at a head injury rehabilitation hospital and manager of utilization services at Group Health Cooperative in the Seattle area. She currently applies her abilities to raising their child. Lani married Rodrick Xuereb of Detroit, Michigan on May 11, 1985. Rod graduated from Wayne State University School of Medicine and did his residency in anesthesiology at the University of Washington, Seattle, Washington. He is currently managing partner of the anesthesiology group serving the Valley Medical Center in

Renton, Washington. Lani and Rod live in Bellevue, Washington and have one child, Linnea Shea (born May 8, 1989 in Seattle, Washington).

Leslie (born May 12, 1960 in Ypsilanti Michigan) graduated from the University of Michigan, Ann Arbor with a BS biology summa cum laude and from Wayne State University School of Medicine, Detroit, Michigan. She did her residency in obstetrics and gynecology at Sinai Hospital in Detroit and is currently a partner in an obstetrics and gynecology practice in Hinsdale, Illinois. Leslie married Donald D. Thomas II of Ann Arbor at Greenfield Village, Dearborn, Michigan on December 21, 1985. Don has his BS biology and MD from the University of Michigan, Ann Arbor and did his residency in general surgery at the Detroit Medical Center. He did his fellowship in Cardio-Thoracic Surgery at the University of Washington in Seattle, Washington. Don is currently a partner in a practice that serves several hospitals in the Chicago Metro area. Leslie and Don live in Burr Ridge, Illinois and have two children: Caroline Leigh (born March 30, 1989 in Detroit, Michigan) and Weston Andrew (born April 13, 1991 in Seattle, Washington).

Shirley and Ralph currently have a home in Mill Creek, Washington, where they moved after retirement to be near their two daughters and families who both lived in the Seattle area at that time. They also maintain Shirley's childhood home in Hale, Michigan where they visit in the spring and fall each year. Shirley is an avid supporter of animal rights and environmental groups.

STANTON FAMILY.

The history of the Stanton Family of Wilber Township originates in England where Esther Eleanor Heal married William Samuel Stanton II. A few years later they made plans to leave England with their small daughter Sarah (born 1845) and make their home in Canada. The sailing vessel they were aboard was shipwrecked and the passengers and crew were marooned on an island for several months before they reached Paris, Ontario, Canada in August of 1846.

In 1846, a son, William Samuel Stanton III, was born in St. George, Ontario, Canada. When he was a little over 2 years of age, his father died. A few months later, a daughter, Anna Stanton was born to Esther Eleanor Heal Stanton. Esther remarried Anthony Ocha (see Ocha family) and the family moved from Canada to Port Hope, in the thumb area of Michigan.

When William Samuel III was 22, the family moved to East Tawas, Michigan and settled in Baldwin Township where William's parents kept a half way house for the stage coaches that ran between AuSable and East Tawas before the Green Railroad was in operation. He met Charlotte Thomas, who was born 1852 in St. Thomas, Ontario, Canada and lived in East Tawas with her brother's family,

William and Charlotte were married in 1871. The spring of 1874, they moved from East Tawas to Wilber Township and homesteaded land with the other families living in the township at that time. They built their home on the corner of the property they homesteaded on Sherman and Esmond Road.

Charlotte (Thomas) and William Samuel Stanton III, 50th wedding anniversary ca. 1921.

The couple had 11 children: Esther, Francis and Enoch died in infancy; Anthony died at 14 and Guy at 2; William Jeremiah (born 1873) married and lived in Bay City, Michigan; James Edward (born 1879) married Vanetta Bielby who died, and he remarried and made his home in Bay City also; Penelope Pauline (born 1881) married Joseph R. Misener (see Misener family) and the couple made their home in East Tawas, Michigan; Mary Charlotte (born 1883) married William Russell Misener (1st cousin to Joseph R. Misener) and the couple made their home in Bay City for 12 years, then moved to Portland, Oregon; Frederick Augustus (born 1887) married and made his home in Sault Ste. Marie, Michigan; Benjamin John (born 1891) married and made his home in Bay City.

Along with the Stantons, other families were the Burcham, Moore, Wilber, Kingsland, Scott, Marshall, Symes, Stevenson, Corner, Falls, Rodman and Abbott. They all worked together to develop the community.

Charlotte and Mrs. Stevenson were midwifes and surrogate doctors for many in the community and William Samuel was Constable and helped to oversee the state of the roads, which at that time were "slab roads and winding trails" and a trip to East Tawas was a long days journey. Charlotte and William Samuel were charter members of the Wilber Methodist Church that was dedicated in 1887 and are buried in Wilber Cemetery. *Submitted by Marilouise (Nelem) Pershon.*

ALBERT "BERT" and ANITA STOLL.

Bert (born 1902, died 1968) and Anita Ione Stoll (born 1902, died 1985) came to the East Tawas area in 1937. Bert was a University of Michigan graduate. He did some writing for the *Cleveland Plain Dealer* and the *Battle Creek Enquirer News* prior to coming to Tawas. He worked construction for one year building the Old AuSable Beach Resort just south of Oscoda.

In 1938 he got back into newspaper work. He was employed by the *East Tawas News* (now the *News Herald*). After a short stint, he began writing for the *Bay City Times*. Later he was employed by the eight Booth newspapers. General writing became outdoor writing, his first love. He wrote of hunting and fishing in northern Michigan.

Late in his career he began to free lance, writing for the *Detroit Free Press, Midland Daily News* and *Alpena News*. His folksy columns were popular throughout the state. He won several awards at the state and national levels. His free lance work took him to western Canada several times for stories and 16mm movie work. He also accompanied a U.S.O. troop to Korea during the Korean War. He took photos and wrote stories about the trip.

Bert was one of the prime movers of our Silver Valley winter sports area. He helped get the celebrity folks to crown our Silver Valley queens. He was an avid hunter and fisherman. Therefore, outdoor writing was a natural for him.

Anita was a graduate of Ohio State University. She enjoyed being a housewife, and was active in the community. She did a great deal at Christ Episcopal Church and was a member of the Ladies Literary Club.

Anita and Bert loved the Tawas area. They bought a lot on Tawas Beach Road and built their home there in 1947. Their only child, son Peter, and his wife Louisa live in that home today (2002).

PETER and LOUISA STOLL.

Pete was born in Cleveland, Ohio, and came to East Tawas in 1937 with his parents, Albert and Anita Stoll. Pete graduated from East Tawas High School in 1952 and from Michigan State University with BS and master's degrees. He was employed by the Birmingham (Michigan) Board of Education from 1956 until he retired in 1992. First and foremost, Pete was a physical education teacher. He also coached a variety of sports, with basketball his first love. In fact, at this writing (2002) he is still helping son Bill with the Tawas Junior Varsity boys basketball squad.

Pete was the Birmingham Public Schools Teacher of the Year in 1981 and the State of Michigan Pride Teacher of the Year in 1988.

Since moving to the Stoll family home in East Tawas upon retirement, Pete has been active in the Tawas Area Education Foundation, the United Way Drive, coaching, and Christ Episcopal Church.

Louisa is a 1953 graduate of Royal Oak (Michigan) Dondero High School, and received her BS degree from Michigan State University. Lou has been very active in the Tawas area as a member of Quota International of Iosco County, and was named Quotarian of the year in 1996. She also serves on the vestry at Christ Episcopal Church. Her twin sister Emily "Em" and husband Mike O'Reilly live in the house next door on Tawas Beach Road.

Lou and Pete met at Michigan State University. They were married in 1956 and have four children: Bob, Deb, Bill and Rick. All of the children are in the field of education at this writing (2002). They have 11 grandchildren.

Lou and Pete love the Tawas area for its small town feeling, friendly people, and beautiful scenery. They enjoy walking, biking, swimming and sailing.

ELMER STREETER FAMILY.

Elmer was born in Pike, New York on January 28 1869 to Wiley Streeter and Almira Clement Streeter. He had two brothers, Clayton and Merton. They were descendents of Stephen Streeter, who came to Gloucester, Massachusetts from England in 1641, and Ursula Adams Streeter, whose father, Henry, was from Bainbridge, Massachusetts, was an ancestor of John Adams.

Elmer's ancestors fought in both the Revolutionary War and the Civil War. His father, Wiley Streeter, at age 16 was in Company C of the 104th New York Volunteer Infantry during the Civil War from 1861 to 1865. He participated in most of the hardest fought battles of the war. He was wounded and was taken prisoner in the battle at Weddon Railroad. He moved through several prison camps and suffered severe exposure from bad weather, lack of shelter, care and food that affected him throughout his life.

Elmer always liked working with horses. When he was a young man, he went to Virginia and helped break and train horses for the army under General White.

Elmer and Nellie

In 1892, Elmer married Nellie May Hetchler who was born in Gorham, New York. Nellie was the daughter and only child of Simon and Louisa Giesy Hetchler. Elmer and Nellie had two sons, Glenwood Elmer (born 1893 in Perry, New York) and Forrest Simon (born 1896 in Pike, New York). Glenwood married Fern Yawger, granddaughter of E.V. Esmond, in 1923 and they had one daughter, Dorothy. Forrest married Pearle Rahl in 1922 and they had one daughter, Shirley.

In February 1900, the family of Nellie, Elmer, Glenwood and Forrest along with Simon and Louisa Hetchler came to Hale by train into Emory Junction (National City). On the same train were William and Kate Rahl with Jennie, Otto and Gladys. The three families settled less than one-half mile apart with the Hetchlers on Ora Lake Road, Streeters on north M-65 and the Rahls on Webb Road.

Some of the older photos of the village show that there were very few trees and the roads looked rough with deep ruts. Business dealings included "trading" their farm goods such as eggs and butter for cloth, flour, and other staples. For some, times were hard and so was the work. Forrest told of his dad, Elmer, feeling sad because he didn't have the few cents in cash to buy a stamp to mail a letter to his parents back in Pike, New York.

Nellie Streeter passed away at 34 years of age on April 25, 1906 leaving her husband Elmer; sons Glenwood (age 12); Forrest (age 10); and her parents, Simon and Louisa Hetchler. The day before Nellie died, she was driving their team of horses, pulling a "stone boat" with stones she had lifted from the field. Elmer continued to farm, raise and train horses, and also became a livestock broker buying and selling sheep and cattle.

In January 1908, Elmer married Nancy Katherine Cook in Tawas City, Michigan. She was born October 22, 1884 in Unionport, Ohio. They bought a store on the main street in Hale and moved into the living quarters in 1919. In 1921, Elmer bought the Perlman store on the southwest corner

of the "Hale Four Corners" and moved into the living quarters there.

Elmer and Katie

Elmer and family spent the summer of 1922 living in the Kokosing Resort where they ran the grocery store. Their daughter Olive was 8 years old and she remembers going down the stairs part way in her nightgown and watching the dancers in the social hall. Later in 1923, they moved to Long Lake where they had a grocery store with dry goods, gas station, rental cottages, boat rental, icehouse and post office for many years. They continued to own the farm on M-65 that was run by their son Morris. Katie was always busy managing the post office, grocery store and the children.

Elmer and Katie were early members of Hale Masonic Lodge and Eastern Star and Elmer was a 32nd Degree Mason. They also belonged to the Gleaners and Elmer was a member of the Hale school board.

Their children, spouses and grandchildren are: Morris Merton Streeter (born 1911, died 1991) married Leone Sperling—child, Nancy Lee; Olive Mary (born 1914) married Eddie LaBerge—children: Gary, Alan, and James; Nellie Louise (born 1916, died 1999) married Wm. Zavitz—children, Linda and Robert; Gertrude Almira (born 1918) married Chester Zbikowski—children: Karen, Mary Jane and Evelyn; Wiley Louis "Bud" (born 1919) married Margaret Webb—children: Katherine "Kay," Wiley and Robert; Izalda Marie (born 1923, died 1975) never married.

Elmer enjoyed visiting with his friends. Each day they would congregate in the store by the pot-bellied heating stove (Elmer with his white "store apron" on) and they would discuss local and national politics, farming, price of gas, fishing, ailments and war.

Their home was always bustling with activity of the family children and a steady stream of friends in and out. There was ice-skating, sledding and ice fishing in the winter, with boating and swimming in the summer. There was always a family Sunday dinner with fried chicken, mashed potatoes, macaroni and cheese and homemade ice cream made with cream from the farm.

Katie, Olive and Nellie worked the kitchen preparing the food; Morris turned the handle on the ice cream freezer, while Elmer always made a large pot of "his special coffee." Elmer and Katie frequently entertained their friends. One cold winter evening, they had an oyster stew supper and invited the entire Masonic and Eastern Star group from the Hale Lodge. Always after dinner, there were tables set up to play the "500" card game which is still played in Hale.

Elmer and Katie retired in 1945 and moved into their lake-front home on Long Lake. Katie died in 1942 and Elmer died in 1954. They are buried in the Esmond Evergreen Cemetery at Hale.

FORREST and PEARLE STREETER.
Forrest Simon Streeter was born March 20, 1896 in Pike, New York. His parents were Elmer Streeter and Nellie Hetchler Streeter. Forrest was a descendent of Stephen Streeter, who came to Gloucester, Massachusetts from England in 1641, and Ursula Adams whose father, Henry, of Braintree, Massachusetts was an ancestor of John Adams.

Forrest left Perry, New York in early 1900 when he was 4 years old with his family and grandparents, Simon and Louisa Hetchler. They came to Michigan on the train to Emory Junction (National City). Coincidentally, on that same train was the Rahl family: William, Kate, Jennie, Otto and Gladys, moving to Hale from Samaria, Michigan. They settled less than one-half mile from each other. In 1902, Nellie Streeter came with Forrest to see the new baby girl (Pearle) at the Rahl farm. Nellie asked Forrest if he would like to take the new baby home. He said "no!" He married Pearle 20 years later.

Forrest and Pearle Streeter

Forrest's mother Nellie passed away April 25, 1906. She was 34 years old and her two sons, Forrest and Glenwood, were 10 and 12 years old. She was the only child of Simon and Louisa Hetchler.

Forrest went to the Hale school and graduated from the 10th grade. He attended Eastern Michigan University for a period of time, then enlisted in the Army in World War I. He was a sergeant and drove an ambulance for a base hospital in France until discharged in July 1919. In 1919, his father had bought a store on main street in Hale and also bought what is now known as the "Perlman Store" where Forrest worked. He then took a mechanic course in Detroit after which he worked at Stacy Yawger's garage.

Forrest married Pearle Beatrice Rohl on June 14, 1922 at Otto and Ida Rahl's home in Hale. Pearle was the fourth child of William and Kate Rahl born on February 21, 1902 at the Rahl farm in Hale on Webb Road.

Pearle was always busy. As a child, she loved to help her parent's garden, paint and wallpaper. She told of the many times she ran the sewing machine needle through her index finger as she sewed doll clothes. She was an excellent student, always punctual and well prepared for her classes. She graduated from the Hale school 10th grade in 1918. For about a year she lived in Whittemore with her brother Otto, his wife Ida (Herr), and their young son Bill. She was the operator for the Whittemore telephone central that was in Otto and Ida's ice cream store. In 1920 her parents had bought the confectionery store in Hale from Dr. Cowie. She and her sister Alice ran the store for a year or so until their parents moved from their farm into the living quarters of the confectionery store.

After Forrest and Pearle's marriage on June 14, 1922, they lived at Loud Dam where he was the dam operator. They lived in a log cabin, which was near where the company houses are now located. He loved to fish and they both loved to dance. One winter Saturday night, they came to Hale in their new Ford roadster to attend a "dance club" at the Hale Town Hall. They left the dance during a blizzard. When they started on the two-rut road going into Loud Dam, they became stuck. They walked for several miles in the deep snow with no boots, Pearle following in Forrest's footsteps. Their shoes and stockings were frozen to their feet when they finally arrived at their cabin home. And to further the problem, the oil line to the stove was frozen so there was no heat until they had thawed the line out. Their roadster was left in the woods until the spring thaw.

In the spring of 1923, they bought the main street store that Forrest's father had previously owned. Shirley was born June 8, 1925 in the living quarters there. That store set just east of the old Hale bank.

On October 19, 1924, Forrest was shot in the neck and chest at close range while hunting. It was four hours before he was carried out of the woods and driven to Bay City in an open sided, canvas top touring car by his brother-in-law, Jim McKeen.

Later, Otto Rahl and Forrest became partners with Otto running the dry goods and clothing store on the south side of Main Street by the bank building, while Forrest and Pearle ran the grocery and meat store on the north side of Main Street where the new post office built in 2002 now stands.

Pearle and Forrest moved into their new home at 218 West Main or Esmond in the spring of 1926 which Mr. Ezra Armstrong and Forrest had built.

In 1928, Forrest started his freight line, picking up groceries, hardware, etc. in Bay City or Saginaw and delivering them north to Hale and South Branch. The railroad was no longer running. When Forrest would go to Bay City/Saginaw to pick up his freight, he almost always took someone with him. He would buy their lunch, drop them off and pick them up if they needed to shop or run errands for free because he enjoyed the company. One person said that if it hadn't been for Forrest, her brother would have never been anywhere but Hale. During World War II, he sold his freightline and then only hauled livestock. Later, he became Plainfield Township Treasurer for three terms. Through these years, Pearle was busy with their large vegetable garden and flower gardens. There was always canning to do and fresh flowers to pick for the house. She also had a crochet, sewing, tatting or knitting project underway at all times.

In 1932 when Forrest began to hunt again, Pearle hunted with him. Her father, Wm. Rahl, and several other members of the family took part in bird and deer hunting. They also spent many hours along the area streams fly fishing for brook trout. Pearle became the most ardent fly fisher of all and was still fishing in the last year of her life.

Forrest and Pearle were early members of the Hale Masons and Eastern Star. They were also instrumental in starting the American Legion Post where Forrest was the second commander and Pearle was very active in the Legion Auxiliary. Pearle also belonged to a 500-card club for many years.

Forrest passed away January 19, 1963 at 66 years old. Pearle lived until May 11, 1975 when she passed away at her home on Mothers Day. They are both buried in the Esmond Evergreen Cemetery at Hale.

WILLIAM F. TILLEY.
William (born 1859, died 1926) was the eldest son of Alfred and Luchanne (Smith) Tilley. Alfred came from England and settled in Canada. Wife Luchanne was born in Allegany County, New York; they married sometime between 1851 and 1861. William was born in Ontario, Canada, and lived primarily in Romney Township, Kent County. Siblings in the family included Hannah (Thomas Christie), Alfred (Ettie Oldham), Henry (Elizabeth Riesner), Emma (Charles Redmon/Edward Hunter), Hattie (Melbourne Batchelor) and Luchanne. Luchanne died when she was very young, but the others eventually came into Michigan during the 1880s.

William F. Tilley on Slosser Road homestead farm in 1908

William's father died at Leamington, Ontario, in 1879. William's mother married George Middleton in 1880 and stayed in Canada until George died in 1890. She came into Michigan shortly after that and lived in DelRay near Detroit through 1897.

William's older sister Hannah and husband Thomas Christie settled in Iosco County during the mid-1880s. The Christies had a farm on Towerline Road in Plainfield Township for many years. They had five children: Emma (Earl Coulter), Charles, Pearl (Fred McIntyre, Harry and Hattie (John Berry/ Milford Vaught). Thomas was a successful farmer, but general economic conditions forced the family to move to Genesee County by 1910 and then to Detroit where they owned and operated a saloon until Thomas died in 1928. Hannah passed away in 1941.

Charles Tilley, age 7 and Alfred Tilley, age 4 in 1910

William came to the U.S. during the 1880s and married Elizabeth Landgraff in 1885. They lived in Detroit for several years and had four children: Charlotte (Albert Chatterson), Frederick (Irene Boots), Mamie (Ernest Sigler) and Lucy Ann. He and Elizabeth divorced, and he married Mae (Kleehammer) Parent. In 1903 William and Mae homesteaded a farm in Iosco County on Slosser Road in Plainfield Township and lived there for the next 15 years where he labored as a farmer.

Mae and William had two children:

Charles (Pauline Pankhurst) and Alfred (M. Myrtle Pickett); Mae's children from a previous marriage to Dennis Parent were part of the household also. They included Robert (Pauline Horning), Mae (Verney Malo), and George (Helen Anderson/ Kate Bruns). William and Mae divorced in 1918. Health conditions required that William relocate to a drier climate, so he and older son Charles moved to Arizona where he worked at various jobs. He died at Phoenix in 1926 and is buried there. Charles returned to Michigan and today his children: Nathan (Carol Burbo), Shirley (Ed Winters), and Sharon (Norman Winter) have a cottage in Iosco County on Britt Road.

Charles Tilley in 1930

Mae stayed in Iosco, County and married Peter Sawyer of Whittemore. William's younger son Alfred stayed on the Sawyer farm with his mother until Peter died in 1924. Mae then married Burt White of Hale and lived on Curtis Road until her health declined in the 1930s. She moved to Birch Run, Michigan, to be with her son George and died there in 1949. Son Alfred continued to farm the homestead land his parents had occupied on Slosser Road in Plainfield Township. Today that land is maintained by Alfred's son William Gary Tilley (Janet Thoms). M. Myrtle Tilley, Major Lois Tilley (Ret.), and Kay Tilley also maintain homes on Slosser Road.

Alfred Tilley on Slosser Road homestead farm in 1930s.

CHARLES CHRISTIAN TIMRECK III.

He comes from a family with a long history in Iosco County. His grandparents, Charles and Ida Timreck, immigrated from Germany between 1881 and 1882. They settled in Tawas City. Charles and Ida had nine children, eight of which were born in Tawas City. Charles Jr. "Charlie" was born in Tawas City in 1890. He married Matilda Green "Tillie" in 1912. Charlie and Tillie had two sons, Harold, born in east Tawas in 1913, and Charles III, born in Tawas City in 1921.

Charlie and Tillie first purchased the "home farm" in 1920. The farm was at the corner of what is now Timreck Road and Wilber Road. The original acreage was around 120. Charlie built the first round-roof barn in Iosco County.

Charles Jr. "Chuck" was raised on the farm in Tawas City. At 5 years of age he would

Chuck holding JoAnn and Stella Timreck

spend his summers driving the horses for the hay wagon. Chuck went to the East Tawas Public School. He left school in the 10th grade at the age of 15 to be of greater assistance on the farm.

In 1923, the family started the Timreck Dairy Farm. This dairy helped the family through the depression as other local families would barter goods and services for the milk and butter. At the age of 14, Chuck had his own milk route.

During this same period of time, the family was also putting their eldest son, Harold, through medical school at the University of Detroit. In order to raise additional income, the family extended their business to potato farming. This continued until after the Second World War. They purchased their very first tractor, a brand new John Deere, in 1937. It dramatically increased their ability to do the work required to run the farm. Chuck met Stella Hachtel, of Bay City, in February 1939. They were married on January 20, 1940, and settled on the family farm with Charlie and Tillie. At that time, the farmhouse was a small five-room house. In 1942, at the age of 21, Chuck and Stella were added to the deed on the farm with the agreement that they would take care of Charlie and Tillie in their old age. It was at this point that Chuck took over control of the family farm.

Chuck and Stella had two children, JoAnn (born February 1942) and Ronald (born December 1943). In 1946, the family decided that the current living quarters were insufficient for two families. Thus, Charlie and Chuck proceeded to build the three-story (plus basement) brick house that sits on the property today. They had seen a house in Standish that had a "look" that they liked. Chuck drew up the floor plan and the two men began to build. The house was 28 feet wide and 44 feet long (for all four stories), although the attic had limited space due to the rafters. The lumber was cut on the plains and then brought to the farm. With a sawmill on the property, Charlie and Chuck

sawed and dried all of the lumber needed for the house. The flooring was taken to Grayling for finishing. The house had many intricate built in cabinets and closets, as well as beautiful wood floors. It was 11 rooms - quite a bit larger than what they'd been living in for the last several years. In 1948, the house was ready to move into. The only work that had been "hired out" was the plumbing and brickwork.

In 1954 the family built a new milking parlor. This parlor was one of the first of its kind in Iosco County and thus made the newspaper. The original design had three stanchions on either side, with a pit in the center for the people. It had a sanitary Pyrex pipeline which sent the milk directly to a strainer and then into a 1,000 gallon bulk tank. Within two years, the three stanchion design was updated to the herringbone design. This allowed them to double their capacity by having 12 cows milked at once as opposed to the original six. With 125 head of cattle, productivity was important!

Due to the farm and their activities within the community, the family were long time members of the Farm Bureau. In 1958, Chuck was selected to be one of five from Iosco County that traveled to Washington, DC for a tour and observation of "government in action." During that trip, they met Vice President Nixon, as well as the Secretary of Agriculture and several senators and representatives. This trip included Farm Bureau members from all over the United States.

In 1968, the family purchased a home in Holiday, Florida, as a retirement home for Charlie and Tillie. In 1970, Chuck sold the farm to his son, Ronald, and took up part-time retirement himself, spending his summers working the farm and his winters in Florida. In 1975 the farm was sold outside the family and Chuck and Stella moved permanently to Holiday. At the time of sale, the farm had grown from its original 120 acres to over 750 acres.

Chuck and Stella owned the Bright and Clean Laundromat in Holiday between 1978 and 1980. After that, they took up permanent retirement. In 1995 they moved to Jacksonville, Florida. to be closer to one of their grandchildren.

Chuck's hobbies include boating, fishing and hunting, as well as gardening. Chuck and Stella have six living grandchildren (with two deceased) as well as 11 great-grandchildren.

HAROLD A. TIMRECK, M.D. (1913-2001)

The older of two sons of Charles W. Timreck and Mathilda (Green) Timreck Jr.,

Harold was born in East Tawas on August 15, 1913. His maternal grandparents were Christian and Dorthea Betsch Green. They immigrated to the United States from Romania, and settled in East Tawas. Harold's paternal grandparents were Mr. and Mrs. Charles W. Timreck Sr. They were farmers and established the family farm on cold creek, on Wilbur Road between M-55 and Monument Road. 15, 1913. When only a small boy his parents purchased a farm near the Timreck family farm on the corner of Wilbur and Timreck Roads. With his own hands and expertise, his father constructed a large barn. He later added a barn for calves, this became known as The Timreck Dairy Farm. At the age of 16, Harold graduated from the East Tawas High School in 1930. He graduated from the University of Detroit (pre-med) with a BS degree in June 1934; enrolled in Georgetown University School of Medicine and was graduated with a MD degree in June 1938.

Harold A. Timreck

He then married Myrna Lou Sommerfield, from Tawas City, Harold had proposed to Myrna on their first date. She was caring for his maternal grandmother, who was convalescing from pneumonia. Harold had met her only the previous day, his birthday, August 15, 1932. He still had two years pre-med and four years of medical school. She promised to wait for him. Harold interned at Mercy Hospital, Bay City, Michigan. Myrna continued to work that year managing Dr. Orland W. Mitton's Office, in East Tawas. They then opened an office for Harold's practice in Beaverton, Michigan.

Harold held a commission in the army and was called to active duty during the emergency in May 1941. Later, he transferred to the Air Force and graduated from the School of Aviation Medicine as a flight surgeon. With Myrna always with him, they lived all over the south, southeastern and southwestern United States. Harold served 19 months overseas with the 8th Air Force. He volunteered to fly 17 combat missions with his crews, to have a better understanding of what his crew was enduring. Harold received the Air Medal and Soldiers Medal.

Upon his return in November 1945, he joined Dr. Keith D. Couter as an equal partner in the original old Gladwin Hospital.

Harold had been buying into it while in the service. Harold and Myrna had two children, Michael Charles and Pamela Ann.

Michael Charles married Marlene Stauffer and they had an infant son, Charles Anthony, who died shortly after birth. They later divorced. Much later, Michael married Tracey Wilbert and they had a son, Michael Jason.

Pamela married Michael A. Pietrzyk and they have three sons and one daughter: Michael S. married Dora Lynn Stamper and they have one daughter, Anna Marie, and one son, Mathew; Christopher married Julie Waters and they have one son, Riley Waters; Paul married Rose O'Brien; and Amanda is a senior in high school. They all live in Roanoke, Virginia. Michael C. Timreck lives in Sugar Springs, Gladwin.

Harold retired from the practice of medicine in July 1986. In 1976 they sold their house in Gladwin and moved to their hunting lodge on Greenwood Road, Roscommon County. Here they were to live out their lives surrounded by all the beauties of nature and God's wildlife, after years of yachting the Great Lakes, flying their own plane all over this continent, motor coaching, traveling the world. Harold also became an expert Big Game Hunter and Fly Fisherman. He was a perfectionist.

Harold passed away peacefully, November 12, 2001. Myrna had her 90th birthday, the previous day, November 11, 2001. Harold had not been well for the past four and a half years. He was lovingly cared for here at the "Lodge."

BENJAMIN TRUDELL. The U.S. Coast Guard is an elite group of men and women who protect our seas and our lives. The Coast Guard (Lifesaving Service) was established August 4, 1790, under Secretary of State, Alexander Hamilton. Some very important men in this writer's life served in the U.S.

Ben Truedell

Coast Guard: her father, Ernest Larson; her husband, Joseph Landgraf; and her uncle, Benjamin Trudell.

A Grand Maris news article recalls the heroism of Captain Benjamin Trudell, formally of East Tawas, Michigan, in many Great Lakes Rescues. The first "Cutters," known as Revenue Cutters, averaged between 40 and 60 feet in length. Ben Trudell was captain of one of these ships named

the *"Cutter Cook."* He later became the Officer in Charge of Grand Maris Coast Guard Station.

Benjamin Trudell was the son of a local fisherman, Joseph and Emaline Trudell of East Tawas. After his retirement from the United States Coast Guard he and his wife established the Green Shingle Inn in Grand Maris, Michigan.

Joseph and Emaline Trudell had other children: Adelbert Trudell (Olive) of East Tawas, Michigan; Ethel Trudell Gates (Elgin) of East Tawas, Michigan; Mildred Trudell Helmer (Phillip) of Pinconning, Michigan; Bessie P. Trudell Larson (Ernest) of East Tawas, Michigan; Benjamin Trudell (Lena) of East Tawas, Michigan/Grand Maris, Michigan

EDWARD A. TRUDELL. He was better known as Eddie and was born April 13, 1892 in Bay City, the youngest son of Louise M. and Katherine (King) Trudell. His grandfather, John B. Trudell, came from Canada and was the third fur trader on the Saginaw River. Arriving in 1835, he bought property, traded with the Indians and was considered by Bay City to be its first settlers. He later moved to the Banks area and turned to commercial fishing.

Edward A. and Laura (Rodel) Trudell in 1930. He was mayor of Tawas City.

The Trudell's fished many years from the Saginaw River area, when Eddie decided to fish from the Charity Islands, moving to the Charities in the early spring and back in the late fall, fishing for perch, whitefish, and herring. They established a settlement there and some of the remains can still be seen. In 1911, Edward married Laura Rodel who was born May 2, 1894. In 1917, Eddie moved his family, along with his father and mother, by fishing tugs to Tawas. They moved with all their furniture, clothing, and all their worldly possessions. That even included the chickens.

His parents, known as Dada and Kate, built a cottage and only stayed the summer months. Eddie moved his family into part of the fish house, later into the house that was to become the Roxy Roach residence, after Eddie's new home that was built on Tawas Bay, near his fishery. The first house burnt, but was rebuilt behind where Coyle's restaurants used to stand.

Eddie warned the state in 1925 that if a ban was not put on all fishing during their spawning seasons and the size of perch and herring was not limited, that in 20 years the lakes would be depleted of fish. Larger fish companies, with their high priced lawyers and politicians fought against him and his understanding friends. Eddie lost what he fought for, and as everyone knows, in 20 years the fish were gone. During the Great Depression, Eddie again, along with the aide of Fred C. Holbeck, asked the state to open the Tawas River to sports fisherman, so they could provide their needy families with food. This time they won, and the river has been open ever since.

During their lives in Tawas, Eddie and Laura were well known for their great generosity. No one would leave their door hungry. Fish were always available, and the needy always cared for. By the age of 39, Eddie had accumulated a great deal of property. The Trudell fishery, a restaurant well known for it's famous fish sandwiches, a pool hall and game room, the original Kick-A-Poo hunting club, as well as several homes and cottages, always looked ahead for his families future. The Trudells, Coyles, Lixeys, Herricks were all related by marriage. Only the Lixeys remain in the fishing business. Eddie passed away in 1932, at age 40, while holding the office of Mayor of Tawas. His life had only begun. At his death he had thought he left his family well taken care of, but two family lawyers, along with some of his best friends and relatives swindled his wife and six children of most everything. Without Eddie's supervision, the fishery, later known as Coyle's Fish Company, was soon closed and dismantled. His five sons and one daughter moved on to make new lives of their own. Laura passed away April 16, 1944, after moving in with her daughter in Bay City. Theodore, Evelyn, and Robert returned to Tawas and reside at Baldwin Center. Edward, William, and Daniel chose city life.

Theodore passed away August 27, 2001; William passed away on April 30, 2001; Daniel passed away on June 23, 1995; and Edward "Bud" passed away on May 18, 1988.

Presently where the Trudell Fish Company and Coyle's Restaurant once stood are now groups of condominiums.

EVELYN TRUDELL.
She was the only daughter of Edward A. and Laura (Roedel) Trudell. Evelyn went to St. Joseph School and graduated in 1931. In 1939 Evelyn opened one of the first roadside food stands in Tawas. Directly in front of the old Trudell Fishery, it was called "Snow White's," with full size hand painted portraits of the seven dwarfs. She was noted for her homemade fish sandwiches and homemade ice cream. People came from all around just to get a fresh sandwich made by Evelyn. Nothing but the best. Especially knowing that they were only made

Evelyn (Trudell) Pockrandt

from fresh whitefish, menominee, or herring. Nothing but fresh, not frozen.

The "Snow White" was only in operation for a short time, due to an electrical fire near the stove area.

While living in Bay City, Evelyn's brothers, Bob and Teed, and Bill all worked at the Mt. Morris Chevy garage. They had a friend and fellow worker whose name was Fred Pockrandt. They or one of them introduced Evelyn to Fred. Evelyn said "I don't remember whether it was Bobby or one of the others that got us together." After a short courtship, they were married on February 8, 1941. After their marriage, Evelyn moved to Saginaw where her husband was in the auto body business. They later combined into an Auto Parts and Fabric business. After her husband's death in 1970, she built a home in Baldwin Center, moving her business to Oscoda, later to open yet another store near her home. Eventually her health forced her to give up the store near her home, and she sold the store in Oscoda to her daughter Karen.

Evelyn and Fred raised three children: Karen, Thomas and Fred Jr.

ROBERT J. TRUDELL.
He was born December 2, 1920 in the home later to be known as the Roxy Roach residence, and is the son of Edward A. and Laura (Roedel) Trudell. At the young age of 6-10, he peddled his little red wagon around town and sold fish (on Fridays) and other days by request. He made about four trips to and from just to take care of all the customers. He built scooters, just for fun, made from a little bit of small pieces of wood, nails, and with a pair of roller skates.

His father died when he was 11 years old, so he quit selling fish. He then rode around with his uncles on the fishing boat and the fishery truck, when they were making deliveries. He worked for Trudell Fishery at age 16 and was paid $18 per week. With his first paycheck he bought his mother a coffee urn, with sugar bowl and the creamer to go with it, on a silver tray.

He went to school with Bernard Stephanski (later shortened to Stephan), at St. Joseph Catholic School in Tawas City. They were good friends, but he later went to school in Bay City for a while and graduated from Bay City Central in 1939.

Robert was in the auto body repair business until 1942 when he went into the service. After his discharge in 1946, he returned to the auto body repair business. The same year he met Marjorie Doak-Stephan, a widow with a daughter, Sharon Ann. Her husband, Bernard Stephan, was killed in World War II. Robert met Marjorie on a blind date. His brother Bud and wife Marge set it all up. They all went to the Old Buckhorn. It worked out well because after about a year of courting, they were married.

On October 18, 1947 they got their marriage license in Tawas. Then they went to Flint to get married. Marjorie's sister Lois and husband Mike Mikolasik were their witnesses for the wedding. After they were married, they came back to Tawas and spent some time with Bud, Marge, and a few friends at the Barnes Hotel. They had no real wedding reception and their honeymoon night was spent at the Barnes Hotel, in Tawas City, across from the Tawas City Park.

Robert Trudell and triplet daughters, l-r: Jean, June and Jane, age 52

On August 25, 1948 their triplet daughters (Jane, June, Jean) were born. The first in Iosco County. After the girls were a little older, Marjorie worked at the Tawas Flower Shop for Harold Pfeiffer. Robert worked at Ottawa Equipment, Featherlite, Leonard Gas (of which he owned), and some at Trudell Auto Body Shop for his brother Teed. On November 13, 1956, another daughter, Sheryl Lea, was born.

Robert worked a couple of years for Russ and Jane Nelkie (son-in-law and daughter), on a dairy farm. He went into the recreational field and built pickup toppers at home, in his garage. When he retired he got into doing crafts and furniture making.

After his wife's death, he helped run the store "Pockrandts," sold fabrics, collectibles, and costume rentals. Originally started by his sister Evelyn (Trudell) and now owned by Evelyn's daughter Karen.

Marjorie Trudell passed away on October 30, 1981.

THEODORE JOSEPH TRUDELL.

He was born November 23, 1911, the oldest son of Edward A. and Laura (Rodel) Trudell. Known to all as Teed, he grew up in the commercial fishing business, which like his father, he loved. He worked with his Uncle Joe (nicknamed Nibby) for a short while. Soon after his father's death the whitefish dwindled to almost nothing.

Teed had gone to the St. Joseph Catholic School, as well as Augusta C. "Gusty" Cadorette, who was one of his fellow classmates. Teed had taken a liking to her. Always giving her rides home from school every day.

Asking Gusty how she and Teed got together, she said "I da know - it seems like we were always together." "He probably just didn't want to get rid of me - I guess." They were married on April 16, 1931.

Theodore and Augusta (Cadorette) Trudell

Teed and Gusty moved to Bay City with family where Teed worked for the Mt. Morris Chevy garage and learned the auto body trade, opened his own shop for about a year or so. In 1947, the whitefish suddenly returned to Tawas Bay, and Teed followed, moving his family back to Tawas. He opened the Trudell and Sons Fish Company, purchasing "Katie Mae," which has been known in the Tawases. Almost, as soon as the fish returned, they disappeared. Teed returned to the auto body business, building his own shop, Trudell Auto Body Shop, and being one of the first settlers of the new prospering Baldwin Center.

He had his brother Robert "Bob" to help him out quite a bit when not working elsewhere. Until Robert branched off and worked for himself. Bob had Leonard Gas Station right next door to the auto body shop, still helping his brother Teed every chance he had on the side, for a number of years. On occasion his brother Danny was around to help in the janitorial side of

the work. Teed's own sons also frequented the body shop to work on their own cars. Teed's three nieces (Jane, Jean and June) were often around the shop also. They knew that their uncle had goodies around. Uncle Teed usually kept a supply of goodies stashed in the file cabinet, along with his chew. Nasty stuff!! (you'd think we tried it or something). Once in a while Teed would treat us to a cold bottle of R.C. cola or even a candy bar. We'd help pick up the shop by sweeping the floor or cleaning out the disgusting bathroom. The pop was good and cold, cause it came from his water-filled pop machine. Back then pop was $0.10, and a $0.02 deposit, glass bottle too! It was the good old times when everyone stopped to get fish from the many crates of whitefish-herring that were put on ice awaiting to be peddled to many friends or waiting for the smoke house. UUMGOOD!! Teed had the best around. Melted in your mouth. Teed has since sold his business and retired. The former body shop is now Timmy Tire Company.

The *"Katie Mae"* went on to lead a merry and glorious life hosting many new owners, until her last owner let her die on the banks of the Tawas River. But she died at home.

Teed and Gusty were married 70 years on April 16, 2001. They have four children: Theodore Jr., Patricia, Edward and Ronald; many grandchildren and a few great-grandchildren. Teed passed away April 27, 2002.

JOHN JETHROE "JACK" and MARGARET M. TYSON.

Jack was born May 2, 1893 in Memphis, Tennessee to Uriah Dawson Tyson (born Moore County, North Carolina) and Lucy Ellen Able (born Shelby County, Tennessee). He first visited the Curtisville/South Branch area in the early 1920s as a guest of the Detroit Hunting and Fishing Club, a group of Detroit businessmen who owned a lodge in South Branch.

Margaret "Peg" Sinclair was born February 22, 1907 in Curtisville to William and Christine (MacColeman) Sinclair, who were the caretakers of the HandR Ranch there. Peg's grandparents were all Scottish-born emigrants and early settlers in Curtisville. William was born in 1880 to Duncan and Jenny (Martin) Sinclair. Christine was born in 1886 to Peter and Christine (Shaw) MacColeman. Both families were involved in farming and logging.

Jack and Peg were married June 29, 1923 and embarked on what would be a long series of business ownership. Two

of those businesses were located in Iosco County: The Chain Lakes Hotel and the Oasis Tavern.

The Chain Lakes Hotel was acquired in the early 1930s. In addition to the hotel there was a tavern and a dance hall which could be converted into an open-air pavilion by lifting hinged wall panels. The dance hall was also used to host prize fights.

Jack Tyson's Oasis on M-65, Glennie, MI

The Oasis Tavern (located in northern Iosco County at M-65 and West Kings Corner Road) was built in 1937 by Ray Smith and his sons, Robert and Eugene. The entire structure was made from logs harvested on site. The rustic building boasted a dance hall that measured 64 feet by 40 feet and two fieldstone fireplaces.

Jack and Peg purchased the Oasis and the surrounding 80 acres in 1943. Two years earlier they had acquired a large farmhouse with an additional 80 acres on West Kings Corner Road. Initially, the Oasis was limited to an eight month resort license allowing only beer and wine sales. Alcohol was added to the license after World War II. In 1945 Jack and Peg added a stockroom and also created a new serving bar by sawing lengthwise one of the 40-foot logs that previously formed the north wall. The Oasis was host to many Saturday night dances with "live" music, Sunday afternoon square dances, wild game dinners, and wedding receptions. The Oasis burned to the ground under suspicious circumstances in June 1964 and Jack Tyson died two months later on August 17.

Peg Tyson died in 1955. She and Jack are buried in Curtisville cemetery. They leave behind three children: Betty Jean (Joseph) Smith and their son, Robin; John Jethroe (Evelyn Tait) Tyson Jr. and their children Valarie (Barton) Fredrickson, Dennis (Deborah), John J. (AKA Jet) III, and Albert; and Marie (Robert) Jardine and her children Christine (Albert) Shaffer, Bradley (Jan) Price, Neil Price, Earl Mason, and Margaret (Kurt) Pierce. A son, Richard Dawson, drowned while still a child.

All of Jack and Peg's children and grandchildren have at one time called Iosco County home. Three descendant families:

Tyson, Smith and Pricestill, live on West Kings Corner Road.

WILLIAM and SYLVIA UPTHE-GROVE.

William (born 1868, died 1957) was born in 1868 during the Harding Administration in the Thumb area and spent his youth there. Coming from a family of 13 children, he quit school at an early age to help support the family. He married Sylvia DeLong (born 1879, died 1959) at Mt. Pleasant in 1902 and during their first years of marriage he worked as a logger on the AuSable River while living in the town of AuSable. They purchased 160 acres of land in Reno Township and moved their home from AuSable in 1908.

Other farm buildings were built as they could be afforded and enough land was cleared to begin farming. Occasional trips to town, five miles away, were made for necessary supplies by horse and buggy or wagon. Not until the early twenties did a used auto arrive on the scene to make it easier. Due to bad road conditions, the car was usually parked on top of the hill about a half mile from the house except in very dry weather. Many times the faithful team was hitched up to pull the jalopy through the mud. Summer days were long from sun up till sun down with no vacations. Grains were harvested and ended with a threshing bee with help of all the good neighbors.

No children were born to this union, but a daughter, Laura, was adopted and two young boys, George and William McKenzie, spent several years on the farm after they lost their parents due to an accident. The boys were later taken in by relatives and moved to Flint, but were always frequent visitors.

Plans had been made for much needed repairs on the buildings when the depression came. William was on his way to Prescott to withdraw his savings from the bank when met by a neighbor telling him that the bank was closed. Many years passed before those repairs were finally made. Purchases were made only in the amount of the small weekly sales of eggs and cream. Every cent possible from the yearly sales of grain, wool, and livestock was saved to pay the taxes and other necessities.

William continued farming until about 1950 when due to ill health at the age of 80 he was unable to do so. They moved to Hale, but made frequent trips and short stays at the old home until the time of their deaths.

RUSSELL "MIKE" AND AVIS (KOEHN) VANCE.

Both Russell and Avis were born in Arenac County, Turner, Michigan. They were married May 31, 1941 in Maple Ridge and honeymooned one night at the Greenbush Inn. About a week after they were married, he was inducted into the Army and left to serve in World War II.

Russell and Avis Vance

In 1945 they returned to Turner, but for lack of employment in that area, they moved to East Tawas. They built their first home on Main Street in 1947. Russell and Avis have four children: Sona lives in Oscoda; Lyna lives in Wisconsin; Kharla lives in Tawas City; and Bill lives in Tawas City. Except for four years in the 1950s when they lived in Montrose, the Vances have been residents of Iosco County and currently live on Tawas Lake Road. They recently celebrated their 61st wedding anniversary.

Russell worked as a mechanic for Ottawa Equipment and Avis retired from the Iosco County Courthouse, Equalization Department They never got rich here, but the area riches have been a blessing to them. They value their many friends, their church family, beautiful Lake Huron, and the privilege of being able to call Iosco County their home.

VAUGHAN FAMILY.

The Vaughan family first appeared in Iosco County in 1853 when Sylvester Vaughan came north from Saginaw as a fisherman. He was the son of Roderick W. Vaughan and Clarissa Stebbins. Originally the family came from New York State. They are descendants of John Vaughan of Lebanon County.

Sylvester married Laura Hubbel

Warren Payne "Win" Vaughan

on July 5, 1862. Their children were Frank, Eva Maud, Charles L., Warren Payne, and Edward. All are buried in Oscoda.

Warren Payne was born November 9, 1872 in Oscoda. He married Mary Ann Cartwright January 12, 1897. They had four children: Winifred, Charles, Daisy and Mina. Warren was a lumberman and a deputy sheriff in Oscoda. He died July 23, 1957 and is buried in Pinecrest Cemetery in Oscoda. His grandchildren still have a cabin on the old Vaughan farm property.

ALEXANDER LARSSON WARG/WARGSTROM.

He was born in 1847 to Swedish-speaking parents, Lars Mattsson Warg and Brita Magdalena Eriksdotter Kallis in Karleby parish, part of the Swedish-speaking western coast of Finland called Swedish Osterbotten. Alexander probably was recruited in Finland in 1872 by an American lumber company from Michigan to work in a mill in Ausable. He married there October 20, 1879 to Maria Sofia Jonasdotter Eklund (born 1852, died 1917) from Pedersore, Finland, daughter of Jonas Johansson Rif and Brita Lena Larsdotter Tarvonen. Maria emigrated in 1879; her brother Frans emigrated in 1881 and was a carpenter in Oscoda. In 1882 he married Brita Johanna Mattsdotter Warg, niece of Alexander Wargstrom. Frans and Brita had four children born in Oscoda; in 1894 they moved to Minnesota to homestead in Palisade.

Alexander Wargstrom Family ca. 1904. Standing in rear l-r: Carl Victor, Alexander Emil, Anders William; seated: Edith Cecelia, Maria Sofia, Selma Victoria, Alexander, Estella Alexandra; seated in front is Alice Maria

Alexander and Maria had eight children born in AuSable in a house rented from the lumber company. One child died in infancy; the other children were as follows:

1) Selma Victoria (born 1881, died 1956) married 1901 in AuSable to Arthur Spring (Adolf Carlsson Kallstrom) (born 1878, died 1969) from Karleby, Finland. Arthur, his brother Edward (born 1875, died 1959) and their mother Maria (born 1833, died 1919) emigrated in 1886 from Finland and lived in East Tawas. The family took the surname Spring during emigration. Arthur and Selma lived on Lake Street, Oscoda until their house was burned in the 1911 fire. They moved to a farm in Alabaster but moved to East Tawas when the Gypsum company claimed their land. Their children were Arthur, Lillian (Bowles), Lorena (Volz) and Carl.

2) Alexander Emil (born 1883, died 1930) never married. It is understood that he posed for the figure on the left side of the Lumberman's Monument. Emil was a

daring riverman on the AuSable during the logging period until his death of pneumonia at age 47.

3) Anders William (born 1885, died 1966) moved to Eveleth, Minnesota and operated one of the first dry cleaning plants on the Mesabi Range. He was involved with a jitney service that eventually become the Greyhound Bus Company. William married Inez Nyberg-Newberg (born 1886 in Oscoda) and they moved to Virginia, Minnesota. They had one child, Inez (Schmidt).

4) Carl Victor (born 1887, died 1977), known as Charles, moved to Eveleth, Minnesota and worked in one of the ore mines, later becoming superintendent of a mine. He married Laura Levine from Sweden; had one child, Harriette (Tabelle).

5) Edith Cecelia (born 1890, died 1938) married Anders Pelo and moved to Flint, Michigan where they had four children: June, Robert, Ruth and Lorraine (Freas). They probably never knew they were related to each other many, many ways through one of their great-grandmothers, Anna Enksdotter Warg.

6) Alice Maria (born 1892, died 1952) married Otto Alexander Ottosson Haglund (born 1878, died 1955) from Finland. They lived in Oscoda and had six children: Edwin, Joyce (Stewart), Marion (Hopcroft), Natalie (lives in Oscoda), and Ann (Gembarski). Alex's brothers (Immanuel) John and (Anders) William also lived in Oscoda for a while.

7) Estella Alexandra (born 1895, died 1977) married Elmer Holder (born 1891, died 1971) and they lived in Oscoda with one child, Janice (Miller). *Submitted by June Pelo.*

WELCH. Harley Samual (born 1907, died 1985) and Bernice Anna Rasmussen Welch (born 1913) moved to East Tawas in 1940 from Bamboo, Wisconsin with their two children, Lorraine Caroline (born 1937) and Spencer Allen (born 1938, died 1996). Harley's uncle, with whom he was employed, got the plumbing and heating contract for the new Federal Building on Newman Street. He liked the town so much that when he was offered the job of custodian he quickly accepted.

During World War II the family moved back to Wisconsin while Harley was in the Navy, and Bernice worked in a munitions plant near Madison. At war's end they returned to East Tawas where Harley's postal job was waiting for him and from where he retired in 1969. Their third child, Darrell Peter, was born in 1946.

Bernice worked at Gifford's Restaurant (which is now Geniis) and in early 1950 purchased the Harbor Lights Restaurant which they owned until the mid-60s. Bernice then worked in the school cafeteria for several years and also managed the Tawas Beach Club for several years. They moved back to Wisconsin until Harley died in 1985, at which time Bernice moved back to Michigan where she is presently residing at Maple Tree Apts. She is now 98 years old.

Lorraine married William Ferguson in 1960, and they have three daughters and seven grandchildren.

Spencer passed away from bone cancer in 1996, leaving six children and nine grandchildren.

Darrell is unmarried and living in Denver, Colorado. *Submitted by Lorraine Ferguson.*

GEORGE AMBROSE WHITNEY FAMILY. George was born January 25, 1866, in the town of Percy, Ontario, Canada, to Joseph Whitney of Antwerp, New York and Mary Mac Evilly of County Mayo, Ireland.

At the age of 14, and after the death of his mother, he emigrated to Rosebush, Isabella Township, Michigan. It was there that he met and married the lovely, gracious, and young (indeed, she was 18 years younger than George). Lily Ellen Conway, daughter of James Conway and Catherine Trainor Conway,

In 1913, George and Lily Ellen "Nellie," along with their three oldest children: John Ambrose, Mary Catherine and Francis Edwin, settled in Tawas City, Iosco County, on a farm they purchased on what is now called Miller Road. George and Lily Ellen, members of St. Joseph Church, were proud of their Irish and Catholic heritage. They farmed to support their growing family and Nellie also worked as a mid-wife and helped to bring many babies of this area into the world.

Because George knew so many of his neighbors (neighborliness has always been a family trait) and also knew all the roads in the area, he worked for one day on a long ago census for which he was paid $1.00, a healthy sum of money in those long ago days.

Their next three children: Leonard James, Lily Ellen and Earl Nathaniel, were born in Tawas City and died during the flu epidemic of 1918 within four days of each other at the ages of 3, 2 and 8 months respectfully.

Their family grew with the births of Joseph Howard, Raymond Charles, George Edmund and Clara Agnes.

The two oldest sons, John and Francis, moved to Green Bay, Wisconsin, where they married and raised their families. John married Alice Heim and raised five sons; Francis married Ophelia Platkowski and raised two daughters.

Mary Catherine married Leo Wellna from a neighboring farm. They farmed the Wellna family farm until their deaths raising their five children, two of whom still reside in Tawas City.

Joseph Howard married Rosemary Klenow of a neighboring farm and moved to Saginaw, where he raised his five daughters and one son.

Raymond Charles married Barbara Heckman and raised five sons and three daughters in Saginaw, returning to East Tawas upon his retirement. The Whitney name is still present here as his wife Barbara still lives here. His sons Edward and Dale also returned to raise their families in East Tawas.

George Edmund married Virginia Panico in Saginaw where they raised two daughters and two sons.

Clara Agnes married Bernard Kapala and also moved to Saginaw where she raised one daughter and three sons.

THOMAS WHITFORD. Thomas (born 1844, died 1919) immigrated to the United States from Canada (Lambton County) in 1878 with his wife, Elizabeth Sykes, three of his children and brother Hugh, leaving behind his parents and siblings. Coming across the St. Clair River from Sarnia, they settled in White Rock (Huron County) Michigan until 1893 when they migrated to Whittemore, Michigan (Burleigh Township). Thomas, son of George and Nancy (McIntyre) Whitford, had eight siblings Jane (Little), George, John, William, Robert, James, Susan and Hugh.

Thomas was a farmer most of his life and a member of the Reorganized Church of Jesus Christ of Latter Day Saints Church of Whittemore when he was said to have been a preacher. Tom and Elizabeth had eight children: George (born 1873, died 1942); Ruth (Wm. Vaughan) (born 1975, died 1917); Walker (Viola Earhardt) (born 1877, died 1969); Bessie (Jack Paradise) (born 1879, died 1956); Sadie (Martin Cataline) (born 1881, died 1968); Phebe (Bill Scott) (born 1883, died 1970); Robert (Rhoda Anderson) (born 1886, died 1971); Jason (born 1887, died 1918).

WALKER AND VIOLA WHITFORD. Walker and Viola were married in Cheboygan, Michigan in 1905. From this union was seven children: Velma (born 1906, died 1906); Wilford (Helen Stoddard) (born 1908, died 1993), Leome (Hazen Lawrence) (born 1911, died 1992); Elva (Orville Youngs); Robert (Marion Beckley) (born 1914, died 1973); Lloyd (Marion Beckley) (born 1916, died 1994); Shirley (Lucille Lawhorn) (born 1919, died 1994). Living in Cheboygan, Fibre, Onaway and Flint in the early years of marriage and by 1930s they had settled back in Whittemore Reno Township. Walker had bright red hair and was a logger most of his life.

WILFORD WELLINGTON WHITFORD.

Wilford married Helen Stoddard on January 10, 1931 in Hale, Michigan (Iosco County). From this union was 10 children: Gary, Sherry, Roger, Patricia, Ronald, Laurel, Katie, William, Dennis and Terrence. Wilford following in his father's footsteps was a logger most of his life also. He and Helen were married for 62 years and resided in Iosco County for all of those years.

DURIN H.T. WILLIAMS.

Durin, a Civil War veteran (born in 1831, died 1896), and Rachel Wolfen (born 1831, died 1899) never lived in Iosco County, but they did have three children that settled near Whittemore. They were parents of seven children: Emily (born 1852, died 1921); Eva (born 1857, died 1858); Martin (born 1859, died ___); Durin Judd (born 1861, died 1910); Sarah; Daniel Sanborn; and Dorman Ross (born 1868, died 1927).

Emily moved to the area in November 1893 with her husband James L. Cataline (born 1849, died 1929) and children: Durin (born 1872, died 1957); Sarah (born 1873, died 1956); Martin (born 1886, died 1954); Herbie (born 1879, died 1883); and Frances "Frankie" (born 1890, died 1971). Judd was married to Jessie and had a son, Stanley. Sarah

Rachel (Wolfen) and Durin H.T. Williams

was married and had two children: Rachel and Ross Griswold. For a few years, these children lived with Emily and James Cataline. Ross was married to Clara and had Vesta, Willard, Vera, Mary and Eva. Descendants, of these children remain in the Iosco County area today.

TAWAS ST. JOSEPH HOSPITAL
1953-2003

It all started with a tornado...

It was June 1953, when a tornado ripped through Iosco County, killing four area residents and injuring nine others - and forcing the just-built Tawas Hospital into service a couple weeks ahead of schedule. The health-care facility first envisioned by the Tawas Hospital Association and its founder, Dr. John LeClair, was now a reality. And in essence, on that night of June 8, 1953, St. Joseph Health System was born.

St. Joseph Health System is now comprised of Tawas St. Joseph Hospital and various outlying clinics and services. Our main campus, which includes the hospital, is at the corner of U.S. 23 and the M-55 highway in Tawas City, on Michigan's beautiful "Sunrise Side."

Within view of the lovely Lake Huron, you'll find a full array of specialties and services at Tawas St. Joseph Hospital, including anesthesiology, emergency medicine at our 24-hour emergency room, pathology and radiology. Our telemedicine component links our emergency room with the ERs at Standish Community Hospital and Saint Mary's in Saginaw. Our rehabilitative services include physical therapy, occupational therapy and speech language pathology.

Inside the Medical Arts Building at the back of the hospital, our Internal Medicine Clinic has a staff of board-certified physicians who can diagnose and treat a wide variety of illnesses. The orthopedics department features board-certified surgeons who do knee and hip replacements weekly. We also offer knee and hip replacement patients the St. Joseph Joint Replacement Center, opened in September 2002, a redesigned, dedicated area of the hospital that is unique in northeast Michigan.

In spring 2002, St. Joseph Health System was proud to open the Seton Cancer Institute of Tawas, our local branch of a larger network devoted to oncology treatment.

Our health system also offers a sleep lab, sleep clinic and CPAP clinic to diagnose and treat sleep disorders.

On the same campus as

Seton Cancer Institute is affiliated with Saint Mary's of Saginaw and the U. of M.

Tawas St. Joseph Hospital, you'll find the St. Joseph Home Health and Hospice and Home Medical Equipment headquarters. This branch of our health system offers registered nurses, home health aides and staff specialized in speech, occupational and physical therapy. Our Home Health and Hospice program serves Iosco, Alcona, Arenac, Ogemaw and Oscoda counties.

Also on the main campus in Tawas City is the Huron Family Medicine Clinic, where board-certified physicians offer care to patients of all ages. Down the road, on M-55, the Tawas St. Joseph Women's Clinic features board-certified physicians who specialize in all aspects of obstetrical and gynecological care.

St. Joseph Health System serves the larger communities of Oscoda, Fairview, Hale and AuGres with its outlying clinics: Oscoda Health Park (featuring lab work, radiology, orthopedics, mammography, bone density, physical therapy and after-hours care), Great Lakes Family Medicine Clinic in Oscoda, AuSable Valley Health Center in Fairview, Hale St. Joseph Medical Clinic and AuGres St. Joseph Family Clinic (with the added specialty of sports-injury management). All of St. Joseph Health System's outlying clinics offer local residents the same quality health care as our main campus - close to home.

Another service of our health system in all of these communities is the Courtesy Coach. Started in 1997, the Coach provides transportation to and from health-system appointments to those individuals unable to drive.

St. Joseph Health System is part of Ascension Health, a national, Catholic-based health-care organization. Rooted in the ministry of Jesus as healer, we are committed to the values of service of the poor, reverence, integrity, wisdom, creativity and dedication. We're very proud to be serving our communities in northeast Michigan since 1953!

The Joint Replacement Center takes a "team" approach to healing, with family members serving as coaches.

THE IOSCO COUNTY ABSTRACT OFFICE
Still going strong after 135 years!

The Iosco County Abstract Office has been serving the property title needs of Iosco County since 1869 when established by Silby G. Taylor. Nicholas C. Hartingh purchased the business in 1887. Hartingh, an attorney who moved to the area from Bay City, continued in the abstract office until his death in 1950 when the business was passed on to his grandson, Carl B. Babcock. Carl had been associated with the abstract office since 1927. Carl (Sr.) was joined by his son, Carl B. Babcock, Jr. in 1960 who succeeded to the family business following his father's demise in 1971. The office continues to serve the title needs of the county under the management of Carl. Jr.

To celebrate its 100 years as a family operation, Carl B. Babcock

Nicholas C. Hartingh and Carl B. Babcock, 1938.

Jr., moved his office directly across the street from its initial location to facilitate the expansion of the Tawas City Park and to provide larger more modern facilities for the growing title needs of the community. The business has come a long way since the days when his great-grandfather, "Nick" Hartingh, operated a one-man office producing abstracts written in longhand. Today, the Iosco County Abstract Office employs eight persons. It is equipped with sophisticated computer and word processing systems, fax and copy machines which aid in the efficient production, duplication and transmission of title searches and title insurance policies, which, for the most part, have replaced the old abstracts of title. The Abstract Office also offers escrow and closing services.

Carl B. Babcock Jr. believes that the community pride shared by the residents and the spirit of cooperation which exists between Tawas City and East Tawas will continue to help facilitate the coordinated and considered growth of this beautiful water-winter wonderland. *"I would like to see the area continue to grow"* Babcock says. The conscientious acquisition of beachfront property and adjacent areas by the cities and the state for the use and enjoyment of our residents visitors will ensure the future of the area as a great place to live and work.

Robbins E. Babcock was born in Sanilac County, Michigan, served in the Civil War near St. Petersburg, Virginia and also saw action in the Battle of Gettysburg before settling in East Tawas. He settled in East Tawas with his wife, Margaret (Hamilton) Babcock and their young son, Erastus Robbins Babcock, who had been born in Port Huron in 1880.

Erastus Robbins Babcock married Winnifred Hartingh in 1907. Winnifred was the daughter of Nicholas C. Hartingh, then attorney and owner/operator of the Iosco County Abstract Office. By his marriage with his beloved wife, Winnifred, they had three

(3) children, Carl B. Babcock, Winnifred (Babcock) Hatton, and Hartingh Babcock.

His love of the water took Erastus (Rasty) on the freight boats of the Great Lakes as a young man. This led to his remarkable rescue from the whaleback barge #115 which went on the rocks during the terrific Lake Superior storm of December 12 and December 13, 1899.

Following this episode, he entered the employ of the D&M Railroad.

Erastus' wife, Winnifred, met her early demise in 1912 while the children were still young. Following the loss of his wife, Erastus moved to Detroit in 1915 to work with the Ford Motor Company taking his oldest two children, Winnifred and Hartingh, leaving his very young son, Carl B. Babcock, with his maternal grandfather, "Nick" Hartingh.

Carl Babcock was raised by his grandfather, and graduated from the Tawas City High School with his senior class of seven members in 1929. Carl went to work. in the Iosco County Abstract Office with his grandfather, N.C. Hartingh, and married Oka Millard of West Branch in 1935. Carl and Oka (Millard) Babcock had four (4) children, Carl B. Babcock Jr., Nicole, Cheryl and Brent.

Carl Babcock Jr. joined his father in the Iosco County Abstract Office in 1960 and still operates the family business. Nicole joined the Civil Service with the Wurthsmith Air Force Base working in procurement and contracting, ultimately retiring from the Williams Air Force Base in Chandler, Arizona upon its closure in 1995. Cheryl retired from her position as an executive secretary with Dow Chemical. Brent Babcock followed in the footsteps of his great-grandfather becoming an attorney and continues to maintain a general practice of law in the Tawas area specializing in property law in conjunction with his family's title company.

IOSCO COMMUNITY CREDIT UNION

"Providing financial services to members and their families since 1958."

Above: The Iosco Community Credit Union in Oscoda.
At right: The Iosco Community Credit Union in Tawas.

The Iosco Community Credit Union was organized early in 1958 through the efforts of Paul Renner, a teacher at the Oscoda Area Junior High School. Along with Tom Stalker, the late Duane London, and the late Bob Ensgtrom, Mr. Renner's early organizational work resulted in a charter issued by the State of Michigan on March 10, 1958. The Credit Union was originally named Oscoda Area School Employees Credit Union and the field of membership included the employees of the Oscoda Area Schools. Mr. Engstrom served as the first manager from March 1958 to January 1960. The office was maintained at the Oscoda High School from 1958 until 1965.

The Credit Union has had five managers in its 45 years of existence. James Howse served from January 1960 to January 1962. William Martin served from January 1962 to March 1966. John Kuenzlie served from March 1966 until August 1970. Paul Fredenburg has served as General Manager/CEO from August 1970 to the present (2003).

The Credit Union was moved from the Oscoda High School to 5226 N. US 23 (the former Wharf Building) in 1968. The office was moved again in 1970 to the Bank Avenue Apartments Building and remained there until March 1980. In 1980 it was moved to the Dexel Building at 103 S. State Street (corner of River Road and U.S. 23) which is still the sight of today's main office in Oscoda. The Credit Union purchased the building from Dexel Realty in 1986 and purchased the adjoining parking lot in the rear from Dexel Realty in 1995.

The Credit Union has amended its field of membership several times. The first was in 1976 when the charter was expanded to include all educational institutions operating in Iosco County. That also brought about a name change. The new name was Iosco School Employees Credit Union. In 1994 the National Gypsum Employees Credit Union from Tawas City, which served the employees of National Gypsum and Jefferson Trucking, was merged into the Iosco School Employees Credit Union. One result of the merger was the establishment of a branch office in Tawas City. The next charter expansion came in 1996 when the credit union became eligible to serve non-school employee and association groups located within a 25-mile radius of either office. The most recent charter change came in 2001 when the State of Michigan granted the credit union a field of membership that includes anyone who lives or works in Iosco County. That also brought about another name change. The Credit Union became the Iosco Community Credit Union.

The Credit Union added a two-lane drive-thru to its Oscoda facility in 2001. The new drive-thru is open Monday through Saturday. An ATM was installed in the main entrance of the Oscoda office and is available to the general public 24 hours a day, 7 days a week. The Tawas Branch is presently located in Brugger's Plaza, which is, conveniently located at 324 W. Lake Street (U.S. 23) in Tawas City.

The Credit Union currently serves 4,732 members and has assets totaling over $26,400,000. The organization was established by volunteers, and 45 years later, it is still governed by volunteer officials. It is still locally owned and controlled right here in Iosco County. Thanks to Paul Renner and all the volunteer leaders who have served the credit union since 1958.

Paul R. Fredenburg
General Manager/CEO

Iosco County Medical Care Facility

Iosco County Medical Care Facility

In November 1959 the County Board of Supervisors of Iosco County appointed a special committee to investigate how the county could care for its sick elderly population. During 1960 the committee's efforts were directed toward finding private investors with an interest in building a suitable nursing home in Iosco County. Despite extensive efforts to entice private investors none could be found and the committee decided to study the feasibility of a county owned and operated medical care facility. On December 11, 1961 the proposed $550,000 medical care facility was placed on the ballot and defeated by voters

Clarence Everett, often referred to as the "father of medical care in Iosco County," was instrumental in the realization of Iosco County having its own medical care facility. Mr. Everett was chairman of the County Welfare Committee. After the initial defeat of the medical care facility Mr. Everett made it his mission to speak to any group he could to promote the need of Iosco counties own medical care facility.

Most medical care for the elderly was provided at home. Iosco County had established a "Poor Farm" to take care of the indigent and infirmed. Voters approved the initiative on the second try by a 2 to 1 margin and a federal loan was obtained to build the Medical Care Facility.

On July 31, 1966 the Iosco County Medical Care Facility opened as a state of the art 50 bed skilled nursing facility which featured an in-house pharmacy along with a well equipped physical therapy department and diversional therapy department which made available an efficient rehabilitation program. The facility also had its own beauty and barbershop along with its own large modern laundry and kitchen, the facility also provided outpatient physical therapy available to residents of the county. In 1968 a 14-bed addition was added due to increasing needs for services making it a 64-bed facility. The private pay room rate was set at $13.00 a day. On May 21, 2001 the Medical Care Facility began the construction of the only architecturally designed 28 bed Alzheimer's Unit in northern Michigan. Called the "Woodlands" to continue to meet the health needs of the residents of Iosco County.

The Iosco County Medical Care Facility is the only area facility that has 100% of its beds certified Medicare and Medicaid. The Iosco Medical Care facility is a non-profit agency and its mission is to serve all those needing medical care regardless of payment source. Over 3,249 residents have been admitted to the facility since it opened in 1966.

The facility has over 100 employees. Licensed nurses on duty 24 hours a day. In house physical, occupational and speech therapy is offered. The facility currently has five dining rooms for intimate dining, a large airy lobby for visiting along with a beautiful atrium with aquariums, bird aviary and fountain for our residents enjoyment. The Iosco County Medical Care facility has been caring for the residents of Iosco County for over 36 years and will be here for many more to provide the care the residents of Iosco deserve.

GFWC Ladies' Literary Club-East Tawas, Inc.
Organized 1885 – Federated 1896

The GFWC Ladies Literary Club of East Tawas, pictured here in 1901, is one of many clubs with one hundred years or more of history.

Carved out of the Michigan forest by the booming lumber industry, the harbor town of East Tawas nestled between thick forests of towering white pines and the Sweetwater Sea, as the Indians named Lake Huron, was undergoing a series of rapid changes. By 1885, the success of timber-related industries and the resulting influx of population ushered in an era of prosperity and enlightenment.

In this fertile climate of adventure and opportunity, five women gathered together on October 29, 1884 at the home of Mrs. Mary White, the wife of a lawyer, to explore the possibility of meeting to study and exchange ideas. The group also included a banker's wife, two schoolteachers and a 19- year-old high school graduate. Three months later, on January 2, 1885, 14 ladies met to effect a permanent organization with Mary White (Mrs. Robert) as president. Mary White died in 1910 after years of devoted service. And the youngest of this little group, Alice Dimmick King, died in 1947.

When the club became a member of the General Federated Women's Clubs of Michigan, now know as GFWCMI, it began an affiliation with other federated clubs that continues to this day. A federated county organization, the Women's Federated Clubs of Iosco County, also brought opportunities for widened horizons. Over the years these clubs worked hand in hand to accomplish larger goals. It is no longer in existence, and of the six clubs in the county federation, only the GFWC Ladies' Literary Club-East Tawas remains.

Affiliation with clubs outside their own coupled with their own growing confidence generated an interest in civic welfare. Around the turn of the century and into the next there was increased involvement is such affairs. In 1897 they went on record as being in favor of allowing female physicians and nurses in the insane asylums. They consulted the Health Officer and Board of Education, published articles in the city newspapers, sponsored community welfare days, and attended city council meetings. And there was Ezoa (Mrs. H.G.) Thomas, who, through here zeal and enthusiasm, was credited for bringing about a public library in 1901. Several members served as the first librarians. Mrs. Thomas died in 1943, having been a member since 1889 and serving as president for nine years.

In 1910, the club incorporated in order to purchase a building formerly used by the public school. This humble abode, dearly loved, was to be home for the Literary Club for almost 70 years until the burden of its upkeep became to much to bear

Now well over 100 years old, the GFWC Ladies' Literary Club-East Tawas, Inc. continues to support local organizations and agencies that are focused on improving community resources, health, child and family welfare, education, conservation, art, and history. It continues to provide annual scholarships, and encourages volunteerism in the local, state, and world community.

EAST TAWAS MARKET

East Tawas—Step inside Klenow's Market and step back to the days of the corner grocer. Pass through the narrow food aisles to a glass meat counter filled with fresh steaks, home-made sausages and bins of seasoned, smoked meats.

Behind the tempting display, store owner Steve Klenow and his butchers greet the parade of customers with a friendly "Hello" or the simple question, "What's for dinner tonight?

Gourmets and meat lovers find the old-fashioned atmosphere irresistible. So it's no wonder the family-owned market is thriving as it gets ready to celebrate its 100th anniversary.

"Anytime you see a business around for 100 years, you know they must be doing something right. I have a lot of people tell me that," Klenow said.

The 49-year-old Klenow is the fourth generation of his family to own and operate Klenow's Market at 201 Newman St., in the heart of the East Tawas business district.

Loren H. Klenow, the son of Polish immigrants who farmed in Iosco County, opened the original store at that location in April 1900. The business passed to his son, Henry, then to grandson J. Henry, and now to great-grandson Steve.

The market has changed over the years - doubling in size to take up building space it once shared with the post office and a pizza parlor. But the same tin ceiling is still there, and so is the same cozy feeling inside.

J. Henry Klenow's sister, Mary Jeanne, recalls how the store was in the old days.

"When I worked in the store, we sold vinegar out of a barrel and the sugar was in a big bin. We had twine strung overhead to the cash register and you would pull some down to wrap things," she said.

The butchering area didn't have a lot of fancy equipment back then, either, recalls J. Henry "Hank" Klenow, 74, who ran the store from 1953 to 1975 and worked there as a child.

"All we had were knives and hand saws. We didn't get our first band saw until after World War II and even then one, of our butchers wouldn't use it," he said.

Air conditioning came in 1965, which was a blessing to the store employee and kept the wheels of cheese from melting in the summer heat

Hank Klenow said the store's customer base has changed over time and so have its products. Klenow's once stocked items like chicken feed and kerosene to sell to the area's many farmers, who would often trade fresh eggs and milk for merchandise at the store, he said.

Customers today are largely a mix of tourists and non-farming area residents. Steve Klenow said satisfying year-round residents is his top priority.

"The tourists are important, but we don't depend on them. We learned a long time ago that you can't rely only on tourists. You have to cater to the local people," he said.

Since Steve Klenow took ownership in 1975, he has expanded the meat counter's offerings to include things like three types of marinated chicken breasts and many types of smoked meats. He also purchased a vacuum-packing machine that seals meat in plastic, which is very popular with customers.

But some traditions continue at Klenow's, such as buying hanging beef and pork and processing it at the store. Some butcher shops purchase their meat already cut in smaller sections, Steve Klenow said.

"Nobody's got short ribs and soup bones, but we do because of that reason. I guess we're kind of old-fashioned that way," he said.

The meat counter has pet treats such as dog bones and pig ears on one end and hunks of cheese on the other. In between are all sorts Of steaks and roasts, homemade salami sticks, pork cutlets and cut-up chickens.

The store still delivers groceries to elderly people in the area who have difficulty leaving their homes, and a few regulars keep running accounts at the market.

While times have changed, the basics that keep Klenow's in business are the same: good service, quality products and owner dedication to providing both.

It's a recipe for success that has allowed Klenow's Market to weather competition from a half dozen other local grocery stores and two national grocery chains that once operated on Newman Street. Only Klenow's remains. *by Eric English, Times writer*

LAKE STATE RAILWAY COMPANY

management. In May 2002 Mr. VanBuskirk sold out his interest in the railroad to Mr. George.

At inception LSRC operated approximately 275 miles of track. In May 2000 the line from Alpena to Hawks and branch to Calcite was abandoned and subsequently removed. Currently the railway operates approximately 224 miles of trackage, consisting of two lines. Bay City to Alpena along the Lake Huron shoreline and from Bay City to Gaylord along the I-75 corridor.

Major commodities hauled by the railroad are aggregate, chemicals, cement and forest products.

The Lake State Railway (LSRC) is the successor of the Detroit and Mackinac (D&M) which originally started out as a logging railroad. In 1878, the railroad started at a point south of Tawas, Michigan, and ran through the forest as needed. The line was later reorganized as the Detroit, Bay City & Alpena logging road. In 1894 a group of businessmen purchased the assets of the Detroit, Bay City & Alpena Railway and reorganized it as the Detroit and Mackinac Railway Company. They operated through trains from Bay City north to Cheboygan, to connect with boats carrying passengers for Mackinac Island. Passenger business declined over the years and was discontinued in 1951.

From the 1920s through 1992 the railroad was family owned and operated by the Pinkerton's for three generations. In 1992 the operating properties were leased by and subsequently sold to Mr. George and Mr. VanBuskirk, two vice presidents of D&M's

The Lake State Railways General office is located at 323 Newman Street, East Tawas, Michigan.

MOONEY'S BEN FRANKLIN
East Tawas

Mooney's Ben Franklin, East Tawas.

In 1944, Lyle D. Mooney and his wife Margaret "Peg" borrowed $16,000 and purchased the Ben Franklin store from Earnest Leaf. Tired of the rigors of running a coffee shop, Lyle and Peg ventured into the world of the "five and dime" variety store. The adventure continues today as Lyle's grandson Mike owns and operates Mooney's Store Inc. with his wife Laura.

In the mid-1940's, variety stores were popping up all over the Midwest and Lyle and Peg were in the right place at the right time. With the help of their sons, Bill and Don, Mooney's Ben Franklin built a reputation based upon impeccable cleanliness and outstanding variety at value prices. In the rare instance Lyle didn't have what the customer wanted, he would special order it. Lyle, an avid coin collector, was a well-respected businessman who was most comfortable out on the floor where he could greet his customers.

By 1957, Lyle and Peg were joined in the business by their son Don. After graduating from Notre Dame in 1952, Don joined the Air Force and was stationed in Topeka, Kansas. While in Kansas, Don met his wife Jan who was nearly finished with a nursing degree. After Jan's graduation, they were married, had a daughter and relocated to East Tawas. In 1959, Mooney's Ben Franklin was bursting at the seams and they purchased the old Carlson Grocery at the northeast corner of Newman St. and Westover. There they built a modern facility that is still the home of Mooney's Ben Franklin.

In 1967, Don purchased the store from his parents. Peg retired shortly thereafter. She and Lyle enjoyed spending their winters in Florida as Don assumed the reigns of the family business. Don and Lyle worked side-by-side until his retirement in the late 70s. By this time, Don and Jan had seven children of various ages that grew up working at the store. All the grandchildren share fond memories of pricing glassware with old ink stampers, while Grandpa Mooney taught lessons about saving money.

In 1973, Don purchased the adjacent Tawas Time Shop and added on to the store. Over the years there were many "re-lays" of the store as its' image and offerings changed to meet the needs of the townspeople and the ever growing tourist population. Nationally, Ben Franklin was a burgeoning franchise that was very successful. Don guided the Ben Franklin through its' hey day of the 70s enjoying being closed on Sunday's and having every Thursday afternoon off. He followed in Lyle's footsteps, keeping a well-stocked, clean store that specialized in customer satisfaction. As times changed, the call to be open seven days a week was met by an experiment. Don decided to open the store on the Sunday of Labor Day Weekend. The workers that day would consist of Don, Jan and the kids. The reward for this hard day's work was to be a new color television. Business that Sunday was so good, the store was permanently open for business on Sundays the following summer.

After graduating from Lake Superior State College, Don's oldest son Mike went to work within the Ben Franklin franchise. In 1992, Mike joined his dad and immediately took over the day-to-day operation of the store. Nationally, the Ben Franklin franchise was experiencing growing pains from over-expansion and a declining economy. Locally, Mike and Don reinvented Mooney's Ben Franklin; the new look focused on fabrics, crafts and gifts, as well as the variety that made the store famous. As tourism drove the statewide economy, inventory changed often, serving the needs of these valued customers.

Mike and his wife Laura purchased the store from Don in 1996, assuring that the family business will survive well into the 21st century. While the Ben Franklin franchise ceased to exist after 1998, Mike has found a niche that makes Mooney's Ben Franklin one of the most successful independent family businesses in northeast Michigan. Mike and Laura work side-by-side just as Lyle and Peg had done almost 50 years earlier. Their two grown daughters, and many nieces and nephews, Lyle's great-grandchildren have spent their summers working the cash registers and stocking the shelves like so many of their aunts and uncles before them. Mooney's Ben Franklin still operates with the same philosophy, and offers a hometown feel that is reminiscent of the days of the "old five and dime" that started it all in 1944.

Huron Shores Genealogical Society

Alonzo Sherman, Compiler, Researcher, Editor

Huron Shores Genealogical Society was established in 1982 to serve those in Iosco and Alcona County interested in tracing their family history. Initially it was a learning experience for many and the organization served as a mutual aid for members. As time progressed the society began indexing available records and later published these documents and made them available for other s outside the area to use. Brochures were made and sent to other societies and libraries advertising what was available. Some members also attended the annual Genealogical Book Fair in Lansing, which enabled further advertising sales.

As the group grew and expanded our materials, books, etc. were housed at the Robert Parks Library in Oscoda. There the society owns a computer, which may be used for research purposes. We try to have someone available on Saturdays or by appointment to offer assistance.

Our main focus is on Iosco County with many of our indexes posted on the Internet through genealogical links. Our membership is spread across the United States and we have members keypunching records of Iosco County from remote locations. Church records, obituaries, newspaper articles and books and material about Iosco County are listed and sold thereby creating a source of revenue for the society. We have received request from as far away as Australia.

A monthly newsletter is sent to members and to other genealogical societies and libraries including the famous Ft. Wayne Library. Thanks to the dedicated volunteer work of our members we have been able to help many people follow the trail in search for their ancestors.

O'Connor's In Downtown East Tawas

The Pendleton Frontier Shop opened its doors the week of July 4, 1948. The building was previously home to a Hudson and Studebaker dealership, and before that, a horse livery. Its owners, Mr. and Mrs. Rosco Legg had divided building into three separate spaces, totaling 588 square feet each. In one of these compartments, the Pendleton Shop was born.

The business was a traditional men's store, opened by brothers, Joe and Bill McNally. Natives of Pontiac, they hired their longtime friend and associate T. Joseph O'Connor to manage the business.

From its grand opening on that July day, the business steadily expanded. The first addition came in 1952, adding 600 square feet to the structure. With the extra space came increased selection, including women's apparel. Three years later, a second addition allowed the entrepreneurs to add gifts and furniture to their merchandising mix.

By 1959, the McNallys had become interested in selling their business, and partners, Joe O'Connor and John O'Brien, assumed ownership. Upon purchase, the new owners undertook an addition that extended the building to the lot's rear edge. The new space allowed the store to expand its lines once again to offer greater selection to its growing clientele.

To that same end, the partners purchased Oscoda's Stag & Doe Shop in 1961. The expansion continued in 1964, with the opening of a new storefront in Gaylord, and in Traverse City six years later.

The original Pendleton Shop underwent its latest and most extensive expansion in 1974, when it absorbed the remainder of the building's three initial storefronts. The renovation restored the structure to its original breadth, and transformed the store into the open, rectangular space it is today.

In 1977, Joe and Isabel O'Connor purchased O'Brien's interest in the company, and the name was changed to O'Connor's Pendleton Shop. By 1980, the senior O'Connors had retired to their Florida home, and the day-to-day operations were turned over to their two sons, Tim and John.

Over the years, the business has sold its interests in other cities and returned to its East Tawas roots.

O'Connor's celebrated its 50th Anniversary in July 1998, as the store proudly welcomed back its original owners to share in the festivities.

In subsequent years, the business has continued to uphold its tradition of customer service and its commitment to the Tawas area. While proud of its past, O'Connor's looks ever to the future, and to the promise and potential of its community.

SCHAAF LUMBER COMPANY

In 1926, Floyd E. Schaaf Sr. graduated from the Chicago Engineering Works, with a degree in electrical engineering.

He married the former Charlotte McMullen of East Tawas and resided in Flint for awhile before returning to the Tawases. The Schaaf family settled in Wilber Township, where they raised their three children: Floyd Jr., Shirley and Willard.

In 1939, Mr. Schaaf established the family owned business in Wilber known as "Schaaf Log Cabins." These cabins were shipped all over northeast Michigan and as far away as Kentucky. In the early 1940s, you could purchase a Schaaf cabin for approximately $400.00.

The cabin business continued to thrive and in 1953, the business was relocated from Wilber to its present location at 1785 E. US-23 (Baldwin Township), East Tawas, Michigan. In 1955, the business became a Michigan corporation known as, "Schaaf Lumber Company".

The early 1960s saw the family business expand to include the production of wood roof trusses. These roof trusses were first used on their own cabins, earning them the fame of becoming one of the first fabricators of the "pre-fab home" in northeast Michigan.

With the fabrication of pre-engineered wood floor and roof trusses, a dealer network was established in 1971. Schaaf trusses have been shipped and sold through other lumber yards (dealers) to building contractors throughout all of northern Michigan and the upper peninsula.

Schaaf Lumber still remains in the family and is operated by its third generation.

Tawas Animal Hospital

Tawas Animal Hospital in 1980 (top) and 1992 (right).

In 1924 Tawas City constructed a new fire/city hall on US-23. To do this the home of the Whittemore family would have to be razed or moved. This house was originally built in 1864 and for many years was considered one of the premier homes in the area. The owner, Charles Whittemore, became one of the founding fathers and served as mayor of the newly established city of Tawas City. The removal of the home was taken on by Henry Fashect, a part-time farmer and janitor of the East Tawas High School. It was moved to the site of his farm on M-55 (Hemlock Road) four miles west of US-23.

In 1968 the home and farm were sold to Dr. Fred Besancon and his wife. Dr. Besancon came to the area to retire from his practice of veterinary medicine in the Detroit area. He was soon practicing medicine from the home at the urging of local pet owners. He built a small clinic next to the beautiful barn a few yards from the farm house and soon was busier than he ever intended.

In June 1978 Dr. Besancon sold the house, farm and small clinic to Dr. Tim Burg. Dr. Burg is a 1972 graduate of Michigan State University College of Veterinary Medicine. He is a native of Michigan and has always limited his practice to pet animals. The practice continued to be conducted from the small original clinic and, despite two additions over the next eight years grew to a point where, in 1991, a new clinic building was erected.

In 1994, Dr. Burg purchased the Oscoda Veterinary Hospital from the retiring Dr. W.S. "Wink" Carpenter and began operating the business there as an out patient clinic with the Tawas office acting then as a central facility for both practices. Meanwhile, Dr. Burg became an active member of the community, serving on the Tawas area Board of Education for 16 years and serving in a variety of leadership roles at The Tawas Methodist Church.

He has just recently celebrated 30 years of compassionate service to his patients. His two daughters, Brianna and Natalie, graduated from the Tawas area schools and went on to have successful careers in nursing and writing respectively. In 2003, to meet the demand of continued growth, the Tawas office was enlarged and modernized.

VILLAGE CHOCOLATIER

The Village Chocolatier preparing for Christmas.

Presently, the Village Chocolatier, located at 104 Newman Street, East Tawas, is owned by Norman and Marian Charters. They purchased the chocolate manufacturing and retail store from Douglas and Emily Moon on January 2, 2002. Their dream for years was to own a store in the downtown area of East Tawas. After Norman retired from General Motors in 1995, they began looking seriously at businesses that were for sale in this area. Doug and Emily were thinking of retiring from the seven days a week business at that same time. They talked one day while the Charters were shopping in the store, and thus, the purchase was discussed.

The original chocolate shop was called Larry's Sweet Shoppe and was started by Larry Hahn as a retirement business in approximately 1983. The shop was located in AuGres. Joan Borske purchased the shop from Hahn in the spring of 1986 and moved the shop to a location in the middle of AuGres. She also changed the name to its present assumed name, Village Chocolatier. Joan started the sugar free line of chocolates which still exists today and is very popular. In the spring of 1991, she sold the shop to Jan and Don Webber. They purchased several recipes from various locations around the world. They also rehired Larry Hahn, the original owner, who worked for them for two years. They moved the store to the second block of Newman where it remained until April of 1994 when Doug and Emily Moon purchased it. The Moon family moved the store the following year to its current location. Because of the larger facility, the Moons were able to expand on the line of chocolates and other candy.

All of the owners developed an extended product line over the 20 years the store has existed. The store has a wonderful array of chocolate delights ranging from chocolate covered fruit to pretzels. The specialty items include chocolate covered creams, truffles, and nuts that delight visitors from all over the world. The shop receives orders from many customers in other states. The owners are so thankful for their many wonderful customers and friends who have supported their "entrepreneur" business.

CENTURY 21-TAWAS REALTY

Century 21 Tawas Reality

Judith L. Thibault bought the Century 21 Franchise in May of 1978. In May of 2003 she will celebrate her 25th year with Century 21.

Prior to owning her own franchise, Judith worked for Margaret Prescott of State Wide Realty for seven years and for Mildred DeBeau of Sunshine Realty for three years, prior to her purchase of the Century 21 Franchise. In 1980 she bought the property at the corner of Bay and Main Streets in East Tawas. The property consists of three tourist cabins. The corner cabin was remolded and is the present office of Century 21. The second cabin was removed, and replaced with a parking lot. This cabin became a hunting cabin. The third cabin was remolded into a beauty shop.

The Tawases and surrounding area have been very good to her. The support that she has received from her loyal friends, family and staff, have made it possible for her business to thrive, even in hard times when interest rates were high. In her career, she has closed on 3000 properties.

She would like to give credit to her mother and father who always believed in her abilities and knew she wasn't a quitter when things got tough. Also, loyal friends who have stayed with her office as they made changes in their lives buying and selling.

Judith is so proud to have been part of the changes in the area and intends to keep working to help the people she cares deeply about and do the best job she can for each and every one of them.

Her newest venture took place three years ago when she and her husband Kenneth bought Townline Campground (previously owned by his parents) now known as Tawas RV Park. Townline Campground was a primitive park with 18 sites and they have made Tawas RV Park into a modern park with 61 sites. They think the park was a much-needed facility and gives a lot back to the community.

Quota Club of Iosco County

The Quota Club of Iosco County was chartered in May 1954 at the Barnes Hotel in Tawas City. In 2004 the club celebrated its 50th Anniversary at the Holiday Inn in East Tawas. Quota is an international service club of business and professional women. The organization's objectives are: To serve the county and community, To promote High Ethical Standards, To emphasis the worth of all Useful Occupations, To develop Ideals of Righteousness, Justice, Mutual Understanding and Good Will.

With the motto, "We Share" the group sponsors projects for hearing and speech, disadvantaged families and community service.

Current large donations have focused on the Classroom Amplification and Shelter, Inc. as well as a variety of other projects in need of support. In prior years the club has raised money for various hearing testing equipment, and worked at an annual hearing testing clinic, and continues to support a variety of projects and donations to help and serve the community.

Nita Greer was the first president of the local club. Current president is JoAnn Lutz. Members Esther Ledsworth and Rosemary Klenow were presented with certificates honoring their more than 25 years of service to the organization, at the 50 year celebration. Club treasurer, Karen Curtis is the daughter of charter member Bertha Montgomery.

FALKER VETERINARY CARE CENTER

Falker Veterinary Care Center, located at 1941 North US 23 in Baldwin Township, was a dream come true in 1998 as the building was designed by Dr. Howard and Karlene Falker and built by Hemphill and Schirmer Construction. The new clinic is a state-of-the-art full-service medical facility, with in-house X-ray and diagnostic equipment, surgery, grooming and boarding. They currently employ one other veterinarian, Dr. James J. King, who graduated from Oscoda High School in 1995 and from Michigan State University in 2002, as well as seven assistants.

Howard William Falker was born June 5, 1947 in Mt. Clemens, Michigan and was raised in Romeo, Michigan on a dairy and poultry farm.

Falker Veterinary Care Center

He was the oldest child of four of Howard and Marjorie Kiehler Falker who were both second-generation Germans.

Howard spent much of his youth involved with 4-H and FFA as well as working on the farm. He was the pianist at the St. John's Lutheran Church in Romeo at a very young age and is a past president of the Luther League. His youngest brother, Mark, still works the family farm on 34-Mile Road.

Karlene, the daughter of Max and Helen Keller Graybiel, was born in the thumb of Michigan on August 24, 1948 and also raised on a dairy and sheep farm in Capac, Michigan. Her parents were both of German descent and she learned to speak German from her mother's parents who lived with them and spoke very little English. The second of five daughters, she also worked on the farm and learned to cook, sew and lead dairy cows through 4-H. She was also very involved in the St. John's Lutheran Church in Capac always singing in the choirs with her father, playing piano and attending Sunday School and Luther League.

It was at one of those youth group roller skating outings that Howard and Karlene met at 15 years of age. Their friendship blossomed while they attended Michigan State University in East Lansing. Howard and Karlene were married September 14, 1968 in Capac, where Karlene worked. Howard graduated in 1969 with a bachelor's degree in dairy science. He earned his doctorate of veterinary medicine in December 1971, soon after their first son, Matthew Howard, was born. His loving and supportive grandfather, William Kiehler, passed away the night of graduation.

In 1972, they moved to Armada, Michigan and Howard worked at Krause Veterinary Clinic for five years, during which their second son, Eric Max, was born. In 1977, the Falkers moved to 1790 North US 23 and bought the Tawas Upholstery Shop from Pat and Edna Johnson and turned it into Falker Veterinary Clinic. The entire family worked at the clinic in front of their residence. Their third son, Todd William, was born in 1981. All of their sons are very involved in music, math and athletics as well as the Tawas United Methodist

Church in Tawas City. The boys have all attended Sunday School, choir and camping, also the youth programs.

Matt, who graduated from Cranbrook High School in Bloomfield Hills and earned his masters degree in jazz studies from the University of Southern California, was recently the assistant director of Purdue University Music Organization. He is now a professor of music at Fullerton-College in Anaheim, California, and the music director at Mt. Sinai Baptist Church.

Eric graduated with high honors in civil engineering from Northwestern University in Evanston, Illinois. After spending one year on a fellowship to Germany, he is now finishing his masters of construction engineering at Purdue University in West Lafayette, Indiana. He will be marrying Katja Schwarz from Magdeburg, Germany in the spring. Eric plays piano and sings with the Praise Team at the University Chapel on campus. Todd is a junior at Albion College in Albion, Michigan where he continues to be an honor scholar, all-conference runner in the Michigan Intercollegiate College Conference, and has just been named Academic All-American in Cross Country. He recently finished an internship in international business and marketing with Saucony Athleticwear in Peabody, Massachusetts where he also taught 5th grade Sunday School at the Old South Methodist Church.

Howard has enjoyed working as a 4-H leader for over 25 years, and has been an active Lions Club member for 26 years. He has also been an officer of the Northeast Michigan Veterinary Medical Association for over 20 years. Karlene spent some years teaching pre-school library hour and nursery school and has been an active member of Quota International Club of Iosco County, including being the past president. Both Howard and Karlene have been very active at the Tawas United Methodist Church; Howard as organist, Karlene as a choir member and Sunday School teacher, also they have served on numerous committees. When they are not at the clinic, they can often by found at their camp in Mikado, where they enjoy building, hunting and relaxing.

IOSCO COUNTY ANIMAL SHELTER

Iosco County Animal Shelter

Wilma Poe and Ila Peters. They were interested in providing better care for the animals at the animal shelter and in the community, so they founded Animal Humanitarians in the fall of 1983. The first goals were to set up an incentive for a spay/neuter program and to improve the conditions at the Animal Shelter. Volunteers picketed the Board of Commissioners for a month to have improvements done at the Shelter. At that time, there was no insulation in the ceiling, no telephone and the Shelter was open for only four hours a week.

Since 1984 many improvements have been made at the Shelter through funds from the county commissioners, donations and fundraising. These have included a self-watering system for the dog runs, insulation, roof over the back outside runs, enclosure of the outside runs, new puppy and cat/kitten pens, washer and dryer, among other things. AHI began donating volunteer hours at the Shelter to enable it to be opened longer hours. Eventually a contract with the county occurred with AHI managing the Shelter with a budget and funding from the county. Donations have helped with other costs and improvements.

Many different fundraising projects have occurred during the years. These include a Christmas House Tour, annual rummage sale, photo contest, Walk-A-Thon, sponsoring a Christmas ornament, and selling various products. Volunteers have gone to elementary schools in the county with their pets to talk to the children about responsible pet ownership. Children have donated food and toys and supplies for the animals at Christmas time.

Volunteers are available for emergency animal rescue during the times when the Animal Control Officer is not on duty.

We have run a spay/neuter rebate program since 1984 and have rebated over $35,000 during that time to have thousands of cats and dogs altered. This has resulted in a gradual decrease in the amounts of unwanted litters arriving at the Shelter. A lot of this funding has come from collecting Carter's receipts. At one time Glen's Market also participated. AHI also runs a SNAP program for low-income families willing to repay a no interest loan for altering their pet or emergency care.

One big community project is the Habitats for Hounds dog house-building project which started in 1993. This is done in conjunction with Make-A-Difference Day. Between 40-50 doghouses are built annually for distribution by the ACO to families who cannot afford a doghouse for their outdoor dog. Some are sold to assist in the cost of the lumber. Carl Pritchett has been instrumental in cutting out the pieces for the builders, who consist of boy and girl scouts, National Honor Society children, and other school children. Recently the Shelter has become computerized and an internet site portrays available animals for adoption. People come from all over the state for a particular animal.

AHI has had as President Ila Peters, Terri Whitford, Annajean Elvey and Marsha Hummel. Animal control officer is Steve Messenger, Shelter Manager is Dan Benjamin and assistant manager is Pam Goettel. Through the hard work of many volunteers, the adoption/return to owner rate of animals is over 50%.

Tawas Area Presbyterian Church

2095 E. US-23 at intersection of Aulerich Road
East Tawas, Michigan

A Presbyterian Church was started in Tawas in 1869 but was dissolved in 1933. The church returned to the Tawas area in 1986 after an absence of 53 years. Dr. William Bos, a retired Presbyterian minister, moved to East Tawas from Florence, Oregon and started a summer worship program. Arrangements were made to rent the Odd Fellows Lodge, located in East Tawas, as a place to conduct worship. Services began May 4, 1986 with 18 people.

Dr. Bos had to leave in May 1987, to return to the church he founded in Florence. The Rev. Janice Pestrue was appointed by the Presbytery of Lake Huron to be coordinator on a part-time basis. Interest in the church grew and on May 31, 1988 the Presbytery voted funds to support a full time pastor. The Rev. Pestrue was called to fill that position. Through her leadership the church grew to more than 80 members. The church was chartered by the Presbytery on October 27, 1991. The First Presbyterian Church of Bay City is fondly looked upon as our "mother church" because of the support they have given over the years.

Property for a building project was purchased in 1991 and construction on a new $490,000 sanctuary began early in 1993. Members voted to build an octagon shaped facility that would seat approximately 300 and have space for fellowship and Christian education. The first worship service was held in the new sanctuary on Sunday, December 19, 1993. The church property extends in an "L" shape from US-23 to Aulerich Road. Therefore space is available to add to the present sanctuary for continued growth.

The Rev. Pestrue was called to another congregation in 1999 and the Rev. Kenneth Tousley became the interim pastor during the search for a new pastor. The Rev. G. Richard "Rick" Vogeley was called by the congregation to be the 2nd full time installed pastor on September 24, 2000.

T.A.P.C. is part of the Presbyterian Church U.S.A. denomination. The local church is governed by a Session made up of 12 elders elected from the congregation, which conduct all the corporate and ecclesiastical business of the church. A Board of Deacons, consisting of 14 members, focus on service and mission.

Since 1986 the Tawas Area Presbyterian Church has grown in spirit and body. Today nearly 170 active and dedicated members are involved in the life of this church, serving a large area (50 mile radius) on the coast of Lake Huron.

Tawas United Methodist Church

In the fall of 1861, Rev. J.P. Merchant was appointed by the presiding elder of the Port Huron District to travel the Lake Shore from Tawas to Alpena and preach the Gospel of Christ to the few people that were then scattered along the shore at different points. It has always been characteristic of Methodism to pioneer into new countries and raise up the gospel standard among the people.

In April 1866, George P. Smith and his wife organized a Methodist Sunday School for religious instruction in East Tawas. By 1867 the Tawas Circuit was organized with class meetings being held in Tawas City. The Tawas Circuit was organized by Rev. George Smith, presiding elder of Flint District, Detroit Conference assisted by Jared Copeland, a local preacher transferred from Wenona Charge and appointed by the presiding elder to serve the people the remainder of the year. At the annual session of the Detroit Conference of 1867, Rev. Alonzo Whitcomb was appointed to Tawas Circuit for the coming year. In 1868, a regular Methodist Society was organized and held services in the Old Whittemore store of Tawas City. Five years later, in 1873, the original building was erected to house the Tawas City Church. In February of 1873, the East Tawas Methodist Church was dedicated.

In September 1877, the Rev. Edward Bancroft was appointed to serve the Tawas City church as its first full time pastor. At various times the church was part of a circuit which included Town Line, Wilber, Alabaster and East Tawas.

Both churches continued to serve the people of the Tawas area. In 1962 the East Tawas Methodist Church celebrated its 100th year anniversary. Six years later, 1968, the Tawas City Methodist Church celebrated its 100th year anniversary.

In 1967, a Study Committee was appointed to investigate the possibility of the merger of the Tawas City and East Tawas churches. After much study and consideration, it was voted to become known as the Tawas United Methodist Church, actual merger becoming effective May 5, 1968.

On September 3, 1969, a charge conference was held to consider the purchase of about three acres of land located at the corner of 5th Avenue and M-55, Tawas City, Michigan. The vote was 84 in favor of purchase and 15 opposed. Soon after the land was purchased attention was focused on the construction of a new church.

On April 14, 1974, Easter Sunrise, the ground breaking service was held for the new building. A few months later, on October 6, 1974, the congregation gathered for the laying of the cornerstone. The construction of the new church was completed in March 1975. On March 16, 1975 the congregation worshipped in their new sanctuary for the very first time. The participants in the consecration service included Dr. Ralph Janka, Superintendent of the Saginaw Bay District; Mrs. Diane Knight, choir director; Mrs. Kaye Phelps, organist; Miss Deborah Knight, acolyte; and Rev. Kenneth Tousley, pastor.

During the late 1970s and early 1980s the church continued to grow. More room was needed for classrooms. Plans were made under the leadership of Rev. Ralph Churchhill to construct a new education wing. In 1985, led by Rev. Ron Carter, the addition was completed and dedicated.

The next pastor to serve the church was Rev. S. Joe Robertson. In his tenure a new ministry focus towards nonbelievers was adopted. A new "praise style of worship was implemented to attract those unfamiliar with church.

To help further serve the needs of the congregation and the community another construction project was approved. A new gym, called a family life center, kitchen, large gathering area and expanded office space was dedicated in 1998.

In 2002, under the leadership of Rev. David Huseltine and the Church Council, the Sunday morning schedule was changed. Though controversial, this decision was made to reach the unchurched.

Tawas United Methodist Church currently has 475 members. The church's purpose is to help connect people to God through Jesus Christ for now and forever.

LAKE HURON COMMUNITY CHURCH

On April 25, 1976 some 38 believers gathered together and formed a community church with basic biblical teachings. Lake Huron Community Church, henceforth LHCC, was organized according to uncompromising simplicity of God's Holy Scriptures for the establishment of His church. On May 17, 1976 LHCC was legally incorporated according to the Michigan Department of Commerce.

For the first two years the congregation of LHCC was small and met in homes in East Tawas. The children met at the home of Ned and Kathy Moffit on Tawas Street for a junior church type of meeting, while the adults met some five blocks away at the home of Terry and Cathie Montgomery on Church Street. This arrangement continued until the congregation became too large in number for either home to adequately provide space for the meetings.

For the next few months the congregation met at the East Tawas Community Building. It was during this time that Mel Miller, a professor from LaTourneau Collage in Texas began to shepherd the flock and trained men from the fellowship to become the pastor/elders. This type of leadership has continued down through the history of LHCC with Larry Stimson and Ned Moffit being the leaders still at the time of this writing.

The fellowship felt a need for a place to worship and meet when necessary and began to rent a building on Pine Street in East Tawas. This rental agreement continued for the next two years. Again the size of the congregation was growing in attendance and need arose to find a larger facility. September of 1980 LHCC became the new owners of 402 W. Lincoln Street, East Tawas. This was formerly the site of the first St. Joseph Catholic Church built in 1883 and was purchased from them after they built their new facilities. During the past 22 years several renovations have been made to the building to continually meet the needs for the growing congregation.

Today LHCC has a heavy emphasis on the biblical structure of the family unit and missionary support. The congregation of LHCC is furthering the Kingdom of Christ by becoming helping hands where needed, and being active throughout the community.

EMANUEL LUTHERAN CHURCH

Emanuel School, Parsonage, and Church, circa 1907.

At right: Emanuel Luthern Church, 1988.

Founding

Early settlers in Tawas area arrived during the lumber and fishing boom, coming from southern Michigan, eastern states, Canada and a sizeable number from Europe. Farming soon followed as an additional major operation.

In the early days Lutheran missionaries from southern Michigan visited the area to give spiritual aid to the German immigrants who had settled there. On August 5, 1877, Emanuel congregation was founded at East Tawas, Michigan with Pastor William Reuter of Bay City assisting in the organization. Monthly services were held April through October and every other month during the winter with services alternating between members homes in the Tawases. When the pastor was not present, sermons were read by the deacons. Yearly dues were $5.00.

Church

In 1880 a house was purchased and remodeled to serve for services as well as a temporary home for the missionary. Plans for the original church building were approved in 1881 and construction completed in 1882. A bell was purchased in 1885. The present bell having been purchased in 1932 after the old bell cracked. A pipe organ in 1919 replaced the old reed organ. An electric organ was purchased 1948 and in 1952. A bolt of lightening, demolished the church steeple in 1941 necessitating a replacement. A new church was built on the North Street property adjoining to the

school in 1989. The stained glass windows from the old church were incorporated into the new church design. The old church was demolished on the Second Street property next to the parsonage in spring of 1996. The demolition was done by a few members and family members (Mike Coyle and his son Scott, and Wade Vadnais, husband to Kelly Coyle Vadnais).

School

A small Christian day school was erected in 1883. In 1892 plans were adopted for a new school completed in 1893. This school was located on the Second Street church property next to the parsonage. The present school located on North Street, was built in 1958-59.

Parsonage

The first parsonage purchased by the congregation was remodeled and enlarged to fit the needs of the pastor. In 1898 a home was purchased at AuSable, and this building was dismantled and rebuilt on church property in Tawas City. On July 5, 1903, fire broke out in horse sheds near the rear of the parsonage and the parsonage burned to the ground. The congregation immediately proceeded to build a new brick parsonage. This is the existing parsonage.

Emanuel Lutheran congregation numbers 593 souls including 83 voting members. Pastor Michael Zuberbier has been serving Emanuel since December 1995 replacing Pastor James Rockoff who served Emanuel since 1964.

Grace Evangelical Lutheran Church (ELCA)
East Tawas, Michigan

Grace Evangelical Lutheran Church

Swedish emigrants originally organized Grace Lutheran Church in the spring of 1886. Twenty-two charter members were recorded in June of that year. The first structure at the east end of State Street, was constructed during the lumber and sawmill days of 1886 and 1887, but was not dedicated until 1896.

In 1939, the name was changed from Abigail Evangelical Lutheran to Grace Evangelical Lutheran Church. The original church was built at a cost of $1,000.00 and had a membership of 70 adults and 69 children. Church records indicated that in 1888, annual dues were $4.00 for each male and $2.00 for every female member. Anyone not belonging to the church could be buried from there for a fee of $1.00. In 1895, the total annual budget was $190.00.

In the early 1890s, the Ladies Aid purchased the bell for the church with money earned at ice cream socials and at regular meetings. In 1916, the old steeple was torn down and a new one erected. At this time, the Ladies Aid contributed $75.00 to the redecoration of the church's interior.

In the old days, a stable was located at the rear of the church where farmers could keep their horses during services. As late as 1900, money was budgeted each year to maintain the stables.

The original church was used until the 1950s when the present site at the corner of Main and Lincoln Streets was purchased and construction began on a new church. Until the entire structure was completed in 1956, the basement was used for services and congregational meetings. Memorial stained glass windows and the bell from the old church were installed into the new structure. A new tri-level brick parsonage adjacent to the church was built in 1963 at the corner of Newman and Lincoln streets.

Grace Evangelical Lutheran Church observed its 100th year of proclaiming Christ in 1986. Further additions to the church, including offices, pastor's study, youth rooms, and nursery took place in the following years. A large parking lot was acquired on Main Street.

A member of the Evangelical Lutheran Church in America (ELCA), Grace Evangelical Lutheran Church, now over 100 years old, continues to minister to the needs of its members, the community, and the whole church of God.

TAWAS CITY SEVENTH DAY ADVENTIST CHURCH
Tawas City, Michigan

One of the earliest records indicate that there was a transfer of membership of a lady from Flint, Michigan, to the church in East Tawas. It was signed by the church clerk, Agnus Kuerbitz. The date was 1957. Her husband Carl and herself were asked to move to Tawas from Glennie to help establish a church in Tawas City.

The earliest available record is a transfer of membership of Kenneth Sherman to the East Tawas Church is dated June 27, 1956. Anna White transferred on July 23, 1956. There are some records from the treasurer and they were signed by Vivian Howe. She was the wife of the Pastor Howe, apparently the first pastor of the church in East Tawas.

They were joined by Ray Deniss (a watch-repairman) and his wife Pearl and their children, who came from the Maple Ridge Seventh-Day Adventist Church. They were also joined by the Mr. and Mrs. Kipp and their two daughters, Wanita and Wanda, from Skidway Lake. There were also other members who transferred to the East Tawas Church, Betty J. Johnson, Fay Johnson Nov. 24, 1958. Lorretta and Hank Lutsky, and the Rollens family. The Maple Ridge Church closed most likely around 1956-1958

William White was baptized by H.L. Alexander July 9, 1960. Gerda Harms was baptized by Pastor H. Musgrave June 23, 1963 and Wayne Harms by Pastor D.B. Meyers August 23, 1963. Others who became members were baptized by Pastor Wenberg in August of 1964; Wanda Nellie Burns, Dean K. and Joyce R. Hinton, Todd J. and Marie W. Wesley. Lola Van Deusan and her husband Shirely transferred on October 3, 1966. Some time later Elzie F. Beaver and his wife Muriel from Bay City joined the small group of believers on July 11, 1967.

They purchased a church building from the Swedish Lutherans who had remodeled an old house. It was located on the north east corner of State St. and Adams. Some folks still remember the old theater seats in the church and the old pump organ. Also one persons recalls an old gentleman who played the violin. The church was sold to the Latter Day Saints for approximately $10,000 sometime between 1969-72.

The church members also operated a community service center located at 314 Newman St., downtown East Tawas. This center was eventually sold to Thomas B. Huck, P.C., Attorney at Law, on May 4, 1982 for $25,000.

Sometime between 1969-71 the church and community service center had been in the process of relocating and purchasing the Methodist Church located on 327 Whittemore St. and 4th St. in Tawas City. It was deeded to the Michigan Conference Association of Seventh-Day Adventists on July 12, 1973.

Over the years the church records indicate the East Tawas Church has been pastored by Pastor Howe, Pastor H. Muskgrave 1963-69. And then during the transition of the church to Tawas City was pastored by Pastor D.B. Meyers 1967-69, then by pastors Kenneth Wenberg 1964-75, Don Siewert 1975-76, Russell Booth 1972-77, Karl Reibow 1977-78, Charles Danforth 1978-84, Gordon

Tawas City Seventh Day Adventist Church

Stecker 1985-91, D. Charles Mackintosh 1991-97, Karl Tsatalbasidis 1997-2000, and currently Pastor Richard P. Mendoza 2000-03 with 33 members.

The Tawas City Seventh-Day Adventist Church continues with their mission of spreading the gospel of Jesus Christ. They continue to serve Iosco County (and adjacent areas) by operating their Community Service Center where they provided food and clothing at no cost or obligation to those who we struggling with poverty. They also box clothes to ship overseas to other countries for Adventist Development & Relief Agency (A.D.R.A.).

The church is just one of the many churches here in Michigan which make up the Michigan Conference of Seventh Day Adventists, established in 1860 in Battle Creek, MI. The Conference is one of the many which form the sisterhood of the World Church of Seventh Day Adventists (General Conference established in 1863 also at Battle Creek), with congregations located in every nation of the world, with the exception of a very small minority.

This is all part of their world-wide mission to take the everlasting gospel of the Three Angels' Message of Revelation 14:6-12 to every nation, kindred, tongue, and people. They hold to the Bible as the only rule of faith and practice and therefore have accepted the Bible's teaching that the seventh day of the week, Saturday, is the Christian Sabbath, the Lord's Day, of both the Old and New Testaments (see Exodus 20:8-11, Mark 2:27-28, Hebrews 4:1-12), and they observe the seventh day Sabbath as a memorial of creation from sundown Friday to sundown Saturday according to the Bible, participating in sacred activities and excluding secular ones, attending Sabbath School and Worship Services, and doing deed of kindness which minister to the needs of humanity. They strongly believe that the only answer to man's problems is being saved by grace through faith in Jesus Christ, accepting Him as Lord, and preparing for His Second Coming to take all who trust in Him to His Father's House in Heaven.

CHRIST EPISCOPAL CHURCH
East Tawas

Christ Episcopal Church

In 1876, the first Episcopal services were held in the Court House in Tawas City with Reverend Dr. Schetky officiating. The canonical organization of Christ Church Missions was started in 1880. That same year, Reverend A. Butler of Bay City came by boat to East Tawas and baptized seven children of Mr. and Mrs. W.H. Warren.

In 1888, Reverend Knox of Alpena came occasionally to celebrate the Blessed Sacrament. Services were held in Joslin Hall and sometimes in the Baptist Church.

April 2, 1893 on Easter Sunday, the present church was dedicated. Reverend R.T. Webb was the pastor during the construction. Mr. George Oakes was the contractor and the cost was $3,000.

September 10, 1907, the church building was consecrated. The present Parish Hall was completed in 1949.

On February 2, 1955, Christ Church was admitted as a parish in union with the Diocese of Michigan.

In 1965 All Saints Hall was added to the rear of the church; 1972, Clarence Everett electronic chime system was installed; 1974, Centennial of the Congregation marked with the bricking of the church, addition of the spire, and laying of a cornerstone; 2002, the addition of a new Greeting Room was completed, adjustments were made to make the church handicap accessible including a lift and rail rider, also improvements made to the Kitchen in Undercroft, and the re-siding of the steeple.

Clergy who have served the church are Reverend Dr. Schetky, 1876; Reverend W.C. Pearson, 1881; Reverend John Evans, 1883; Reverend R.T. Webb, 1889; Reverend Edward H. Earle, 1895; Reverend J. Orson Miller, 1896; Reverend George W. Wye, 1897; Reverend Frank A. Saylor, 1903; Reverend Nassau Stephens, 1907; Reverend Denham H. Quinn, 1908; Reverend W.R. Blachford, 1911; Reverend A.W. Darwall, 1917; Reverend Goodrich, 1918; Reverend Charles E. Edinger, 1919; Reverend Herbert Wilson, 1937; Reverend John R. Colby, 1939; Reverend H.R. Ziegler, 1946; Reverend Warner L. Forsyth, 1949; Reverend Richard P. Jennings, 1954; Reverend Paul E. Sutton, 1957; Reverend E.N. Kemp, 1961; Reverend Robert Morrison, 1962; Reverend Alfred W. Saulsbury, 1968; Reverend Kenneth M. Near, 1978; The Right Reverend James Sorenson, 1985; The Right Reverend Robert McKay III, 1995 and Reverend Mary Short, 2002.

TRINITY LUTHERAN CHURCH

Trinity Lutheran Church began in 1958 as an extension of Zion Lutheran Church, Tawas City. The first worship service and Sunday School were held on September 28, 1958 in the old Oscoda community building. Before long, we were needing a building of our own, and a decision was made to purchase the present piece of property and to buy the old Methodist church which was moved to our location. Only the roof needed to be dismantled for travel and then reconstructed on our property, which is now 5625 North, US 23.

1963—As we continued to outgrow this building, a need for a new one was under construction. It would have a parish hall, education room, and a kitchen. This building was dedicated in October 1963.

1973—Because of the growth and paper work, a secretary was added. She had no office until later when the cloakroom was remodeled.

1981—A fund was started to enlarge and blacktop the parking lot, along with the need for a nursery and an all-purpose room. By 1985, these things became a reality.

1992—Trinity became a mother congregation to Faith Lutheran in Harrisville.

1994—The stained windows and altar panels were installed and dedicated. We were also blessed at this time with a new pastor, Pastor Tom Boehne.

1995—The ground breaking was done for the eight classrooms, two new restrooms, a new kitchen, secretary's office, and then to revert the old cloakroom back to a new cloakroom.

1996—The new church wing was dedicated with a special service conducted by Rev. Erwin Kostizen and Pastor Boehne. A buffet was served after the service, thanks to the Stewardship Committee. Also during this time the parking lot was repaired and resurfaced.

1997—Trinity now has a beautiful new sign to decorate the church. Many donations and memorials helped to pay for this. It was placed in the ground May 29, 1997.

1998—We purchased land to the West End of the parking lot, connecting to Cedar Lake Rd.

1999—The parking lot was expanded behind the education wing.

1999—Received community service award for our outreach to the community and love of God.

2001—Constructed a new storage barn and new flooring in parish hall thru generous donations. Also thru a donated bell, a bell tower was constructed in our garden.

2002—Rev. Alan R. Stadelman accepted our call to be our new pastor and is serving us at this time.

Trinity Lutheran Church

Interior view of Trinity Lutheran Church

INDEX